FRENCH
for Business

Jacqueline Lecanuet

Hugo's Language Books Limited

'French for Business' is also available in a pack
with four cassettes: ISBN 0 85285 151 0

Written by

Jacqueline Lecanuet
L. ès L., PG Dip. Ling.

Senior Lecturer in French
Department of Modern Languages
South Bank Polytechnic, London

Cover photo (Spectrum): La Défense, Paris

Set in Helvetica 55 & 65 by
Logotechnics Ltd (Sheffield)
Printed and bound in Great Britain by
Courier International Ltd
East Kilbride

PREFACE

"French for Business' is the first in a new series of language courses from Hugo, designed for business and professional people who wish to take advantage of the opportunities offered by the Single European Market. The book will also prove valuable to students for whom French is one of the options on a Business Studies course in colleges of further and higher education. The content is not solely applicable to British users, but will greatly aid any English-speaking person needing to improve his or her French for business purposes.

Anyone completing this Course will have acquired the linguistic competence necessary to deal successfully with most business situations, including one that is becoming more common each day, namely the purchasing of property in France.

This Course is intended for:

a) those who studied French at school some years ago and now need to brush up their (rusty) knowledge and to continue their studies in a business context.

b) those who have already completed Hugo's 'French in Three Months' and now require the language specifically for business/professional reasons.

c) those highly-motivated beginners who are looking for a stimulating, fast-moving and methodical course and who are prepared to devote the necessary time and effort to each Unit.

Method

The method adopted is a very practical one with the emphasis being placed on communication in a realistic context. Every business dialogue in French is accompanied by an English translation, followed by a study of the individual words used (the Checklist), detailed explanatory notes (Checknotes) and abundant examples of grammar 'in action'. Throughout the Course there are numerous varied, lively and contextualized exercises, all with key, offering ample scope for practising the material taught. Most Units include actual, up-to-date French documents in the form of articles, advertisements, letters, etc., which add a certain authenticity and challenge to the exercises. Many of the new words introduced appear in more than one of the vocabulary lists, as it is well known that repetition plays an important role in the language learning process.

Theme of the Units

The majority of the Units are centred around the activities of a British businessman, Mr Jackson, and his French counterpart, Madame Duval, and cover a wide range of business situations (see Contents). It should be noted however that, with the exception of the authentic material, the names of all persons and companies mentioned in the Course are purely fictitious.

Cassettes

In addition to the chapter devoted to pronunciation, the first five Units have been provided with the Hugo system of imitated pronunciation, because we feel it is essential for the student to acquire a correct accent from the outset. Nevertheless, we strongly recommend that you obtain the four audio-cassettes which accompany the Course, as these will make the lessons so much more interesting and entertaining and will, of course, accustom your ear to French as pronounced by native speakers.

We hope that you will enjoy 'French for Business' and we wish you every success in your studies.

ACKNOWLEDGEMENTS

I am very grateful to Rémi and Monique Lecanuet, Michel Lecanuet and in particular to my mother, Hélène Lecanuet, for all their help during the preparation of this Course. I would also like to say a special thankyou to my niece, Isabelle Lecanuet, for reading through the manuscript and making some very useful suggestions.

Thanks are also due to Crédit Agricole and to all those others who have kindly allowed the reproduction of extracts from their copyright material.

CONTENTS

The pronunciation of French

French is a pleasant language to listen to, but it can sometimes be difficult for English-speaking people to pronounce, which is why we have used Hugo's imitated pronunciation for the first five Units. You can therefore, if you wish, turn immediately to Unit 1 and begin the first lesson. On the other hand, you will certainly find it useful to read the following general rules fairly rapidly and, then, to refer back to them as you proceed through the Course. Always remember - French is more phonetic than English! If, of course, you can obtain the accompanying cassettes so much the better, as you will then be able to listen to perfect pronunciation whenever you wish. But, first, make yourself familiar with the few, simple comments regarding the imitated pronunciation.

Imitated pronunciation

Pronounce all syllables as if they were part of an English word, but note the following:

ng (in italics)	must never be pronounced; these letters indicate that the preceding vowel has a nasal sound
er (r in italics)	pronounce like 'er' in 'her' (but don't sound the r)
zh	like 's' in 'measure'
ü	say 'ee' with rounded lips
o	like 'o' in 'not'
oh	like 'o' in 'note'
y	always like 'y' in 'yes'

Liaison

The French like to link their words together, so that the language flows smoothly. This is called liaison which means carrying over the last letter of one word to the beginning of the next. For example:

Monsieur Jackson est arrivé.
Mr Jackson has arrived.

Madame Duval vous attend dans son bureau.
Madame Duval is waiting for you in her office.

When carried over in this way, **s** and **x** sound like **z**; **d** sounds like **t**; **f** sounds like **v**.

8

The French sounds

Imitated pronunciation

a	sounds like English 'ah', but shorter: accord commercial (*trade agreement*)	ah-kor ko-mair-syahl
à	as above: à la banque (*at the bank*)	ah lah bah*ng*k
â	sound like English 'ah': câble (*cable*)	kah-ble*r*
ai	like 'e' in English 'let': les économiquement faibles (*those in the lower-income bracket*)	lay zay-ko-no-meek-mah*ng* febble*r*
ail	at the end of a word sounds like 'ah-ee': travail (*work*)	trah-vah-ee
aim	like 'ang' in English 'sang': grève de la faim (*hunger strike*)	grev de*r* lah fa*ng*
ain	as above: gains considérables (*considerable profit*)	ga*ng* ko*ng*-see-day-rah-ble*r*
am	like 'ahng' (nasal): chambre de commerce (*chamber of commerce*)	shah*ng*bre*r* de*r* ko-mairss
an	as above: mandat international (*international money order*)	mah*ng*-dah a*ng*-tair-nah-syo-nahl
au	like English 'oh': au chômage (*unemployed*)	oh shoh-mahzh
b	as in English: banquier (*banker*)	bah*ng*-kyay
c	before e or i sounds like 'ss': certificat d'origine (*certificate of origin*)	sair-tee-fee-kah do-ree-zheen
c	elsewhere like 'k': capital fixe (*fixed assets*)	kah-pee-tahl feeks
ç	like 'ss': commençons (*let's begin*)	ko-mah*ng*-song
ch	like English 'sh': chèque sans provision (*bad cheque*)	shek sah*ng* pro-vee-zyo*ng*

d	as in English:	
	déclaration fiscale (*income tax return*)	day-klah-rah-syo*ng* fee-skahl
e	in the middle of a syllable sounds like 'ai' in 'fair':	
	personnel (*staff*)	pair-so-nel
e	at the end of syllable sounds like 'er' in 'her':	
	recyclage du personnel (*staff retraining*)	re*r*-see-klahzh dü pair-so-nel
e	silent at the end of a word:	
	baisse de prix (*price reduction*)	bess de*r* pree
é	like 'ay' in 'day':	
	téléphoner (*to telephone*)	tay-lay-fo-nay
è	like 'e' in 'let':	
	grève du zèle (*work to rule*)	grev dü zel
ê	like 'e' in 'let', but longer:	
	être à la tête de (*to be at the head of*)	etre*r* ah lah tet de*r*
eau	like 'oh':	
	réseau de distribution (*distribution network*)	ray-zoh de*r* dee-stree-bü-syo*ng*
ei	like 'e' in 'let':	
	la Reine (*the Queen*)	lah ren
eil, eille	like 'ay-ee':	
	appareils électriques (*electrical appliances*)	ah-pah-ray-ee ay-lek-treek
ein	like 'ang' in 'sang':	
	plein chargement (*full cargo*)	pla*ng* shahr-zher-mah*ng*
em	like 'ahng':	
	emprunt bancaire (*bank loan*)	ah*ng*-pru*ng* bah*ng*-kair
en	as above:	
	engager des employés (*to engage staff*)	ah*ng*-gah-zhay day zah*ng*-plwah-yay
er	at the end of a word of two syllables or more sounds like 'ay' in 'day':	
	financer (*to finance*)	fee-nah*ng*-say
eu	like 'er' in 'her':	
	exportateur (*exporter*)	eks-por-tah-te*rr*

euil	like 'er-y' in 'her yacht': seuil de rentabilité (*break-even point*)	s*er*-y d*er* rah*ng*-tah-bee-lee-tay
ez	at the end of a word sounds like 'ay': télécopiez-le (*fax it*)	tay-lay-ko-pyay-l*er*
f	as in English: forces du marché (*market forces*)	forss dü mahr-shay
g	before e or i sounds like 's' in measure': gestion (*management*)	zhess-tyo*ng*
g	elsewhere like 'g' in 'go': garantie (*guarantee*)	gah-rah*ng*-tee
gn	like 'ni' in 'onion': signer (*to sign*)	see-nyay
h	is silent: homme d'affaires (*businessman*)	om dah-fair

Although h is always silent in French, in certain words this letter is treated as if it were like any other consonant, for example:

	l'homme d'affaires (*the businessman*)	lom dah-fair
	BUT	
	le hall d'exposition (*the exhibition hall*), see Checknote 3	l*er* ohl deks-poh-zee-syo*ng*
i	like 'ee' in 'meet': crédit illimité (*unlimited credit*)	kray-dee ee-lee-mee-tay
ien	like 'yang': biens de consommation (*consumer goods*)	bya*ng* d*er* ko*ng*-so-mah-syo*ng*
im	like 'ang' in 'sang': importations (*imports*)	a*ng*-por-tah-syo*ng*
in	as above: industrie aéronautique (*aircraft industry*)	a*ng*-dü-stree ah-ay-ro-noh-teek

The English word 'van' sounds very much like the French word **vin** (wine), but the latter is pronounced with a nasal sound.

j	like 's' in 'measure': Veuillez trouver ci-joint … (*Please find enclosed …*)	ver-yay troo-vay see-zhwa*ng*

k	as in English, but rare in French: krach (*financial crash*)	krahk
l	as in English: fabriqué sous licence (*manufactured under licence*)	fah-bree-kay soo lee-sah*ng*ss
m	as in English: moderniser (*to modernize*)	mo-dair-nee-zay
n	as in English: négociations (*negotiations*)	nay-go-syah-syo*ng*
o	like 'o' in 'not': monopole (*monopoly*)	mo-no-pol
ô	like 'o' in 'note': entrepôt (*warehouse*)	ah*ng*-tre*r*-poh
p	as in English: publicité (*advertising*)	pü-blee-see-tay
q, qu	like 'k': quartier des affaires (*business district*)	kahr-tyay day zah-fair
r	the sound we make when gargling: rémunération (*salary*)	ray-mü-nay-rah-syo*ng*
s	at the beginning of a word sounds like 'ss': syndicat (*trade union*)	sa*ng*-dee-kah
s	between two vowels sounds like 'z': informatiser (*to computerize*)	a*ng*-for-mah-tee-zay
t	as in English: traite bancaire (*banker's draft*)	tret bah*ng*-kair
u	this sound doesn't exist in English; say 'ee' with rounded lips: usine (*factory*)	ü-zeen
v	as in English: voiture de fonction (*company car*)	vwah-tür de*r* fo*ng*k-syo*ng*
w	sometimes like English 'w' and sometimes like 'v': a) Washington b) wagon de marchandises (*goods van*)	wah-shi*ng*-ton vah-go*ng* de*r* mahr-shah*ng*-deez

x	a) like 'gz' when initial and followed by a vowel or h:	
	exempt de droits de douane (*free of customs duty*)	eg-zah*ng* de*r* drwah de*r* dwahn
	b) occasionally like 'ss': dix (*ten*)	deess
	c) occasionally like 'z': deuxième (*second*)	de*r*-zyem
	d) elsewhere like 'ks': expert-comptable (*chartered accountant*)	eks-pair ko*ng*-table*r*
y	like 'ee': hypothèque (*mortgage*)	ee-po-tek
z	as in English: zone industrielle (*industrial estate*)	zon a*ng*-dü-stree-yel

IMPORTANT: With the exception of c, f, l and r, consonants coming at the end of a word are not usually pronounced:

effecti̶f̶ (*workforce*), industrie̶l̶

BUT: crédi̶t̶, entrepô̶t̶

The French alphabet

This is the same as in English, but k and w are rare. You must know how to pronounce the alphabet as you will certainly have to spell your name in French. For example: JACKSON = zhee ah say kah ess oh en.

A	(ah)	H	(ahsh)	O	(oh)	V	(vay)
B	(bay)	I	(ee)	P	(pay)	W	(doobler-vay)
C	(say)	J	(zhee)	Q	(kü)	X	(eeks)
D	(day)	K	(kah)	R	(air)	Y	(ee-grek)
E	(er)	L	(el)	S	(ess)	Z	(zed)
F	(ef)	M	(em)	T	(tay)		
G	(zhay)	N	(en)	U	(ü)		

Looking for an agent (1)

> *Study this conversation in French for a few moments, then compare it with the English translation which follows. At this stage you only need to have a general idea of the meaning.*
>
> Mr Jackson, a British businessman, has an appointment with Madame Duval in Paris. As he enters the office he's greeted by Madame Duval's secretary.

Secrétaire:	Bonjour, Monsieur.
Mr Jackson:	Bonjour, Mademoiselle. Je suis Monsieur Jackson.
Secrétaire:	Pardon? Monsieur...?
Mr Jackson:	Jackson ... de la société britannique Excel-Equip. Voici ma carte. Je suis le directeur des ventes. J'ai rendez-vous avec Madame Duval à onze heures.
Secrétaire:	Ah, oui. Monsieur Jackson. Bien sûr. Vous avez téléphoné hier. Madame Duval vous attend. Elle est dans son bureau. Voulez-vous passer ici, s'il vous plaît? ... Attention à la marche.

TRANSLATION

Secretary:	Good morning (Monsieur).
Mr Jackson:	Good morning (Mademoiselle), I'm Mr Jackson.
Secretary:	Sorry? Mr ...?
Mr Jackson:	Jackson ... of the British company Excel-Equip. Here's my card. I'm the sales manager. I have an appointment (*literally* 'I have appointment') with Madame Duval at eleven o'clock.
Secretary:	Oh, yes, Mr Jackson. Of course. You telephoned yesterday. Madame Duval is expecting you. She's in her office. Will you come this way (*lit.* 'Will you pass by here') please? ... Be careful of the step.

Checklist 1

Masculine nouns:

1	le	*the* (used with masc. nouns)
2	le directeur	*the manager; director*
3	le rendez-vous	*the appointment*
4	le téléphone	*the telephone*
5	le bureau	*the office; desk*

Feminine nouns:

6	la	*the* (used with fem. nouns)
7	la directrice	*the manager; director*
8	la société	*the company*
9	la carte	*the card*
10	la vente	*the sale*
11	la marche	*the step*
	l'	*the* (see Checknote 3)
12	l'heure	*the hour*

Plural forms:

13	les	*the* (used with plural nouns)
14	les ventes	*the sales*

Adjectives:

15	britannique	*British*
16	mon (*m.*), ma (*f.*)	*my*
17	son (*m.*), sa (*f.*)	*his/her*

Verbs/verbal expressions:

18	je suis	*I am*
19	j'ai	*I have*
20	nous avons	*we have*
21	vous avez téléphoné	*you telephoned*
22	elle vous attend	*she's expecting you*
23	il/elle est	*he/she is*
24	Voulez-vous …?	*Will you …?*
25	passer	*to pass*

Other words/expressions:

26	pardon	*sorry*
27	voici	*here is/are*
28	bien sûr	*of course*
29	s'il vous plaît	*please*
30	attention (à)	*be careful (of)*
31	avec	*with*
32	dans	*in*
33	par	*by*
34	ici	*here*
	par ici	*this way*
35	hier	*yesterday*
36	de	*of, from*
37	du = de + le	*of the*
38	des = de + les	*of the (pl.)*
39	à	*at, to*
40	au = à + le	*at, to the*
41	onze	*eleven*
42	oui	*yes*
43	non	*no*
44	bonjour	*good morning/ afternoon*
45	Monsieur	*Mr* (also polite form of address to a man)
46	Madame	*Mrs* (also polite form of address to a married lady)
47	Mademoiselle	*Miss* (also polite form of address to a single lady)

Imitated Pronunciation: If you don't have the cassettes and you'd like help with the pronunciation of the words in this Checklist, turn to the Imitated Pronunciation section at the back of the book; the numbers against each word cross-refer.

CHECKNOTES

1 Greetings

As well as **bonjour** ('good morning' or 'good afternoon') you'll also need to know **bonsoir** ('good evening') and **bonne nuit** ('good night', said just before going to bed).

2 The verb **être** ('to be')

This verb is very important; it is also irregular - i.e. the various parts don't follow a clear-cut pattern - so you must learn it carefully. As shown in the Checklist, 'I am' is **je suis;** the rest of the present tense is as follows:

he is	**il est**
she is	**elle est**
we are	**nous sommes**
you are	**vous êtes**
they are	**ils sont**
they (*f.*) are	**elles sont**

3 The gender of French nouns

In French all nouns are either masculine or feminine, and words used in connection with nouns must reflect their gender.

'The' is expressed as follows:

le	(m. singular)	le contrat	*the contract*
la	(f. singular)	la banque	*the bank*
l'	(m. & f. sing. used before a vowel and normally before h)	l'achat	*the purchase*
les	(m. & f. plural)	les exportations	the exports

Unfortunately, there are few rules that can help you to determine the gender of French nouns. The best rule of all is to learn each noun and its gender together. Generally speaking, -e and -ion are feminine endings, although there are exceptions. Nouns denoting male persons are masculine and those which refer to female persons are feminine.

4 The plural

The plural in French is formed as follows:

a) By adding **s**: vente → ventes; banque → banque**s**.
b) By adding **x** to words ending in -au or -eu: bureau → bureaux.
The **s** and **x** are not pronounced, so the plural form sounds just like the singular.
c) By changing the ending -**al** to -**aux**: journal ('newspaper') → journaux.

Words already ending in -**s** or -**x** do not change: fois ('time') → fois ('times'); prix ('price') → prix ('prices').

5 The position of adjectives

In English you say 'the British company' but in French this is expressed as 'the company British'. In other words, the adjective usually comes <u>after</u> the noun. Note also that adjectives denoting nationality take a small letter in French:

la société britannique	*the British company*
un produit français	*a French product*

6 **Mon/ma/mes** ('my')

The French for 'my' also has to change according to the gender of the thing possessed and whether this noun is singular or plural:

mon bureau (*m.*)	*my office*
ma carte (*f.*)	*my card*
mes échantillons (*m. pl.*)	*my samples*

Note that the possessor's gender is immaterial. (See also Checknote 14, 'his/hers'.)

7 **Du/des, au/aux** ('of the', 'to the')

The words **de** and à combine with the definite article **le/les** as follows, with example sentences:

de + le   = **du**
de + les = **des**
à + le   = **au**
à + les   = **aux**

les termes (*m.*) du contrat	*the terms of the contract*
le directeur des ventes	*the sales manager*
au téléphone	*on the* (lit. *'at the'*) *telephone*
aux États-Unis	*to the United States*

8 The verb **avoir** ('to have')

J'ai ('I have') comes from **avoir**, another very important and irregular verb. Here's the rest of the present tense:

il/elle a	*he/she has*
nous avons	*we have*
vous avez	*you have*
ils/elles ont	*they have*

9 Numbers

Here are the numbers from 1 to 19:

1	**un**	7	**sept**	13	**treize**
	(une, *f.***)**	8	**huit**	14	**quatorze**
2	**deux**	9	**neuf**	15	**quinze**
3	**trois**	10	**dix**	16	**seize**
4	**quatre**	11	**onze**	17	**dix-sept**
5	**cinq**	12	**douze**	18	**dix-huit**
6	**six**			19	**dix-neuf**

Un/une is also used to express the English 'a/an'; note that the feminine form **(une) is** to be used with feminine nouns.

10 The time

Use the word **heure** to express the English 'o'clock', remembering that (unlike English) you shouldn't leave it out of the full phrase when expressing times:

(Il est) une heure	*(It's) one o'clock*
deux heures, etc	*two o'clock*
cinq heures et quart	*a quarter past five*
six heures et demie	*half past six*
sept heures moins le quart	*a quarter to seven*
huit heures dix	*ten past eight*
neuf heures moins cinq	*five to nine*

Note the following new words used in these phrases: **et** ('and'), **demi/demie** *f.* ('half'), **moins** ('minus', 'less'). Make a note also of:

à neuf heures du matin	*at nine o'clock in the morning*
à neuf heures du soir	*at nine o'clock in the evening*
à deux heures de l'après-midi	*at two o'clock in the afternoon*
À quelle heure?	*At what time?*

11 Verbs ending in -er

In French dictionaries you'll find thousands of verbs ending in **-er**, which is the equivalent of the English 'to'. Here are some examples:

parler	*to speak*	organiser	*to organize*
importer	*to import*	commander	*to order*
exporter	*to export*	installer	*to install*
téléphoner	*to telephone*	proposer	*to propose*

11a The present tense of -er verbs

This is how verbs ending in **-er** perform in the present tense. Learn this pattern thoroughly - it will pay great dividends. The regular endings are underlined.

je parl<u>e</u>	*I speak* or *am speaking*
il/elle téléphon<u>e</u>	*he/she telephones* or *is telephoning*
nous command<u>ons</u>	*we order, etc*
vous import<u>ez</u>	*you import, etc*
ils/elles export<u>ent</u>	*they export, etc*

11b The past tense of -er verbs

In the conversation with Mr Jackson the secretary said 'Vous avez téléphoné hier' ('You telephoned yesterday'). This is the past tense of the verb **téléphoner.** Verbs ending in **-er** form their past tense like this:

j'ai parl<u>é</u>	*I have spoken* or *I spoke*
Il/elle a import<u>é</u>	*he/she has imported* or *he/she imported*
nous avons export<u>é</u>	*we have exported, etc*
vous avez organis<u>é</u>	*you have organized, etc*
ils/elles ont install<u>é</u>	*they have installed, etc*

Study this past tense very carefully - you'll be using it all the time in business conversations with French people.

12 Verbs ending in -re

As we have pointed out, thousands of French verbs, in their dictionary form, end in -er. Thousands, yes - but <u>not all</u>. Some end in **-re** like **attendre** ('to expect') and **vendre** ('to sell'). These **-re** verbs have their own special pattern, shown in Checknote 12a.

12a Present/past tenses of **vendre, attendre**

Present:

j'attends	*I wait* or *I am waiting*
il/elle attend	*he/she waits* or *he/she is waiting*
nous vendons	*we sell, etc*
vous vendez	*you sell, etc*
ils/elles vendent	*they sell, etc*

Past:

j'ai attendu	*I have waited* or *I waited*
il/elle a attendu	*he/she has waited, etc*
nous avons vendu	*we have sold, etc*
vous avez vendu	*you have sold, etc*
ils/elles ont vendu	*they have sold, etc*

13 Some object pronouns (1)

In English you say 'he exports them', 'we order it', 'she sells them', but in French the object pronoun comes <u>before</u> the verb:

he exports them	il <u>les</u> exporte (lit. he <u>them</u> exports)
we order it	nous le/la commandons
she sells them	elle les vend
I'm expecting you	je vous attends

14 **Son/sa/ses** ('his/her')

These work in the same way as **mon/ma/mes** (see Checknote 6):

son télex (*m.*)	*his/her telex*
sa commande (*f.*)	*his/her order*
ses ventes (*pl.*)	*his/her sales*

Note that, when **ma** (my) and **sa** (his/her) come before a feminine word beginning with a vowel or silent **h**, they take the <u>masculine</u> form **mon** and **son**; this sounds much nicer to the French ear: **mon** entreprise (*f.*), **son** intention (*f.*). You'll find an example of this in Fluency Practice 11.

Comprehension Practice 1

Re-read or listen again to the conversation between the secretary and Mr Jackson at the beginning of this Unit, and then say whether the following statements are true (vrai) or false (faux). Just before you begin, study the following:

New words:

la carte de visite	the visiting card
la publicité	the advertising
allemand (allemande, *f.*)	German

Ready?

1	Monsieur Jackson a une carte de visite.	vrai/faux
2	Monsieur Jackson est le directeur de la publicité.	vrai/faux
3	Il a rendez-vous avec Madame Duval à neuf heures.	vrai/faux
4	Excel-Equip est une société allemande.	vrai/faux
5	Madame Duval est dans son bureau.	vrai/faux
6	Elle attend Monsieur Jackson.	vrai/faux

FLUENCY PRACTICE 1

We're going to ask you now to introduce some of your colleagues, but first learn the French for four important posts:

le chef du personnel	*the head of personnel*
le directeur de la publicité	*the advertising manager*
le président-directeur général (le P.-D.G.)	*the chairman and managing director*
l'analyste en études de marché	*the market research analyst*

N.B.: Both men and women would say 'Je suis le chef ...', 'Je suis le président-directeur général'.

Now introduce your colleagues like this: 'Voici David Smith, le directeur des ventes'.

1 Mary Green, the head of personnel.
2 Peter Brown, the advertising manager.
3 Rosalind and Amanda, the two secretaries.
4 Barbara White, the market research analyst.
5 Yourself, the chairman and managing director.

And now, answer these questions (**Qui** asks 'Who'):

6 Qui est Mary Green?
7. Qui est David Smith?

8 Qui sont Rosalind et Amanda?
9 Et qui êtes-vous?

FLUENCY PRACTICE 2

Imagine that you and your colleagues have just received a delivery of office equipment from France. The equipment is as follows: 10 calculators, 8 micro-computers, 6 word processors, 4 fax machines. The French clerk telephones you to check that you've received the correct number of items. Answer the questions. But first, learn these French words:

le micro-ordinateur	*the micro-computer*
le traitement de texte	*the word processor*
le télécopieur	*the fax machine*
la calculatrice	*the calculator*
combien (de)	*how much/many*

Ready for the exercise ...?

1 Combien de calculatrices a David?
2 Combien de micro-ordinateurs a Mary?
3 Combien de traitements de texte ont Rosalind et Amanda?
4 Combien de télécopieurs avez-vous?

Bon, c'est juste alors!   Good, it's correct then!

FLUENCY PRACTICE 3

You'll be pleased to hear that you can often guess the meaning of a French word just by looking at it. This is because thousands of French and English words have identical or very similar spellings. The pronunciation, however, is usually <u>very</u> different!

In this exercise we'd like you to concentrate on pronunciation. With the help of the Key at the back of the book, practise saying the following French words - but make sure they sound like French words, not like their English equivalents. Say them aloud if possible.

banque	signature	catalogue	compétitif	production
crédit	compagnie	brochure	industrie	distribution
contrat	firme	importations	client	garantie
agent	robot	exportations	chèque	finances
photocopieuse	marchandises	qualité	ingénieur	signer

FLUENCY PRACTICE 4

Complete the following sentences, but study these words first:

du, de la, de l', des	some
bon (m.), bonne (f.)	good
le (la) commerçant(e)	the shopkeeper
le fonds (de commerce)	the business
l'exposition (f.)	the exhibition
l'usine (f.)	the factory

1 Nous (organize) l'exposition.
2 Ils (order) deux photocopieuses*.
3 Vous (import) les télécopieurs français
4 La société (sells) des marchandises de bonne qualité.
5 L'ingénieur (has telephoned) à l'usine.
6 Je (signed) le contrat.
7 Le commerçant (has sold) son fonds.
8 Les clients (waited) une heure.

*Both photocopieur and photocopieuse exist but the latter is more usual.

FLUENCY PRACTICE 5

Imagine you have an appointment with Monsieur Martin at three o'clock. Take part in the following conversation with his secretary. You'll need to learn these three words first: **merci** ('thank you'), **votre** ('your'), **la tête** ('the head').

Secretary: **Bonjour, Monsieur.**
You: Good afternoon (Madame). I'm John Brown. I have an appointment with Monsieur Martin at three o'clock.
Secretary: **Oui, Monsieur. Avez-vous une carte de visite, s'il vous plaît?**
You: Yes, here's my card.
Secretary: **Merci.**
You: I'm the chairman and managing director of Brown Engineering Ltd.
Secretary: **Oui. Voulez-vous passer par ici, s'il vous plaît, Monsieur Brown.**
You: Thank you.
Secretary: **Attention à votre tête!**

Looking for an agent (2)

Now that your recollection of the French you learned some years ago is reawakening, it looks like being easier than you imagined. Be positive! But don't rush things; if you find the Fluency Practice exercises slow you down, go through the Checknotes again. Unit 2 tells you about adjectives and how they must 'agree' with the noun, the past tense and making requests.

The secretary takes Mr Jackson along to Madame Duval's office. She knocks on the door ...

Mme Duval:	Oui, entrez.
Secrétaire:	Monsieur Jackson de la société Excel-Equip est arrivé.
Mme Duval:	Tiens, il est déjà onze heures? Comme le temps passe vite. Entrez, entrez, Monsieur Jackson!
Mr Jackson:	Bonjour, Madame Duval. Enchanté de faire votre connaissance.
Mme Duval:	Enchantée, Monsieur Jackson. Asseyez-vous. Vous prenez un café?
Mr Jackson:	Volontiers. Un café crème, s'il vous plaît, sans sucre ... j'ai apporté ma sucrette.
Mme Duval:	Eh bien, nous avons déjà parlé au téléphone de votre intention d'exporter vos produits sur le marché français, n'est-ce pas? Pouvez-vous me parler un peu de votre entreprise?
Mr Jackson:	Oui, bien sûr. Nous nous spécialisons dans la bureautique. Nous fabriquons des calculatrices, des machines à écrire électroniques, des micro-ordinateurs, des télécopieurs, des traitements de texte, etc ... c'est à dire tout le matériel pour l'entreprise de l'An 2000.
Mme Duval:	Je vois que vous vous spécialisez vraiment dans la technologie de pointe. Mais pourquoi avez-vous décidé d'exporter vos produits en France?

TRANSLATION

Mme Duval:	Yes, come in.
Secretary:	Mr Jackson from the Excel-Equip company has arrived.
Mme Duval:	Oh, is it already eleven o'clock? How quickly time passes. Come in, come in, Mr Jackson!
Mr Jackson:	Good morning, Madame Duval. Delighted to make your acquaintance.
Mme Duval:	How do you do, Mr Jackson? Sit down. Will you have a coffee (*lit.* 'You take a coffee')?
Mr Jackson:	With pleasure. A white coffee please, without sugar ... I've brought my sweetener.
Mme Duval:	Well, we've already talked on the telephone about your intention to export your products onto the French market, haven't we? Can you tell me (*lit.* 'speak to me') a little about your firm?
Mr Jackson:	Yes, of course. We specialise in office automation. We manufacture calculators, electronic typewriters, micro-computers, fax machines, word processors, etc ... that's to say, all the equipment for the company of the Year 2000.
Mme Duval:	I see that you really specialize in advanced technology. But why have you decided to export your products to France?

Checklist 2

Masculine nouns:

48	le temps	*time*
49	le café	*coffee*
50	le sucre	*sugar*
51	le produit	*product*
52	le marché	*market*
53	le matériel	*equipment*
54	l'an	*year*

Feminine nouns:

55	la connaissance	*acquaintance*
56	la sucrette	*sweetener*
57	la bureautique	*office automation*
58	la machine à écrire	*typewriter*
59	la technologie de pointe	*advanced technology*
60	la crème	*cream*
61	l'intention	*intention*
62	l'entreprise	*firm, company*
63	La France	*France*

Adjectives:

64	enchanté	*delighted*
65	électronique	*electronic*
66	votre (*m. & f. sing.*)	*your*
67	vos (*pl.*)	*your*
68	tout (*m.*), toute (*f.*), tous (*m. pl.*), toutes (*f. pl.*)	*all*

Adverbs:

69	vite	*quickly*

70	volontiers	*with pleasure*
71	vraiment	*really*

Prepositions:

72	sans	*without*
73	sur	*on, onto*
74	de	*of, from, about*
75	en	*in, to*
76	pour	*for*

Other words/expressions:

77	un peu	*a little*
78	Pourquoi ...?	*Why ...?*
79	tiens	*oh (as an expression of surprise)*
80	comme	*how, as*
81	eh bien	*well*
82	n'est-ce pas?	*isn't it? aren't you?, etc.*
83	asseyez-vous	*sit down*
84	déjà	*already*
85	c'est à dire	*that's to say*
86	que je vois que ...	*that I see that ...*
87	mais	*but*

Verbs:

88	entrer	*to enter*
89	arriver	*to arrive*
90	passer	*to pass*
91	apporter	*to bring*
92	fabriquer	*to manufacture*
93	décider	*to decide*
94	se spécialiser	*to specialize (see Checknote 20)*

Irregular verbs:

95 faire (*to do, make*)
present: je fais, il fait, nous faisons, vous faites, ils font *I do, he does, etc.*
past: j'ai fait *I have done, I did, etc.*

96 prendre (*to take*)
present: je prends, il prend, nous prenons, vous prenez, ils prennent
I take, he takes, etc
past: j'ai pris *I have taken, I took*

97 pouvoir (*to be able*)
present: je peux, il peut, nous pouvons, vous pouvez, ils peuvent
I can, he can, etc
past: j'ai pu *I have been able*

98 voir (*to see*)
present: je vois, il voit, nous voyons, vous voyez, ils voient. *I see,*
he sees, etc
past: j'ai vu *I have seen, I saw*

Remember - if you're unsure of the pronunciation of any word, check it against our imitated system at the back of this book. Or, listen to the tape!

CHECKNOTES

15 Agreement of adjectives

Adjectives in French have to agree with the noun they're linked to. If, for instance, the noun is feminine and plural, then the adjective must have the feminine, plural form. To make an adjective feminine we normally add -e (unless it already ends in -e):

important (*m.*) → **importante** (*f.*)
urgent (*m.*) → **urgente** (*f.*)

Examples:

un document important	*an important document*
un télex urgent	*an urgent telex*
une lettre importante	*an important letter*
une télécopie urgente	*an urgent fax*

To make an adjective plural we usually add -s (unless it already ends in -s):

des employés compétents	*(some) competent employees*
des machines performantes	*(some) efficient machines*

Remember that adjectives in French usually come after the noun (but not always!).

When you have time, study these additional rules for forming the feminine of adjectives:

a) adjectives ending in -x change the -x to -se:

dangereux (*m.*), dangereuse (*f.*) *dangerous*

b) final **-f** changes to **-ve**:

    compétitif (*m.*), compétitive (*f.*) *competitive*

c) final **-er** becomes **-ère**:

    dernier (*m.*), dernière (*f.*) *last*

d) final **-et** becomes **-ète**:

    secret (*m.*), secrète (*f.*) *secret*

16 Making requests

If you want to tell someone to do something, just drop the **vous** of the present tense:

Entrez.	*Come in.*
Fixez un rendez-vous.	*Arrange an appointment.*
Téléphonez à la filiale.	*Telephone the subsidiary company.*
Vendez toutes les calculatrices.	*Sell all the calculators.*

Of course, you can make your request more polite (and probably get the task completed more quickly), by using one of the following expressions:

Voulez-vous ...?	*Will/Would you ...?*
Voulez-vous bien ...?	*Would you kindly ...?*
Pourriez-vous ...?	*Could you ...?*

Examples:

    Voulez-vous organiser une réunion ?
    Would you arrange a meeting?

    Pourriez-vous commander dix disquettes?
    Could you order ten floppy disks?

17 The past tense (2)

In Checknotes 11b and 12a you learned how to talk about the past. You'll remember that you have to use part of the verb **avoir** ('to have'), together with the verb ending **-é** or **-u** (the past participle). See also Checknote 22. Here's a reminder - but first note these new words:

le chiffre	*figure*	**la lettre**	*letter*
le magnétophone	*tape recorder*	**les affaires** (*f.*)	*business*

    J'ai dicté trois lettres.
    I have dictated three letters.

La société a doublé son chiffre d'affaires.
The company has doubled its turnover.

Nous avons vendu douze magnétophones.
We sold twelve tape recorders.

However, there's a small group of verbs, many denoting motion, that form their past tense with **être** ('to be'). The following, some of which are irregular, are the most important:

arriver *to arrive*	je suis arrivé *I arrived/have arrived**
retourner *to return*	il est retourné *he returned**
monter *to go up*	elle est montée *she went up**
rester *to remain*	nous sommes restés *we remained**
aller (irreg) *to go*	vous êtes allé *you went**
partir (irreg) *to leave*	ils sont partis *they left**
venir (irreg) *to come*	elles sont venues *they (f.) came**
revenir (irreg) *to come back*	je suis revenu *I came back**

*Remember that the past tense can be expressed by 'he has remained', 'she has gone up', etc.

The past participle of these verbs requires an **-e** when the subject is feminine, and an **-s** when the subject is plural:

Le directeur général est allé à la foire commerciale.	*The managing director has gone to the trade fair.*
La facture est arrivée hier.	*The invoice arrived yesterday.*
Je suis arrivée à cinq heures.	*I (f.) arrived at five o'clock.*
Les deux secrétaires sont restées au bureau jusqu'à huit heures.	*The two secretaries remained at the office until eight o'clock*

18 Enchanté de ('delighted to'), content de ('pleased to'), etc.

Some adjectives in French require **de** to express the English 'to'. Study the following:

Je suis enchanté de faire votre connaissance.	*I'm delighted to meet you.*
Nous sommes contents d'avoir reçu** votre commande du 2 janvier.	*We are pleased to have received your order of the 2nd January.*
Nous sommes désolés de vous informer que ...	*We are sorry to inform you that ...*

Note that **de** becomes **d'** before a vowel or silent h.

Learn the verb **recevoir ('to receive'):

Present: je reçois, il reçoit, nous recevons, vous recevez,
  ils reçoivent
Past: j'ai reçu

Make a note also of:

heureux de	*happy to*
triste de	*sad to*
avoir l'intention de	*to intend to*
avoir l'occasion de	*to have the opportunity to*
avoir le plaisir de	*to have pleasure in*
il est possible de	*it is possible to*
il est impossible de	*it is impossible to*
il est temps de	*it is time to*

19 To me/to you/to him, etc

Study the following:

Pouvez-vous me donner la date exacte du télex?	*Can you give me (to me) the exact date of the telex?*
Nous pouvons vous livrer ces marchandises (*f. pl.*) le mois prochain.	*We can deliver these goods to you next month.*
Est-il possible de nous envoyer des échantillons (*m. pl.*) aujourd'hui?	*Is it possible to send us (to us) some samples today?*
Je lui ai parlé hier de notre nouveau modèle.	*I spoke to him/to her yesterday about our new model.*
Nous pouvons leur accorder une remise de 10%.	*We can grant them (to them) a discount of 10%.*

You'll see from the above examples that:

'to me' is expressed by **me** (**m'** before a vowel or silent h)
'to you' by **vous**
'to us' by **nous**
'to him/her' by **lui**
'to them' by **leur**

Note the position of the above words in the French sentence.

Comprehension Practice 2

*Re-read the conversation at the beginning of this unit (or listen to it again on the cassette), note the new words below and then answer the questions - **vrai ou faux?** - true or false?*

New words:

le thé   tea
Japonais   Japanese

1 Monsieur Jackson est arrivé à huit heures.
2 Il est enchanté de faire la connaissance de Madame Duval.
3 Il prend un thé avec du sucre.
4 Monsieur Jackson a déjà parlé à Madame Duval au téléphone.
5 La société Excel -Equip se spécialise dans la bureautique.
6 Monsieur Jackson a l'intention d'exporter son matériel sur le marché japonais.

FLUENCY PRACTICE 6

New words:

l'ordre (*m.*) du jour	*agenda*
les cadres (*m.*)	*managerial staff*
à Londres	*in London*
préparer	*to prepare*
mais bien sûr	*(but) of course*

Using the expression **Pourriez-vous ...?** ('Could you ...?'), ask your secretary:

1 to telephone Mr Jackson in London.
2 to prepare the agenda for the meeting.
3 to arrange a meeting with all the managerial staff
4 to bring you a coffee.
(The secretary) Mais bien sûr, Monsieur!

FLUENCY PRACTICE 7

New words:

l'acheteur (*m.*) potentiel	*potential buyer*
l'atelier (*m.*)	*workshop*
la standardiste	*the switchboard operator*
visiter	*to visit*

Complete these sentences:

1 La standardiste (arrived) à onze heures.
2 Le Directeur (has left) visiter les ateliers.
3 Les acheteurs potentiels (have gone) à la foire commerciale.
4 L'ingénieur (came back) de l'usine aujourd'hui.

FLUENCY PRACTICE 8

New words:

l'employé (*m.*)	*employee*
nécessaire	*necessary*
aider	*to help*
annuler	*to cancel*
se recycler	*to retrain (oneself)*

Complete the following:

1 Notre entreprise (intends to) importer tout le matériel nécessaire.
2 Le chef du personnel (is happy to) aider les employés à se recycler.
3 (It's impossible to) annuler la commande.
4 Nous (have pleasure in) vous informer que nous pouvons vous
   accorder une remise de 10%.

FLUENCY PRACTICE 9

Cover up the translation and then put all the English examples in
Checknote 15 back into French IN WRITING.

FLUENCY PRACTICE 10

Cover up the translation and then put all the French examples in
Checknote 19 back into English ORALLY.

FLUENCY PRACTICE 11

One of your colleagues has accidentally spilt some of his coffee
over part of a report which has just arrived on your desk. The
report is a little difficult to read now. Can you decipher the
missing words and syllables?

Monsieur Jackson est --- au bureau de Madame Duval à onze ---.
Il a --- de la société Excel - Equip. La société --- tout le --- pour
l'entreprise de l'An 2000, c'est à dire des cal ---, des machines à
--- ---, des micro-ordinateurs, des --- copieurs, des traitements de
texte, etc. Monsieur Jackson a parlé de son intention d' --- ses
produits sur le marché français.

UNIT 3

Reaching agreement

> Unit 3 introduces the -ir verbs and reflexives ('I – myself'), simple
> negatives, comparisons and question-forming.
>
> Mr Jackson continues his conversation with Mme Duval and
> explains why he wants to market his products in France.

Mr Jackson:	Eh bien, comme je vous l'ai déjà mentionné, notre entreprise est en pleine expansion. Nous avons des filiales dans tout le Royaume-Uni et je suis certain que nous avons une bonne réputation. Notre société mère est basée aux États-Unis, à New York, et le programme d'expansion est en partie financé par les Américains. Nos produits sont performants et nos prix sont compétitifs. Bref, nous sommes bien établis sur le marché britannique. Mais notre chiffre d'affaires n'augmente pas beaucoup en ce moment à cause de l'inflation et des difficultés économiques du pays.
Mme Duval:	Vous pensez donc qu'il est temps de commencer à exporter en France?
Mr Jackson:	Oui, c'est ça. 1992 est une occasion à ne pas manquer et les Français sont nos voisins les plus proches ... du moins géographiquement!
Mme Duval:	Oui, vous avez raison. Il faut franchir les frontières. Comme vous le savez, notre société vend des produits de fabrication française, similaires aux vôtres. Mais nous pouvons certainement intégrer la technologie britannique à notre gamme de produits ... avec les modifications nécessaires, bien sûr. Après tout, les Français sont déjà familiarisés avec la terminologie anglo-saxonne, c'est à dire avec le franglais ... avec le fax, le marketing, le management, le business, etc.

TRANSLATION

Mr Jackson:	Well, as I've already mentioned to you (*lit.* 'mentioned it to you'), our firm is expanding fast (*lit.*'is in full expansion').

We have subsidiary companies throughout (*lit.* 'in all') the United Kingdom and I'm certain that we have a good reputation. Our parent company is based in the U.S.A., in New York, and the expansion programme is being partly financed by the Americans. Our products are efficient and our prices are competitive. In a word, we're well established on the British market. But our turnover isn't increasing much at the moment because of inflation and the economic difficulties of the country.

Mme Duval: You think therefore that it's time to begin to export to France?

Mr Jackson: Yes, that's right. 1992 is an opportunity not to be missed (*lit.* 'an opportunity not to miss') and the French are our nearest neighbours ... at least geographically!

Mme Duval: Yes, you're right. One must cross (*lit.* 'It is necessary to cross') frontiers. As you know (*lit.* 'As you know it'), our company sells products (*lit.* 'some products') of French manufacture, similar to yours. But we can certainly add British technology to our range of products ... with the necessary modifications, of course! After all, the French are already familiar with Anglo-Saxon terminology, that's to say with Franglais ... with 'fax', 'marketing', 'management', 'business', etc.

Checklist 3

Masculine nouns:

99	le pays	*country*
100	le voisin	*neighbour*
101	le moment	*moment*
102	le franglais	*Franglais*
103	le Français	*Frenchman*

Feminine nouns:

104	la réputation	*reputation*
105	la difficulté	*difficulty*
106	la frontière	*frontier*
107	la fabrication	*manufacture*
108	la technologie	*technology*
109	la terminologie	*terminology*
110	la gamme	*range*
111	la modification	*modification*
112	l'expansion	*expansion*
113	l'inflation	*inflation*
114	l'occasion	*opportunity*

Countries:

115	le Royaume-Uni	*United Kingdom*

Adjectives:

116	anglo-saxon, -onne (*f.*)	*Anglo-Saxon*
117	plein	*full*
118	certain	*certain*
119	économique	*economic*
120	proche	*near*
121	similaire	*similar*
122	nécessaire	*necessary*
123	familiarisé (avec)	*familiar (with)*
124	bon (*m.*), bonne (*f.*)	*good*
125	mauvais	*bad*

34

Adverbs:

126	géograph-iquement	geograph-ically
127	certainement	certainly

Other words/expressions:

128	beaucoup	much/many
129	à cause de	because of
130	donc	therefore
131	ne (n') ... pas	not
132	bref	in a word
133	plus	more
134	c'est ça	that's right
135	du moins	at least
136	après tout	after all

137	bien établi	well established
138	en ce moment	at the moment
139	le/la vôtre	yours
140	les vôtres	yours (pl.)

Verbs:

141	mentionner	to mention
142	augmenter	to increase
143	penser	to think
144	commencer	to begin
145	manquer	to miss
146	intégrer	to integrate
147	franchir	to cross
148	avoir raison	to be right
149	avoir tort	to be wrong

Irregular verbs:

150 falloir *to be necessary*
   present: il faut *it's necessary*
   past: il a fallu *it was necessary*
151 savoir *to know*
   present: je sais, il sait, nous savons, vous savez, ils savent *I know, he knows etc.*
   past: j'ai su *I have known/I knew*

CHECKNOTES

20 Reflexive verbs

Préparer means 'to prepare' but **se préparer** means 'to prepare oneself'. Verbs that have this **se** attached to them are called reflexive verbs. The present tense set out below will show you the words for 'myself', 'himself' etc.

je me prépare	*I prepare myself*
il/elle se prépare	*he/she prepares himself/herself*
nous nous préparons	*we prepare ourselves*
vous vous préparez	*you prepare yourself/yourselves*
ils/elles se préparent	*they prepare themselves*

Note that **se** becomes **s'** before a vowel or silent h.

It's easy to understand why verbs like **se préparer**, **se recycler** ('to retrain oneself'), **s'organiser** ('to organise oneself') have the **se**

attached - it means 'oneself'. But sometimes a verb will be reflexive when you wouldn't have expected it to be so.
For example:

se spécialiser (dans)	to specialize (in)
se reporter (à)	to refer (to)
se documenter (sur)	to obtain information (about)
s'élever (à)	to amount (to)

An important thing to remember about reflexive verbs is that, like the group of verbs mentioned in Checknote 17, they form their past tense with **être**:

Le directeur commercial s'est documenté sur le nouveau copieur.
The sales manager obtained information about the new copier.

Nous nous sommes spécialisés dans la bureautique.
We specialized in office automation.

The past participle of reflexive verbs agrees in gender and number with the preceding direct object. For example:

nous <u>nous</u> sommes spécialis<u>és</u>
elle <u>s</u>'est recycl<u>ée</u>.

21 Colours

Here are some useful colours; remember that they are adjectives and so must agree with their noun (see Checknote 15):

bleu	blue
vert	green
gris	grey, gray
jaune	yellow
blanc (*m.*) blanche (*f.*)	white

22 Verbs ending in -ir

In Checknotes 11 and 12 we talked about verbs which end in **-er** and **-re** when you look them up in French dictionaries. Some verbs, however, have **-ir** as their 'to' -form (the infinitive). This is how **-ir** verbs perform:

Present tense: **établir** *(to establish)*

j'établis I establish, etc.
il/elle établit
nous établissons
vous établissez
ils/elles établissent

Past tense: **établir**

j'ai établi *I have established, I established*
il/elle a établi
nous avons établi
vous avez établi
ils/elles ont établi

Here are some more important **-ir** verbs:

finir (*to finish*)
choisir (*to choose*)
bâtir (*to build*)
franchir (*to cross*)

23 The negative

To form the negative in French we place **ne** (**n'** before a vowel or silent h) in front of the verb and **pas** after:

> Les machines ne sont pas performantes.
> *The machines are not efficient.*

> Nous ne sommes pas bien implantés sur le marché français.
> *We're not well established on the French market.*

> Notre chiffre d'affaires n'augmente pas beaucoup.
> *Our turnover isn't increasing much.*

Note the position of the **ne** and **pas** in the past tense (**la lettre**, 'letter'; **répondre**, 'to reply'):

> Ils n'ont pas répondu à notre lettre.
> *They haven't replied to our letter.*

But **ne** and **pas** do not separate when they're linked to the 'to' -form of a verb:

> 1992 est une occasion à ne pas manquer.
> *1992 is an opportunity not to be missed.*

24 Verbs followed by de

In Checknote 18 we showed that many adjectives in French are linked to the 'to' -form of the verb by **de**:

> Nous sommes contents de pouvoir participer à ce projet.
> *We're pleased to be able to participate in this project.*

(Remember, however, that the normal meaning of **de** is 'of' or 'from').

This same **de** is used to link two verbs. Learn the following:

décider de	*to decide to (do)*
conseiller de	*to advise to (do)*
demander de	*to ask to (do)*
refuser de	*to refuse to (do)*
cesser de	*to stop (doing)*
éviter de	*to avoid (doing)*
proposer de	*to suggest (doing)*
empêcher de	*to prevent from (doing)*

Examples:

Nous avons décidé d'exporter nos produits en France.	*We've decided to export our goods to France.*
Je vous conseille de contacter tous les cadres.	*I advise you to contact all the managerial staff.*
Il faut éviter d'augmenter les prix.	*We must avoid increasing the prices.*

25 Expressions followed by à

As we've already seen, many adjectives and verbs are followed by **de** but there are also quite a few which take **à** to translate 'to' (and sometimes 'in').

Study the following:

être prêt à	*to be ready to*
être disposé à	*to be willing to*
avoir de la difficulté à	*to have difficulty (in)*
avoir du mal à	*to have difficulty (in)*

Note also:

commencer à	*to begin to*
continuer à	*to continue to*
hésiter à	*to hesitate to*
inviter à	*to invite to*
aider à	*to help to*
réussir à	*to succeed (in)*

Examples

Il est temps de commencer à exporter.	*It's time to begin exporting (lit. 'to begin to export').*
Nous sommes disposés à discuter de la possibilité d'une fusion entre nos deux compagnies.	*We're willing to discuss the possibility of a merger between our two companies.*

26 Comparison

In English comparisons are made by adding **-er** to the adjective or by using 'more'/'less'. In French we simply put **plus** ('more') or **moins** ('less') in front of the adjective.

Examples:

Cette usine est grande.	*This factory is large.*
Cette usine est plus grande.	*This factory is larger.*
Ce projet est intéressant.	*This project is interesting.*
Ce projet est moins intéressant.	*This project is less interesting.*

Incidentally, notice how we translate 'this' ('that')/'these' ('those'):

ce (*m.*)	*this (that)*
cet (*m.* before a vowel/silent h)	*this (that)*
cette (*f.*)	*this (that)*
ces (*m.* & *f. pl.*)	*these (those)*

Examples:

ce répondeur (*m.*) téléphonique	*this answerphone*
cet ordinateur (*m.*)	*this computer*
cette télécopie (*f.*)	*this fax*
ces employés (*pl.*)	*these employees*

We translate 'than' by **que**:

Le prix est plus important que la date de livraison.	*The price is more important than the delivery date.*

'Most' or '-est' are expressed by **le/la/les plus**:

Cette imprimante laser est le modèle le plus récent.	*This laser printer is the most recent model.*
Les Français sont nos voisins les plus proches.	*The French are our nearest neighbours.*

The comparison of adverbs follows the same pattern as adjectives:

Le cerveau humain fonctionne plus lentement que les ordinateurs.	*The human brain functions more slowly than computers.*

'Most' or '-est' used with adverbs is always expressed as <u>le</u> **plus**:

Les employés japonais travaillent le plus rapidement de tous.	*The Japanese employees work the fastest of all.*

27 Adverbs (1)

Do you remember the French for 'really', 'rapidly', 'geographically'? The correct answer is: **vraiment, rapidement, géographiquement.** From these you'll have noticed that adverbs in French are usually formed by adding **-ment** to the adjective; this **-ment** is the equivalent of -ly in English. However, if the adjective ends in a consonant, then the **-ment** is attached to the feminine form:

certain	certaine (f.)	**certainement**	*certainly*
immédiat	immédiate (f.)	**immédiatement**	*immediately*
complet	complète (f.)	**complètement**	*completely*
dangereux	dangereuse (f.)	**dangereusement**	*dangerously*

28 Falloir (to be necessary)

Falloir is a very important irregular verb. You'll hear it all the time in your conversations with the French. The form of this verb you meet most often is **il faut** which means 'it's necessary', or '(we, you, they, someone, etc.) must'. For example:

Il faut franchir les frontières.
One must cross frontiers (or frontiers must be crossed).

Il faut augmenter notre chiffre d'affaires.
We must increase our turnover.

Il faut intégrer la technologie britannique à votre gamme de produits.
You must add British technology to your range of products.

Il faut juguler l'inflation.
Inflation must be checked.

The past tense of **il faut** is **il a fallu:**

Il a fallu recruter du personnel supplémentaire.
It was necessary to recruit additional staff.

The negative form **il ne faut pas** means 'one (etc.) must not'.

29 Asking questions

In conversational French questions are often asked simply by using a rising intonation in the voice. Compare the following:

Statement: **Vos prix sont compétitifs.**   *Your prices are competitive.*
Question: **Vos prix sont compétitifs?**   *Are your prices competitive?*

Other examples:

Votre société est en pleine expansion?
Is your company expanding fast?

Votre chiffre d'affaires augmente en ce moment?
Is your turnover increasing at the moment?

See Checknote 31 for other ways of asking questions.

30 Some/any

We saw briefly in Fluency Practice 4 that 'some' is translated by **du, de la, de l', des**. For example:

Nous avons importé du mobilier   *We imported some new office*
de bureau neuf.   *furniture.*

Nous avons acheté des classeurs.   *We bought some filing cabinets.*

Note the new vocabulary in these examples: **le mobilier de bureau**, 'office furniture'; **neuf, neuve** (*f.*), '(brand-) new'; **acheter**, 'to buy'.

'Some' is frequently omitted in English but it must always be expressed in French:

Nous fabriquons des produits   *We manufacture high quality goods.*
de haute qualité.

After a negative, **du/de la/de l'/des** become **de**; in other words, 'any' in a negative sentence is translated by **de**:

Nous ne vendons pas de   *We don't sell any Japanese*
produits japonais.   *products.*

Comprehension Practice 3

Study the new words and then answer the questions. Note that (a)
il/elle *mean 'it' when referring to things, and (b)* ***son/sa/ses*** *mean*
'its' when referring to things.

New words:

le mot	*word*
Pourquoi pas?	*Why not?*
intégrer	*to integrate*
citer	*to quote*

1 La société Excel-Equip est en pleine expansion?

2 Elle a une mauvaise réputation?

3 Ses produits sont bien implantés sur le marché britannique?

4 Son chiffre d'affaires augmente en ce moment?

5 Pourquoi pas?

6 Il est temps de commencer à exporter à l'étranger?

7 Qui sont nos voisins les plus proches?

8 Madame Duval vend des produits de fabrication japonaise?

9 Elle est prête à intégrer la technologie britannique à sa gamme de produits?

10 Vous pouvez citer quatre mots de franglais?

FLUENCY PRACTICE 12

New word:

la formation   *training*

Using the expression **Nous nous spécialisons dans ...**, tell your potential customer that you specialize in:

a) the manufacture of electronic typewriters
b) office automation
c) advanced technology
d) staff training

FLUENCY PRACTICE 13

New words:

le concurrent	*competitor*
le franc	*franc*
le service après-vente	*after-sales service*
la correspondance	*correspondence*
espagnol	*Spanish*

Answer these questions in the same way as the following example, in the person indicated by the pronoun set in parentheses:

Vous vous reportez à votre dernière lettre? **(je)**
Are you referring to your last letter?
Oui, je me reporte à ma dernière lettre.
Yes, I'm referring to my last letter.

1 Vous vous reportez à votre dernière lettre? **(nous)**
2 Votre secrétaire s'occupe de toute la correspondance espagnole? **(elle)**
3 Vous vous êtes documentés sur le service après-vente de nos concurrents? **(nous)**
4 La facture s'élève à 5.000 francs? **(elle)**

FLUENCY PRACTICE 14

New words:

le prix de revient	*cost price*
l'informaticien	*computer scientist*
expérimenté	*experienced*

Match the words in the first column with those in the second:

a) Le directeur des ventes
b) Nous

e) franchissons les frontières.
f) ont choisi l'informaticien le plus expérimenté.

c) La réunion
d) Le Directeur et le chef du personnel

g) établit le prix de revient.
h) a fini à 4 heures.

FLUENCY PRACTICE 15

New words:

les conditions de paiement	*terms of payment*
l'informatique	*computer science, data processing*

Imagine there's a difference of opinion between you and one of your colleagues. When he/she makes a statement, you disagree, like this:

Notre entreprise est en pleine expansion.
Our firm is expanding fast.
Non, notre entreprise n'est pas en pleine expansion!
No, our firm is not expanding fast!

1 Nos concurrents sont bien implantés sur le marché espagnol.
2 J'ai raison.
3 Ils ont répondu à notre lettre.
4 Le prix est plus important que la date de livraison.
5 Nous nous spécialisons dans l'informatique.
6 Le client a accepté nos conditions de paiement.

FLUENCY PRACTICE 16

Cover up the translation and then put all the French examples in Checknotes 24 and 25 back into English.

FLUENCY PRACTICE 17

Cover up the translation and then put all the English examples in Checknote 26 back into French.

FLUENCY PRACTICE 18

New words:

le rapport   *report*
faire un inventaire   *to make an inventory*

Imagine that you need to reprimand some of your staff because certain things have not been done. Do it like this:

Vous n'avez pas contacté les clients.   *You haven't contacted the clients.*
Il faut contacter les clients!   *You must contact the clients!*

1 Vous n'avez pas augmenté le prix.
2 Vous n'avez pas répondu au télex.
3 Vous n'avez pas parlé de la possibilité d'une fusion entre nos deux sociétés.
4 Vous n'avez pas fait l'inventaire.
5 Vous n'avez pas fini le rapport.

Confirmation of agreement:
Letter writing

In this unit we concentrate on letter writing, explain some more question forms, and help you ask about details of commission, delivery and terms of payment.

Mr Jackson, who is now back in London, has received a letter from Mme Duval confirming that their company, France-Burotic, is happy to market Excel-Equip office machines in France. Mr Jackson replies and confirms the main points of their discussions. This is his letter:

EXCEL - EQUIP
LIMITED

400 Regent Street
London W1R 6XZ
Telephone: 071 654 3210 Telex: 1234 Fax: 071 765 4321

A DIVISION OF THE EXCEL—EQUIP CORPORATION, NEW YORK

Vos réfs: HD/12
Nos réfs: PJ/JL

Madame Hélène DUVAL
Directrice des Achats
FRANCE-BUROTIC
rue du Commerce
75015 PARIS, France

Objet: Votre lettre du 28 Mars

Londres, le 3 Avril 1990

Chère Madame,

Nous vous remercions de votre lettre du 28 Mars dans laquelle vous acceptez de représenter notre société et de commercialiser nos produits en France. J'ai le plaisir de vous confirmer par la présente les points essentiels de nos discussions.

Nous vous consentirons une commission de 25% sur toutes les ventes, et ce pourcentage comprendra tous les frais de publicité et la participation à toute foire commerciale éventuelle. Nous espérons qu'il vous sera possible d'organiser une campagne publicitaire très prochainement.

La livraison des marchandises se fera par camion directement à votre entrepôt à Paris franco de tous frais dans un délai de trois à quatre semaines dès réception de la commande. Le paiement des factures sera effectué par virement bancaire à notre banque (NATWEST, Regent Street, Londres W.1) tous les deux mois, déduction faite de votre commission. Nous aimerions recevoir un relevé des ventes mensuel.

Puisque vous serez responsable du service après-vente, nous mettrons immédiatement à votre disposition un technicien bilingue qui pourra organiser un cours de formation dans votre entreprise.

Nous espérons vivement que cette collaboration entre nos deux sociétés sera des plus fructueuses.

Veuillez agréer, chère Madame, l'expression de mes sincères salutations.

Le Directeur des Ventes

Peter Jackson

TRANSLATION

Dear Madame Duval,

Thank you for your letter of 28 March in which you agree to represent our Company and to market our products in France. I now (*lit.* 'hereby') have pleasure in confirming the main points of our discussions.

We will grant you a commission of 25% on all sales, and this percentage will include all advertising expenses and participation in any trade fair that may take place. We hope that it will be possible for you to organize an advertising campaign very shortly.

The delivery of the goods will be made by truck directly to your warehouse in Paris free of all charges within a period of three to four weeks following (*lit.*'from') receipt of order. Payment of invoices will be made by bank transfer to our bank (NatWest, Regent Street,London, W1) every two months, after deduction of your commission (*lit.* 'after deduction made of your commission'). We would like to receive a monthly sales report.

Since you will be responsible for the after-sales service, we will immediately put at your disposal a bilingual technician who will be able to organize a training course in your company.

We hope very much that this collaboration between our companies will be most successful (*lit.* 'will be of the most fruitful').

Yours sincerely

Peter Jackson
Sales Manager

Checklist 4

Masculine nouns:

152	le produit	*product*
153	le plaisir	*pleasure*
154	le pourcentage	*percentage*
155	le camion	*truck, lorry*
156	le délai	*time limit*
157	le paiement	*payment*
158	le virement bancaire	*bank transfer*
159	le mois	*month*
160	le relevé des ventes	*sales report*
161	le service après-vente	*after-sales service*
162	le technicien	*technician*
163	le cours	*course*
164	le point	*point*
165	l'entrepôt	*warehouse*
166	les frais	*expenses*

Feminine nouns:

167	la discussion	*discussion*
168	la lettre	*letter*
169	la commission	*commission*
170	la publicité	*advertising*
171	la participation	*participation*
172	la foire commerciale	*trade fair*
173	la campagne publicitaire	*advertising campaign*
174	la livraison	*delivery*
175	la (les) marchandise(s)	*goods*
176	la semaine	*week*
177	la réception	*receipt*
178	la commande	*order*
179	la facture	*invoice*
180	la banque	*bank*
181	la déduction	*deduction*

182	la formation	training
183	la collaboration	collaboration
184	l'entreprise	firm
185	les salutations	greetings

Adjectives:

186	possible	possible
187	responsable (de)	responsible (for)
188	bilingue	bilingual
189	essentiel, -elle (f.)	essential
190	cher, chère (f.)	dear, expensive
191	éventuel, -elle (f.)	possible, that may take place
192	mensuel, -elle (f.)	monthly
193	fructueux, -euse (f.)	fruitful

Adverbs:

194	prochainement	shortly
195	directement	directly
196	immédiatement	immediately
197	vivement	greatly
198	franco	free

Prepositions:

199	par	by
200	dès	from
201	entre	between

Other words/expressions:

202	par la présente	hereby
203	très	very
204	qui	who,which
205	que	whom, which
206	puisque	since
207	notre, nos	our
208	à votre disposition	at your disposal
209	lequel, laquelle (f.), lesquels(m. pl.), lesquelles (f. pl.)	which (used after preposition)

Months:

210	janvier	January
211	février	February
212	mars	March
213	avril	April
214	mai	May
215	juin	June
216	juillet	July
217	août	August
218	septembre	September
219	octobre	October
220	novembre	November
221	décembre	December

Numbers:

222	vingt	20
223	vingt et un	21
224	vingt-deux	22
225	vingt-neuf	29
226	trente	30
227	trente et un	31
228	quarante	40
229	cinquante	50
230	soixante	60

Cities:

231	Londres	London

Verbs:

232	remercier	to thank
233	accepter	to accept, agree
234	représenter	to represent
235	commercialiser	to market
236	confirmer	to confirm
237	organiser	to organize
238	effectuer	to effect, make
239	aimer	to like, love
240	agréer	to accept
241	espérer	to hope

present: j'espère, il espère, n.espérons, v.espérez, ils espèrent
past: j'ai espéré

242	il/elle sera (être)	*he/she/it will be*	
243	vous serez	*you will be*	
244	il/elle se fera (faire)	*it will be done*	
245	il/elle pourra (pouvoir)	*he/she/it will be able*	
246	nous aimerions	*we would like*	
247	veuillez (vouloir -to want)	*please*	

Irregular verbs:

248 consentir *to grant*
   present: je consens, il consent, nous consentons, vous consentez, ils
      consentent
   past: j'ai consenti

249 mettre *to put*
   present: je mets, il met, nous mettons, vous mettez, ils mettent
   past: j'ai mis

250 vouloir *to want*
   present: je veux, il veut, nous voulons, vous voulez, ils veulent
   past: j'ai voulu
   N.B. je voudrais *I would like*

251 comprendre *to include; to understand*
   see prendre Checklist 2

CHECKNOTES

31 Questions

Further to the very easy, conversational way of asking questions (Checknote 29), consider the following:

a) Another useful and simple question form is to place **est-ce que** (**est-ce qu'** before a vowel or silent h) in front of the statement:

Statement: L'ingénieur a programmé les robots.
   The engineer has programmed the robots.

Question: Est-ce que l'ingénieur a programmé les robots?
   Has the engineer programmed the robots?

b) A more formal way of putting a question is to invert the subject and pronoun, like this:

Statement: Vous offrez un service complet.
   You offer a comprehensive service.

Question: Offrez-vous un service complet?
   Do you offer a comprehensive service?

A **t** is inserted in the third person singular if it ends in a vowel:

Envoie-t-il les documents sous pli séparé?
Is he sending the documents under separate cover?

c) When the question refers to a noun, you can use a combination of noun, pronoun and inversion:
Notre représentant vous a-t-il déjà contacté?
Has our representative already contacted you?

32 How to translate 'what'

a) Linked to the verb 'to be' and a noun, 'what' is expressed by **quel** (*m.*), **quelle** (*f.*), **quels** (*m. pl.*), **quelles** (*f. pl.*):

Quel est le prix?	*What is the price?*
Quelle est la date limite de vente?	*What is the sell-by date?*

b) When 'what' is the object of the sentence, use **qu'est-ce que** or simply **que (qu')**:

Qu'est-ce que vous avez reçu ce matin?	*What have you received this morning?*
Qu'ont-ils expédié?	*What have they dispatched?*

c) As an exclamation - **Quoi!**

Quoi! Vous n'avez pas annulé la commande?	*What! You haven't cancelled the order?*

d) As an exclamation followed by a noun - **quel** (etc):

Quel bon technicien!	*What a good technician!*
Quelle bonne idée!	*What a good idea!*

33 Correspondence

Let's begin by examining the layout of a typical French business letter.

a) *Name and address*

The name and address of the person or company you're writing to should appear on the right-hand side of the letter; **Monsieur, Madame, Mademoiselle,** must be written in full (the abbreviations are **M., Mme, Mlle** - notice no full stop for the ladies).

b) *Date*
This is placed underneath (sometimes above) the address and appears as:

Londres, le 3 Avril 1990
Paris, le 21 Juin 1991
Saint-Lô, le 27 Juillet 1992

Although the month in French normally takes a small initial letter, it is quite common in commercial letters to write it with a capital. Of the eight letters that the author has recently received from France only one had the date typed with a small initial letter.

Incidentally, note that we say in French 'the two January', 'the ten March', 'the twenty June', etc - not 'the second', 'the tenth', 'the twentieth', as in English. The only exception is when the French refer to the first day of the month and say '**le premier juillet**' etc.

c) *References*
These are placed on the left-hand side, and may be abbreviated:

Vos références: **Vos réfs:**   **V/Réf:**
Nos références: **Nos réfs:**   **N/Réf:**

Sometimes you'll see **Références à rappeler:** - here, the expression **à rappeler** means 'to be quoted'.

d) *Re*
This translates into French as **Objet**, and is put below the **Références**:

Objet: Votre commande N° 1234

e) *Beginning the letter*
There's a formal way (**Monsieur/Madame/Mademoiselle**); a less formal way (**Cher Monsieur/Chère Madame/Chère Mademoiselle**); and a very friendly way (**Cher Monsieur Martin/Chère Madame Duval/Chère Mademoiselle Leblanc**).

Remember that the French are often very formal and a letter beginning **Cher Monsieur Jackson** is much less usual in French than 'Dear Mr Jackson' would be in English.

If you don't know whether you're writing to a man or a woman, begin: **Madame, Monsieur**. When writing to a company: **Messieurs**.

f) *Body of the letter*
Here are some useful ways of starting the letter itself:

Suite à ...	*Further to ...*
En réponse à votre lettre du ...	*In reply to your letter of ...*
Nous avons bien reçu...	*We have received ...*
Nous accusons réception de...	*We acknowledge receipt of ...*
Nous vous remercions de votre lettre du ...	*We thank you for your letter of ...*
Nous avons le plaisir de vous informer que ...	*We have pleasure in informing you that ...*
Je vous confirme notre conversation téléphonique ...	*I confirm our telephone conversation ...*
Nous nous excusons de ne pas avoir répondu plus tôt ...	*We apologise for not having replied sooner ...*
Veuillez trouver ci-joint ...	*Please find enclosed ...*
Je vous serais reconnaissant(e), si vous pouviez ...	*I would be grateful if you could ...*

g) *Ending the letter*

'Yours faithfully' or 'Yours sincerely' can be expressed in many different ways in French. Here are some of the most common:

Veuillez agréer, Monsieur, mes (nos) salutations les plus distinguées.

Veuillez accepter, Madame, mes (nos) sincères salutations.

Je vous prie de croire, Mademoiselle, à l'assurance de mes sentiments distingués.

Veuillez agréer, Messieurs, l'expression de nos meilleures salutations.

The author recently received a letter from the subscription department of a French magazine which ended simply: **Sincèrement**.

h) *Enclosures*

If you see P. J. at the top or bottom of the page, you'll know that there are some enclosures. P. J. stands for **pièces jointes** ('documents enclosed') and appears like this: **P. J.: 1 catalogue**.

34 Future tense

The future tense is formed by adding the following endings to the infinitive (the 'to ...' form of the verb):

je	**-ai**
il/elle	**-a**
nous	**-ons**
vous	**-ez**
ils/elles	**-ont**

This is how the future tense of **-er** and **-ir** verbs looks:

consulter (*to consult*)	**je consulterai**	*I will consult*
confirmer (*to confirm*)	**il/elle confirmera**	*he/she will confirm*
expédier (*to dispatch*)	**nous expédierons**	*we will dispatch*
finir (*to finish*)	**vous finirez**	*you will finish*
réussir (*to succeed*)	**ils/elles réussiront**	*they will succeed*

To form the future tense of **-re** verbs, drop the final **-e** before adding the endings:

attendre (to wait (for))	**j'attendrai**	*I will wait*
répondre (to reply)	**nous répondrons**	*we will reply*

There are a number of important verbs which have irregular futures; you should learn them now:

avoir (*to have*)	**j'aurai**	*I will have*
être (*to be*)	**je serai**	*I will be*
aller (*to go*)	**j'irai**	*I will go*
faire (*to do, make*)	**je ferai**	*I will do/make*
envoyer (*to send*)	**j'enverrai**	*I will send*
falloir (*to be necessary*)	**il faudra**	*it will be necessary*
il y a (*there is/are*)	**il y aura**	*there will be*

In conversational French a simpler form of the future tense is often used. This is similar to the English construction 'to be going to do something'. As shown by the examples below it uses the present tense of aller (to go) followed by the infinitive form of the second verb:

je vais verser des arrhes	*I'm going to pay a deposit*
il/elle va profiter de l'occasion pour	*he/she's going to take the opportunity of*
nous allons vendre à crédit	*we're going to sell on credit*
vous allez déduire votre commission	*you're going to deduct your commission*
ils/elles vont investir dans l'immobilier	*they're going to invest in property*
je vais payer comptant	*I'm going to pay cash*
il/elle va payer par traite bancaire	*he/she's going to pay by bank draft*
nous allons payer par chèque	*we're going to pay by cheque*
vous allez payer la facture à 60 jours fin de mois	*you're going to pay the invoice 60 days from end of month*
ils/elles vont payer le solde	*they're going to pay the balance*

Comprehension Practice 4

Study the new words and then answer the following questions which are based on Mr Jackson's letter to Mme Duval. Give complete answers.

New words:

le transport	*transport*
par chemin de fer	*by rail*
de quelle manière	*in what way*
faciliter	*to facilitate*

1 Quelle est la date de la lettre?

2 Quelle commission M. Jackson accordera-t-il à Mme Duval?

3 Qu'est-ce que le pourcentage comprendra?

4 Est-ce que la livraison se fera par chemin de fer?

5 Quel est le délai de livraison?

6 Qui paie les frais de transport?

7 Quelles sont les conditions de paiement?

8 De quelle manière M. Jackson va-t-il faciliter le service après-vente?

FLUENCY PRACTICE 19

New words:

le directeur adjoint	*assistant director*
le Dictaphone	*Dictaphone*
la conférence de presse	*press conference*
livrer	*to deliver*
classer	*to file*
probablement	*probably*

Answer the questions using the future tense, as in the example:

Avez-vous payé?	*Have you paid?*
Non, je payerai demain.	*No, I'll pay tomorrow.*

1 Avez-vous téléphoné?

2 Avez-vous versé des arrhes?

3 Avez-vous parlé du contrat? (*Reply using* nous)

4 A-t-il fixé le rendez-vous?

5 A-t-elle organisé la conférence de presse?

6 Est-ce que j'ai programmé les robots?

7 Ont-ils livré les machines?

8 Ont-elles commandé les marchandises?
9 Avez-vous fini de classer les documents?
10 Avez-vous réussi à contacter le directeur adjoint?
   (*Reply using* nous *and* probablement)
11 A-t-il vendu le dernier Dictaphone?
12 Ont-elles répondu au télex?

FLUENCY PRACTICE 20

We want you to imagine that you work for a book publisher in London. Your company has received the following letter from a French newspaper and you've been asked to translate it because no-one else understands French. To save you looking the words up in a dictionary we've provided a list of all the necessary words.

LA NORMANDIE VERTE
rue du Musée
14404 Bayeux

                                        Happy Books Ltd
                                        St John's Park
                                        LONDON SE3 7TP
                                        (Angleterre)

                                        Bayeux, le 5 Juin 1990

A l'attention de Monsieur John Brown

Monsieur,

Suite à votre lettre du 20 Mai au sujet d'un article paru dans
LA NORMANDIE VERTE du 20 Décembre 1989, nous vous donnons
volontiers, à titre gracieux, notre autorisation de
reproduction.

Nous vous demandons de bien vouloir veiller à ce que toutes les
références d'usage figurent à la fin du texte ainsi que de nous
envoyer deux exemplaires du livre au moment de la publication.

Vous en remerciant, nous vous prions d'agréer, Monsieur,
l'assurance de nos sentiments distingués.

Pierre Martin
SERVICE DES DROITS DE REPRODUCTION

The words you'll need:

le sujet	*subject*	la reproduction	*reproduction*
le texte	*text*	la publication	*publication*
le moment	*moment*	la fin	*end*
le service	*department*	l'autorisation	*authorization*
le droit	*right*	les références	*usual references*
l'article	*article*	d'usage	
l'exemplaire	*copy*		

Expressions:

au sujet de	*concerning*
à titre gracieux	*free of charge*
nous vous demandons de bien vouloir	*we ask you to be good enough*

Verbs:

donner	*to give*	veiller à ce que	*to ensure that*
demander	*to ask*	envoyer (*irreg.*)	*to send*
figurer	*to appear*	paraître (*irreg.*)	*to appear*
remercier	*to thank*	paru	*appeared*
remerciant	*thanking*		

FLUENCY PRACTICE 21(A)

You work for Reliable Engineering Ltd. This morning you've found a letter on your desk, written in French. Your head of department has attached a note to it; he's guessed it must be something to do with the faulty desk lamps which Reliable sent back recently, but wants to know what the French company is going to do about them.

Make a summary of the letter for your boss. You'll need a dictionary; Hugo's pocket French dictionary will be perfectly adequate for this purpose. Check afterwards with the Key.

Here's the actual letter:

56

ETABLISSEMENTS
MARTIN

Promenade des Rochers, 50000 Saint-Lô

V/RÉF:
N/RÉF:RD/DR

Reliable Engineering Ltd
The High Street
Chislehurst
Kent
(Angleterre)

Saint-Lô, le 16 Juillet 1990

<u>À l'attention de Monsieur Sands</u>

Monsieur,

Notre représentant à Londres, Mr Smith, nous a retourné les deux lampes de bureau type AB, qui ne vous ont pas donné entière satisfaction. Nous les avons examinées et devons admettre qu'il y a, en effet, un défaut dans ces marchandises.

Nous vous assurons que c'est la première fois que nous avons des problèmes avec cet article et vous précisons que nous sommes intervenus sur ce point auprès de nos ateliers.

Bien entendu, nous vous reprenons ces deux lampes de bureau et créditerons votre compte en conséquence.

Veuillez agréer, Monsieur, l'assurance de nos sentiments distingués.

Le Directeur des Ventes

R Dupré

FLUENCY PRACTICE 21 (B)

This exercise is also based on the above letter. <u>From memory</u> supply the French for:

1 our representative	12 to assure
2 to return	13 the first time
3 a desk lamp	14 a problem
4 to give complete	15 an article
satisfaction	16 to make clear
5 to examine	17 to intervene
6 we have to	18 on this point
7 to admit	19 the workshop
8 there is/are	20 of course
9 indeed	21 to take back
10 a fault	22 we will credit your account
11 the goods	23 accordingly

FLUENCY PRACTICE 22

New words:

l'incendie (*m.*)	*fire*
identique	*identical*
malheureusement	*unfortunately*
à l'avance	*in advance*
endommager	*to damage*

Imagine that you received a delivery of office furniture a week ago. As a result of an unfortunate incident on your premises, some of the furniture has been damaged and you need to re-order. To crown it all, your word processor has jumbled up the contents of the letter you're writing this morning. Reconstruct the letter in the correct sequence. Here's the letter:

a) des 5 bureaux et des 10 classeurs.
b) a endommagé tous les bureaux à notre entrepôt.
c) Je vous remercie à l'avance.
d Nous vous accusons réception
e) Veuillez agréer , Monsieur,
f) Je vous serais reconnaissant(e), si vous pouviez
g) Malheureusement, un incendie
h) mes salutations distinguées.
i) m'expédier 5 bureaux identiques immédiatement.
j) Monsieur,

FLUENCY PRACTICE 23

Using the replies in the Key to Comprehension Practice 4 as a basis, reproduce the original questions.

Finally, in this Unit:

Note the following fax, just received by Excel-Equip; it contains details relevant to events in Unit 5.

FAX: (1) 45.12.34.56 6.AVRIL.90 14.21 NO. 05 P. 01

FRANCE - BUROTIC
765 rue du Commerce
75015 PARIS

FAX: (1) 45.12.34.56

Date:	6.04.90
De:	Mme H.Duval, France-Burotic
A:	M. P. Jackson, Excel-Equip
No Télécopie:	071 7654321
Nombre de pages:	01

Veuillez m'expédier dans les plus brefs délais:

- 6 traitements de texte (réf. AB)
- 10 agendas électroniques (réf. CD)
- 4 imprimantes laser (réf. EF)

Je vous remercie d'avance.

Salutations

Problems with the equipment delivered: Telephoning (1)

> *Unit 5 includes constructions such as 'this is', 'these are', more numbers, days of the week and other 'time' phrases, comparison, the use of 'me', 'him', 'us' etc., important expressions for use on the telephone - and dictionary practice.*
>
> *The office equipment ordered by Mme Duval has now been delivered to France-Burotic, but there are some problems with the consignment. Mme Duval decides to telephone Mr Jackson in London. Unfortunately, it's 6 p.m and the offices of Excel-Equip are already closed. This is what Mme Duval hears:*

... I'm sorry but there's no-one in the office at the moment. If you'd like to leave your name and telephone number, we'll get back to you as soon as possible. Please speak after the tone ... *peep*

Mme Duval: Allô. C'est Madame Duval à l'appareil ... Je vous remercie Monsieur Jackson pour nous avoir expédié les marchandises si rapidement. Malheureusement, il semble y avoir quelques petits problèmes ... Euh, pouvez-vous me rappeler au bureau demain, mercredi? De préférence entre huit heures et midi. Merci beaucoup.

Wednesday, 11 a.m.   Mr Jackson rings France-Burotic.

Switchboard: Allô, France-Burotic. Bonjour.

Mr Jackson: Bonjour, Madame. Je voudrais parler à Madame Duval,s'il vous plaît.

Switchboard: C'est de la part de qui, Monsieur?

Mr Jackson: Monsieur Jackson ... de la société Excel-Equip à Londres.

Switchboard: Excusez-moi, la ligne est très mauvaise. Pouvez-vous répéter votre nom, s'il vous plaît.

Mr Jackson: Jackson ... J-A-C-K-S-O-N.

Switchboard:	Attendez un petit instant, s'il vous plaît ... Allô, Monsieur Jackson, ne quittez pas, je vous passe Madame Duval ...
Mme Duval:	Bonjour, Monsieur Jackson. Je vous remercie de m'avoir rappelée si vite.
Mr Jackson:	C'est tout à fait normal, Madame. J'ai reçu votre message ce matin. Je suis désolé d'apprendre que vous avez quelques problèmes avec le matériel que nous vous avons livré.
Mme Duval:	Ce ne sont pas des problèmes insurmontables, loin de là, mais je pense qu'il est préférable de les résoudre immédiatement. Après tout, je voudrais donner toutes les chances de succès à notre future collaboration.
Mr Jackson:	Je suis tout à fait d'accord avec vous et je ferai tout mon possible pour essayer de résoudre ces problèmes.
Mme Duval:	Eh bien, la première chose que je voudrais mentionner, c'est l'emballage. À notre avis, l'emballage est insuffisant pour transporter par route des marchandises aussi fragiles que des traitements de texte, des machines à écrire, etc.
Mr Jackson:	Est-ce que le matériel a été endommagé au cours du transport à cause d'un emballage inadéquat?
Mme Duval:	Non,non, il n'y a aucun dommage apparent, mais deux ou trois caisses ont été abîmées et il faudra donc renforcer l'emballage à l'avenir.
Mr Jackson:	Je veillerai à ce que notre service d'emballage et d'expédition fasse le nécessaire. Y a-t-il autre chose que vous aimeriez ajouter?

TRANSLATION

Mme Duval:	Hello. This is Madame Duval speaking (*lit.* 'on the telephone') ... Thank you (*lit.* 'I thank you') Mr Jackson for sending (*lit.* 'for having sent') us the goods so quickly. Unfortunately, there appear to be a few small problems ... Er, can you call me back at the office tomorrow, Wednesday? Preferably between 8 o'clock and midday? Thank you very much.

Switchboard:	Hello. France-Burotic. Good morning.
Mr Jackson:	Good morning. I'd like to speak to Madame Duval, please.
Switchboard:	Who's calling? (*lit.* 'It's on behalf of whom?')
Mr Jackson:	Mr Jackson of Excel-Equip in London.
Switchboard:	I'm sorry, the line is very bad. Can you repeat your name, please?
Mr Jackson:	Jackson ... J-A-C-K-S-O-N.
Switchboard:	Just one moment (*lit.* Wait a small instant') please ... Hello, Mr Jackson, hold the line, I'm putting you through to Madame Duval.
Mme Duval:	Good morning, Mr Jackson. Thank you for calling me back (*lit.* 'I thank you for having called me back') so quickly.
Mr Jackson:	That's the least I can do (*lit.* 'That's quite normal'). I received your message this morning. I'm sorry to hear (*lit.* 'learn') that you're having some problems with the equipment that we've delivered to you.
Mme Duval:	They're not (*lit.* 'These are not') insurmountable problems, far from it (*lit.* 'far from there'), but I think that it's preferable to resolve them immediately. After all, I'd like to give our future collaboration every chance (*lit.* 'all the chances') of success.
Mr Jackson:	I quite agree (*lit.* 'I am quite of agreement') with you and I'll do my utmost (*lit.* 'all my possible') to try and resolve these problems.
Mme Duval:	Well, the first thing that I'd like to mention is (*lit.* 'this is') the packing. In our opinion, the packing is insufficient for transporting by road goods as fragile as word processors, typewriters, etc.
Mr Jackson:	Has the equipment been damaged in transit (*lit.* 'in the course of the transport') because of inadequate packing?
Mme Duval:	No,no, there's no visible damage, but two or three cases have been damaged and it will be necessary therefore to reinforce the packing in the future.
Mr Jackson:	I'll ensure that our packing and despatch department makes the necessary arrangements (*lit.* 'does the necessary'). Is there something else (*lit.* 'other thing') that you'd like to add?

Checklist 5

Masculine nouns:

252	le nom	*name*
253	le problème	*problem*
254	le dommage	*damage; pity*
255	le transport	*transport*
256	le succès	*success*
257	l'instant	*moment*
258	l'emballage	*packing*
259	l'appareil	*machine; telephone*

Feminine nouns:

260	la ligne	*line*
261	la chance	*chance; luck*
262	la chose	*thing*
263	la caisse	*case; cash desk*
264	l'expédition	*dispatch*
265	la (les) march-andise(s)	*goods*

Adjectives:

266	petit	*small*
267	grand	*large*
268	normal	*normal*
269	désolé	*sorry*
270	insurmontable	*insurmountable*
271	préférable	*preferable*
272	futur	*future*
273	premier, première (f.)	*first*
274	insuffisant	*insufficient*
275	fragile	*fragile*
276	inadéquat	*inadequate*
277	apparent	*visible*

Adverbs:

278	rapidement	*rapidly*
279	imméd-iatement	*immediately*
280	malheur-eusement	*unfortunately*
281	vite	*fast*

When?

282	maintenant	*now*
283	hier	*yesterday*
284	aujourd'hui	*today*
285	demain	*tomorrow*
286	après-demain	*the day after tomorrow*
287	ce matin	*this morning*
288	à l'avenir	*in the future*
289	mercredi	*Wednesday*
290	à midi	*at midday*
291	à minuit	*at midnight*

Apologies:

292	excusez-moi	*I'm sorry*

Opinion:

293	à mon/notre avis	*in my/our opinion*

Comparison:

294	aussi fragile que	*as fragile as*

Preference:

295	de préférence	*preferably*

Emphasis:

296	loin de là	*far from it*
297	tout mon possible	*my utmost*
298	tout à fait	*quite, entirely*

Negatives:

299	ne+verb+ aucun	*no*

Other words/expressions:

300	si	*so*
301	euh...	*er ...*
302	allô	*hello (on phone)*

303	donc	therefore
304	que	which, that, whom
305	quelques	some, a few
306	eh bien	well
307	autre chose	something else
308	par route	by road
309	au cours de	in the course of
310	ne quittez pas	hold the line
311	c'est de la part de	it's on behalf of
312	après tout	after all
313	j'ai été [être]	I have been
314	il semble y avoir	there seems to be
315	il y a	there is/are
316	Y a-t-il...?	Is/Are there ...?
317	faire le nécessaire	to do what is necessary
318	fasse [faire]	do/does [This is the present subjunctive, which we'll be studying later]
319	vous aimeriez	you would like

Numbers:

320	soixante et un	61
321	soixante-deux	62
322	soixante-dix	70
323	soixante et onze	71
324	soixante-douze	72
325	soixante-treize	73
326	soixante-dix-neuf	79
327	quatre-vingts	80

Verbs:

328	sembler	to seem
329	quitter	to leave
330	passer	to put through (on phone)
331	penser	to think
332	ajouter	to add
333	transporter	to transport
334	abîmer	to damage
335	aimer	to like, love
336	rappeler	to call back (see appeler p.173)

N.B.:

337 répéter *to repeat*
present: je répète, il répète, nous répétons, vous répétez, ils répètent.
past: j'ai répété.

338 essayer *to try*
present: j'essaie, il essaie, nous essayons, vous essayez, ils essaient.
past: j'ai essayé

339 endommager *to damage*
present: nous endommageons.

340 renforcer *to reinforce*
present: nous renforçons.

Irregular verbs:

341 apprendre *to learn*
present: j'apprends, il apprend, nous apprenons, vous apprenez, ils apprennent.
past: j'ai appris.

342 résoudre *to resolve*
present: je résous, il résout, nous résolvons, vous résolvez, ils résolvent.
past: j'ai résolu.

CHECKNOTES

35 C'est, ce sont (This/it is, these/they are)

Examples:

C'est urgent.	*This/It is urgent.*
Ce sont les connaissements.	*These/They are the bills of lading.*
Ce n'est pas important.	*This/It is not important.*
Ce ne sont pas des problèmes insurmontables.	*These/They are not insurmountable problems.*

36 Days of the week

In French, the days of the week are written with a small letter; **lundi** (Monday), **mardi** (Tuesday), **mercredi** (Wednesday), **jeudi** (Thursday), **vendredi** (Friday), **samedi** (Saturday), **dimanche** (Sunday). Note that, with the days of the week, the English 'on' is not translated.:

Pouvez-vous me rappeler mercredi?	*Can you call me back on Wednesday?*
Les comptes annuels seront prêts mardi.	*The annual accounts will be ready on Tuesday.*
Les fournitures de bureau seront expédiées lundi.	*The office supplies will be sent off on Monday.*

If you want to express 'on Mondays', 'on Tuesdays' etc, use le:

L'inventaire se fait le vendredi.	*The stocktaking (inventory) is carried out on Fridays.*

37 Verbs followed by an infinitive

You'll remember that, in Checknotes 24 and 25, we pointed out that some verbs are followed by **de** (**d'**) and others by **à**, to express the English 'to/in'. For example:

Je vous conseille d'apprendre la sténographie.	*I advise you to learn shorthand.*
Nous avons réussi à renforcer l'emballage.	*We've succeeded in reinforcing the packing.*

We translate 'in order to' by **pour**:

Je ferai tout mon possible pour résoudre ces problèmes.	*I'll do everything possible (in order) to solve these problems.*

But ... some verbs are followed by a second verb without any intervening preposition:

Je préfère parler à Monsieur Jackson.   *I prefer to speak to Mr Jackson.*

Here are some of the verbs that fall into this category (see Hugo's 'French Verbs Simplified' for complete lists), and three example sentences:

sembler   *to seem*
aimer   *to like, love*
préférer   *to prefer*
espérer   *to hope*
vouloir   *to want*
devoir   *to have to/must*
pouvoir   *to be able*

N.B. **préférer**:
     present je préfère, il préfère, nous préférons, vous préférez, ils préfèrent; *past* j'ai préféré.
     devoir:
     present je dois, il doit, nous devons, vous devez, il doivent; *past* j'ai dû.

Nous devons transporter ces marchandises par voie aérienne.
We must airfreight these goods.
Je voudrais* demander une augmentation de salaire.
I'd like to ask for an increase in salary.
Les chômeurs veulent réclamer une indemnité de licenciement.
Those out of work want to claim a redundancy payment.

*N.B.: **Je voudrais** ('I would like') is actually the conditional tense of **vouloir**. We'll be studying this tense later.

38 Useful expressions of time

ce matin   *this morning*
cet après-midi   *this afternoon*
ce soir   *this evening*
cette semaine   *this week*
ce mois-ci   *this month*
cette année   *this year*

la semaine prochaine   *next week*
le mois prochain   *next month*
l'année prochaine   *next year*

39 Comparison (**aussi ... que**, 'as ... as')

Nous transportons des marchandises aussi fragiles que des machines à écrire électroniques, etc.
We transport goods as fragile as electronic typewriters, etc.

Quoi! Les frais de transport sont presque aussi élevés que les frais de production?
What! The transport costs are almost as high as the production costs?

Cet ouvrier travaille aussi bien que les autres.
This workman works as well as the others.

40 Être (**a/ont été**, 'has/have been')

Le matériel a été endommagé.
The equipment has been damaged.

Les stocks de pièces détachées ont été récemment renouvelés.
The stocks of spare parts have recently been renewed.

Le règlement n'a pas été effectué selon les conditions habituelles.
Payment has not been (was not) made according to the usual terms.

41 Il y a ('there is/are')

Malheureusement, il y a un formulaire à remplir.
Unfortunately, there's a form to fill in.

Cette semaine il n'y a pas d'articles en promotion.
This week there are no special offers.

Y a-t-il autre chose que vous aimeriez mentionner?
Is there something else you would like to mention?

En ce qui concerne votre projet, il semble y avoir des avantages et des inconvénients.
As far as your project is concerned, there seem to be advantages and disadvantages.

The expression **il y a** also means 'ago':

J'ai annulé la commande il y a trois semaines.
I cancelled the order three weeks ago.

42 Object pronouns (2)

In Checknote 13 we gave some examples of the use of the direct object pronouns in French: 'He exports them' = **Il les exporte**, 'We order it' = **Nous le/la commandons** (remember to use **le** for masculine nouns and **la** for feminine). Here are some more examples:

(a) Pouvez-vous me rappeler ce matin?
Can you call me back this morning?

(b) Je vous remercie de <u>m'</u>avoir promu (promue, *f.*) au poste de sous-directeur (sous-directrice, *f.*).
Thank you for promoting (having promoted) me to the post of assistant director.

(c) Nous n'avons pas réussi à <u>le</u> contacter.
We haven't managed to contact him.

(d) Vous pouvez peut-être <u>la</u> joindre à l'usine.
Perhaps you can reach her at the factory.

(e) Ils <u>nous</u> ont remerciés pour les fiches techniques.
They thanked us for the specification sheets.

Here's the complete list:

me	**me**	(**m'** before a vowel or silent h)
him, it	**le**	(**l'** before a vowel or silent h)
her, it	**la**	(**l'** before a vowel or silent h)
them	**les**	
us	**nous**	
you	**vous**	

43 Agreement of the past participle

You'll have noticed from examples (b) and (e) that the past participle (**promu, remercié, expédié, acheté, vendu**, etc) must agree with the preceding direct object pronoun. The next examples will make this clear:

je l'ai contacté	*I contacted him*
je l'ai contactée	*I contacted her*
je les ai contactés	*I contacted them (m.)*
je les ai contactées	*I contacted them (f.)*
nous l'avons copié	*we copied it* (speaking about **le document**, for example)
nous l'avons copiée	*we copied it* (for example, **la fiche technique**)

44 Telephoning in French (part 1)

Learn these expressions (together with those in Unit 6), and you'll never have any difficulty speaking French on the telephone.

Talking to the switchboard operator:

Allô. Bonjour, Madame/Monsieur. C'est bien la Société France-Burotic?
Hello. Good morning. Is that France-Burotic?

(a) Je vous appelle d'Angleterre.   *I'm calling you from England.*
(b) Je vous appelle des États-Unis.   *I'm calling you from the United States.*

(c) Je vous appelle du Canada. *I'm calling you from Canada.*
(d) Je vous téléphone de Londres. *I'm phoning you from London.*
(e) Je vous téléphone de New York. *I'm phoning you from New York.*

Je voudrais parler à Monsieur/Madame/Mademoiselle Ricard, s'il vous plaît.
I'd like to speak to M./Mme/Mlle Ricard, please.

Pourriez-vous me passer Monsieur/Madame/Mademoiselle Ricard, s'il
vous plaît?
Could you put me through to M./Mme/Mlle Ricard, please?

Est-ce que je peux avoir le poste vingt-cinq, s'il vous plaît?
Can I have extension 25, please?

Je n'ai peut-être pas le bon numéro.
I may not have the right number.

Possible replies from the switchboard:

(a) Ne quittez pas. *Hold the line.*
(b) La ligne est occupée. *The line is busy.*
(c) Voulez-vous rester en ligne ou *Will you hold on or do you prefer to*
préférez-vous rappeler plus tard? *call back later?*
(d) Ça ne répond pas. *There's no reply.*
(e) Excusez-moi de vous faire *Sorry to keep you waiting.*
attendre.
(f) La ligne est très mauvaise. *The line is very bad.*
(g) Je vous entends mal. *I can't hear you very well.*
(h) Il/Elle n'est pas là; je vais *He/She isn't here. I'll put you*
vous passer sa secrétaire. *through to his/her secretary.*
(i) Je pense que vous vous êtes *I think you have the wrong number.*
trompé de numéro.

Comprehension Practice 5

At this point in the Course the questions become more challenging and we give in brackets an indication of the answer required. Reply in French with complete sentences.

New words:

le contenu	*contents*
la leçon	*lesson*
laisser	*to leave*
s'adresser à	*to go and see*
pourquoi	*why*
difficile	*difficult*
fermé	*closed*
parce que	*because*

1 Pourquoi Mme Duval laisse-t-elle un message sur le répondeur téléphonique de M. Jackson? [*office closed*]

2 Quel est le contenu du message? [*must call back Wed., 8-12*]

3 Pourquoi M.Jackson doit-il répéter son nom? [*line's bad*]

4 Est-ce que les problèmes sont difficiles à résoudre? [*not insurmountable*]

5 Pourquoi M. Jackson veut-il résoudre ces problèmes immédiatement? [*wants to give every chance of success*]

6 Quel est le premier problème que Mme Duval mentionne? [*insufficient packing*]

7 Est-ce que le matériel a été endommagé au cours du transport? [*no visible damage*]

8 Pourquoi est-ce que Mme Duval pense qu'il sera nécessaire de renforcer l'emballage à l'avenir? [*cases damaged*]

9 À quel service M. Jackson va-t-il s'adresser? [*packaging/dispatch*]

10 Y a-t-il autre chose que Mme Duval veut ajouter? [*we don't know and must wait for Unit 6*]

FLUENCY PRACTICE 24

A little arithmetic ... Complete the following, writing your answers in words (and, of course, in French!):

a) 5 + 5 =   i)   16 + 10 =
b) 10 + 10 =   j)   20 + 13 =
c) 15 + 15 =   k) 30 + 11 =
d) 20 + 20 =   l)   40 + 17 =
e) 25 + 25 =   m) 50 + 14 =
f) 30 + 30 =   n) 60 + 11 =
g) 40 + 30 =   o) 50 + 22 =
h) 40 + 40 =   p) 40 + 39 =

FLUENCY PRACTICE 25

Give the French equivalent for:

1 I'm calling you from London.
2 Can I have extension 79, please?
3 I may not have the right number.
4 I think you have the wrong number.
5 I can't hear you very well.
6 The line is bad.
7 I'm sorry to keep you waiting.
8 There's no reply.
9 Do you prefer to call back later?
10 Could you put me through to his/her secretary, please?

FLUENCY PRACTICE 26

New words:

le camionneur	*lorry driver, trucker*
la télévision	*television*
l'avocat	*lawyer (m.)*
l'avocate	*lawyer (f.)*
le directeur technique	*works manager*
consulter	*to consult*
licencier	*to make redundant*
imprimer	*to print*

Answer the questions in the same way as in the following example (1), i.e. in the affirmative and 'this morning':

1 Avez-vous contacté le camionneur? *Have you contacted the truck driver?*
  Oui, je l'ai contacté ce matin.   *Yes, I contacted him this morning.*

2 Avez-vous consulté l'avocate?
3 Avez-vous licencié le directeur technique?
4 Avez-vous imprimé les catalogues?
5 Avez-vous reçu la facture?
6 M'avez-vous vu (vue *f.*) à la télévision?

FLUENCY PRACTICE 27

Study again the names of the letters of the French alphabet (see chapter on pronunciation) and then spell the following aloud:

Smith, Brown, Johnson, Harper, Bournemouth, Norwich, Carlisle, Edinburgh, New York, Miami, Sydney, Toronto

DICTIONARY PRACTICE 1

It's absolutely essential that you should be able to use a French dictionary quickly, easily and correctly. For this reason you should now study the following extract of an article taken from Normandie Magazine (March-April 1990), dealing with a seminar which was held on the importance of 1992 for British businessmen. Look up the words you don't know (or can't guess), so as to get the gist of the text, then answer in English the comprehension questions at the end. Model answers are given in the Key.

Il y a encore des barrières à faire tomber

« L'homme d'affaires britannique doit maintenant penser européen » dit Ken Webb, responsable du développement économique à la mairie de Portsmouth. «Beaucoup d'entre eux jouent encore l'autruche.» «Souvent ils disent "Ce n'est pas mon problème"» confirme David Higham, président du Groupe 1992 de la Chambre de commerce du Sud-Est Hampshire, qui compte sur ce séminaire pour faire sortir les têtes du sable. Il insiste sur la nécessaire prise de conscience: «Si les Britanniques ne font rien, ils seront rapidement confrontés à la concurrence française, italienne et allemande sur leur propre terrain.»

S'aligner sur les normes européennes

1992, c'est le grand chambardement. Les échanges commerciaux dans les différents pays de la CEE seront de plus en plus faciles. Le bras de mer qui sépare le Royaume-Uni du continent n'est plus qu'un problème de langue, une barrière psychologique. La franchir est vital pour le dynamisme des entreprises britanniques. Elles doivent s'aligner sur les normes européennes. En France et en Normandie en particulier, les opportunités sont très avantageuses, ne serait-ce que pour reprendre des entreprises dont le fondateur prend sa retraite (comme l'a montré le colloque tenu sur ce thème à Caen en novembre dernier).

En Normandie, les terrains sont à des prix vraiment avantageux. Les agglomérations font des concessions importantes pour faciliter les implantations étrangères, trop contentes de dynamiser une économie stagnante et de redonner du travail aux chômeurs.

Here are the questions:

1 What is the criticism levelled at British businessmen in the first paragraph?
2 What is the purpose of the seminar?
3 What will happen if British businessmen don't change their attitude?
4 What major change will take place in 1992 within the EEC?
5 What is the main barrier between Britain and the continent that remains to be overcome?
6 What makes setting up a business in Normandy attractive?
7 Why are towns in Normandy welcoming the arrival of foreign companies?

Solving the problems:
Telephoning (2)

You'll get more help with making phone calls and learn the conditional tense of verbs ('I would -'). Further negative constructions are explained and there's more of the all-important dictionary practice.

Mr Jackson and Mme Duval continue to discuss the problems in connection with the goods which Excel-Equip has just delivered.

Mr Jackson: Y a t-il autre chose que vous aimeriez ajouter?

Mme Duval: Oui,nous avons testé les machines à l'arrivée et elles sont toutes en bon état de marche, à l'exception d'une seule. L'imprimante d'un des six traitements de texte fait un bruit insupportable.On croirait avoir un marteau-piqueur au beau milieu du bureau!

Mr Jackson: Vous dites que c'est la seule qui soit défectueuse. Je ne vois pas quelle pourrait en être la cause. Le mieux, c'est que je vous envoie une autre machine immédiatement.

Mme Duval: Oui, je pense que c'est la meilleure solution. La troisième chose, c'est la question des prises de courant. Aucune de vos machines n'est équipée de prise. Or, vous savez qu'ici en France, même le plus petit objet électrique comporte déjà une prise, et il ne reste plus qu'à le brancher.

Mr Jackson: Ah bon? Nous avons bien sûr suivi le système britannique mais je suis d'accord que, pour pouvoir rivaliser au mieux avec les marchandises de nos concurrents, nos devrons nous aligner sur les habitudes françaises. J'en prends note pour l'avenir. Merci de me l'avoir signalé. J'aurais dû y penser. Mais ce n'est pas grave.

Mme Duval: Finalement, il reste la question du mode d'emploi. Il est bien imprimé et bien présenté, mais la traduction en français est, malheureusement, difficile à suivre et parfois maladroite.

Mr Jackson: Ah bon? J'ai fait traduire le texte par un membre de mon personnel. Mais il est crucial que cette traduction soit claire et facile à comprendre. Je la ferai refaire par des traducteurs professionnels le plus vite possible.

Mme Duval: Merci, Monsieur Jackson. Je crois que notre conversation au téléphone ce matin a été bénéfique.

Mr Jackson: Oui, et je vous assure que nous ferons de notre mieux pour vous donner satisfaction et pour rectifer ce contretemps. Au revoir, Madame Duval.

Mme Duval: Au revoir, Monsieur Jackson.

TRANSLATION

Mr Jackson: Is there something you'd like to add?

Mme Duval: Yes, we tested the machines on arrival (*lit.* 'at the arrival') and they are all in good working condition (*lit.* 'in good state of working'), with the exception of one (*lit.* 'of a single one'). The printer of one of the six word processors makes an unbearable noise. One would think one had (*lit.* 'One would think to have') a pneumatic drill right in the middle of the office!

Mr Jackson: You say that it's the only one which is faulty? I can't see (*lit.* 'I don't see') what could be the cause of it (*lit.* 'What could of it be the cause').The best thing is that I send you another machine immediately.

Mme Duval: Yes, I think that is the best solution.The third thing is the question of plugs. None of your machines is fitted with a plug. Now, you know that here in France, even the smallest electrical object includes a plug, and one only has to (*lit.* 'it only remains to') plug it in.

Mr Jackson: Really? (*lit.* 'ah good?'). We,of course, followed the British system but I agree that, in order to compete as well as possible (*lit.* 'to the best') with the goods of our competitors, we'll have to conform to (*lit.* 'fall into line on') customs in France. I'll make a note of it (*lit.* 'I of it take note') for the future. Thank you for pointing it out to me. I should have thought of it (*lit.* 'to it'). But it's not serious.

Mme Duval: Finally, there remains the question of the instruction booklet (*lit.* 'method of use'). It's well printed and well presented, but the translation in French is, unfortunately, difficult to follow and at times clumsy.

Mr Jackson:	Really? I had the text translated (*lit.* 'I have made to translate the text') by a member of my staff. But it's crucial that this translation be clear and easy to understand. I'll have it redone by professional translators as quickly as possible.
Mme Duval:	Thank you, Mr Jackson. I think that our conversation on the telephone this morning has been helpful (*lit.* 'beneficial').
Mr Jackson:	Yes, and I assure you that we'll do our best to give you satisfaction and to rectify this hitch. Goodbye Madame Duval.
Mme Duval:	Goodbye Mr Jackson.

Checklist 6

Imitated Pronunciation: We feel that you should now be fairly confident as far as the pronunciation is concerned and we are discontinuing the imitated pronunciation at this point. If you are still having difficulty with this aspect of the language, and it has to be admitted that French pronunciation does present problems, we strongly recommend that you purchase the cassette recordings which accompany this course.

Masculine nouns:

le bruit	noise
le marteau-piqueur	pneumatic drill
le milieu	middle
le système	system
le concurrent	competitor
le mode d'emploi	instruction booklet
le texte	text
le membre	member
le traducteur	translator
le contretemps	hitch
l'état	condition
l'objet	object

Feminine nouns:

la cause	cause
la solution	solution
la question	question
la prise (de courant)	plug
traduction	translation

la traductrice	translator
la conversation	conversation
l'arrivée	arrival
l'exception	exception
l'habitude	custom, habit

Adjectives:

seul	single, only
meilleur	better
électrique	electric
grave	serious
maladroit	clumsy
crucial	crucial
clair	clear
facile	easy
bénéfique	beneficial
insupportable	unbearable
défectueux, -euse (f.)	defective
professionnel, -elle (f.)	professional

beau (*m.*)	
bel (before *m.* noun beginning with vowel or silent h)	
beaux (*m. pl.*)	
belle (*f. sing.*)	
belles (*f. pl.*)	*beautiful, fine*

faire de son mieux	*to do one's best*
donner satisfaction	*to give satisfaction*
il ne reste plus que	*there only remains*
au revoir	*goodbye*

Adverbs:

finalement	*finally*
parfois	*at times, on occasions*

Other words/expressions:

en	*of it, of them*
y	*to it*
ici	*here*
or	*now*
mais	*but*
même	*even*
mieux	*better*
ah bon?	*really?*
le plus vite possible	*as quickly as possible*
en bon état de marche	*in good working order*
soit (subjunctive of être; see Unit 7)	*be*
pourrait	*could*
nous devrons	*we'll have to*
j'aurais dû	*I should have*
prendre note	*to take note*

Numbers:

premier, -ère (f.)	*1st*
deuxième	*2nd*
troisième	*3rd*
quatrième	*4th*
cinquième	*5th*
sixième	*6th*
septième	*7th*
huitième	*8th*
neuvième	*9th*
dixième	*10th*

Verbs:

tester	*to test*
équiper	*to equip*
comporter	*to include*
brancher	*to plug in*
rivaliser	*to compete*
signaler	*to point out*
imprimer	*to print*
présenter	*to present*
assurer	*to assure*
rectifier	*to rectify*
s'aligner	*to fall into line*

Irregular verbs:

croire *to think, believe*
present: je crois, il croit, nous croyons, vous croyez, ils croient
past: j'ai cru

dire *to say, tell*
present: je dis, il dit, nous disons, vous dites, ils disent
past: j'ai dit

suivre *to follow*
present: je suis, il suit, nous suivons, vous suivez, ils suivent
past: j'ai suivi

CHECKNOTES

45 The conditional tense:

In Unit 4 we met:

> Je vous serais reconnaissant, si vous pouviez …
> *I would be grateful, if you could …*

In Unit 5 we saw:

> Y a-t-il autre chose que vous aimeriez ajouter?
> *Is there something else you would like to add?*

We now find in the dialogue to Unit 6:

> On croirait avoir un marteau-piqueur au beau milieu du bureau.
> *One would think one had a pneumatic drill right in the middle of the office.*

The verbs **serais, aimeriez, croirait** are in the conditional tense which translates the English 'I/you/he, etc. would …, (if)':

je serais   *I would be*
vous aimeriez *you would like*
on croirait   *one would think*

The conditional tense is formed by adding the following endings to the infinitive form of the verb (that's the 'to...' form, the word you look up in a dictionary):

je   -ais
il/elle -ait
nous   -ions
vous   -iez
ils/elles -aient

As with the future tense, omit the final **e** of **-re** verbs before adding the endings: **je vendrais**('I would sell'), **nous répondrions** ('we would reply'). For example:

je commanderais   *I would order*
il importerait   *he would import*
elle exporterait *she would export*
nous fabriquerions *we would manufacture*
vous réussiriez   *you would succeed*
ils attendraient *they would wait*

When a verb is irregular in the future tense, it will have the same irregularity in the conditional:

	future		conditional	
être	je serai	*I will be*	je serais	*I would be*
avoir	j'aurai	*I will have*	j'aurais	*I would have*
aller	j'irai	*I will go*	j'irais	*I would go*
faire	je ferai	*I will do*	je ferais	*I would do*

Examples:

Nous fabriquerions ces produits sous licence, si …	*We would manufacture these goods under licence if …*
Vous augmenteriez les ventes, si …	*You would increase sales, if …*
Quelle pourrait en être la cause?	*What could be the cause of it?*

Finally, note this construction with the verb **devoir** ('to have to'):

j'aurais dû	*I should have*
J'aurais dû y penser	*I should have thought of it*

46 The negative (2)

In Checknote 23 we pointed out that the negative in French is formed by putting **ne** (or **n'**) before the verb and **pas** after:

Leurs prix ne sont pas compétitifs.	*Their prices are not competitive.*

But there are other important negatives that have to be learned:

ne ... jamais	*never*
ne ... rien	*nothing*
ne ... personne	*no-one*
ne ... plus	*no more, no longer*
ne ... plus que	*only, nothing but*
ne ... aucun, aucune (*f.*)	*no*

Examples:

Je ne suis jamais ce système-là.	*I never follow that system.*
Nous n'importons rien.	*We import nothing.*
Nous ne rivalisons plus avec cette entreprise-là.	*We no longer compete with that firm.*
Ils n'ont personne de compétent pour traduire le mode d'emploi.	*They have no-one competent to translate the instruction booklet.*
Est-ce que vous ne testez plus les machines dans vos ateliers?	*Don't you test the machines in your workshop any more?*
Je ne travaille plus pour la Banque de France.	*I no longer work for the Bank of France.*

| Il ne vous reste plus qu'à signer les contrats. | *It only remains for you to sign the contracts.* |

Some of these negatives can begin a sentence:

Rien n'est arrivé.	*Nothing has arrived.*
Personne n'a téléphoné.	*No-one has telephoned.*
Aucune machine ne fonctionne parfaitement.	*No machine works perfectly.*

In the past tense **jamais, rien** and **plus** come before the past participle:

| Je n'ai jamais parlé à votre président. | *I've never spoken to your chairman.* |
| Nous n'avons rien vu de nouveau à la foire du livre. | *We saw nothing new at the book fair.* |

47 On

The French word **on** refers to no-one in particular. It means 'one', 'they', 'people' etc.

Examples:

| En Grande-Bretagne on se prépare pour le Marché unique européen de 1992. | *In Britain they're preparing themselves for the Single European Market in 1992.* |

On is often used in place of the passive:

| On est en train de construire un tunnel sous le Manche. | *A tunnel is being built under the Channel.* |

48 To have something done

When you get something done by someone else, you have to use a construction with **faire**:

| Nous faisons construire une usine en Normandie. | *We're having a factory built in Normandy.* |
| Ils feront traduire le texte en espagnol. | *They'll have the text translated into Spanish.* |

49 En

En means:

a) 'some' or 'any' when not followed by a noun:

| Avez-vous des clients japonais? | *Do you have any Japanese customers?* |
| Oui, j'en ai. | *Yes, I do (Yes, I have some).* |

b) of/about it,them

Avez-vous parlé de la conférence internationale à votre chef de service?	*Have you spoken about the conference to your head of department?*
Oui, j'en ai parlé.	*Yes I've spoken about it.*
J'en prends note pour l'avenir.	*I'll make a note of it for the future.*

50 Y

Y means:

a) 'there':

Vous allez à l'exposition agricole?	*Are you going to the agricultural show?*
Oui, j'y vais demain.	*Yes, I'm going there tomorrow.*

But when actually pointing we say **là** or **là**-bas.

b) 'to it'

Le taux d'intérêt va encore augmenter!	*The interest rate is going to increase again!*
Oui, je sais, mais j'y suis habitué.	*Yes, I know, but I'm used to it.*

51 Telephoning in French (Part 2)

Here are some more useful expressions to use when talking to the French secretary:

Bonjour, Madame. Je m'appelle Peter Jackson, de la société Excel-Equip.
Good morning. My name is Peter Jackson, of Excel-Equip.

Je voudrais parler à M./Mme/Mlle Legras, s'il vous plaît.
I'd like to speak to M./Mme/Mlle Legras, please.

Est-ce que Mme Duval est là, s'il vous plaît?
Is Mme Duval there please?

Serait-il possible de parler à M.Legras, s'il vous plaît?
Would it be possible to speak to M.Legras, please?

Mme Duval m'a demandé de lui téléphoner.
Mme Duval has asked me to telephone her.

J'ai trouvé un message de Mme Duval sur mon répondeur automatique.
I've found a message from Mme Duval on my answerphone.

Est-ce que je peux lui laisser un message?
Can I leave a message for him/her?

Savez-vous quand il/elle sera de retour?
Do you know when he/she will be back?

Possible replies from the French secretary:

C'est de la part de qui?	*Who's calling?*
C'est à quel sujet?	*What is it in connection with?*
Avez-vous déjà été en contact avec Mme Duval?	*Have you already been in contact with Mme Duval?*
Puis-je vous demander d'épeler votre nom?	*May I ask you to spell your name?*
Je vous passe Mlle Legras tout de suite.	*I'm putting you through to Mlle Legras right away.*
Je regrette, il/elle n'est pas là.	*I'm sorry, he/she's not here.*

Now come all the excuses!

Elle est en déplacement.	*She's away on business.*
Il est en réunion.	*He's at a meeting.*
Elle est en conférence.	*She's in conference.*
Il est en vacances.	*He's on vacation.*
Elle est en Angleterre/Italie/Espagne.	*She's in England/Italy/Spain.*
Il est en Allemagne/Belgique.	*He's in Germany/Belgium.*
Elle est à l'étranger.	*She's abroad.*
Il n'est pas disponible.	*He's not available.*
Elle est occupée sur l'autre ligne.	*She's busy on the other line.*
Il sera là cet après-midi.	*He'll be back this afternoon.*
ce soir	*this evening*
demain	*tomorrow*
après-demain	*the day after tomorrow*
la semaine prochaine	*next week*
Voulez-vous laisser un message?	*Would you like to leave a message?*
Je vais lui demander de vous rappeler.	*I'll ask him/her to ring you back.*
Je peux peut-être vous aider moi-même.	*Perhaps I can help you myself.*

When the French give a telephone number, they divide the number up into units of two, like this: 12 34 56 78, saying (twelve, thirty-four, fifty-six, seventy-eight) **douze, trente-quatre, cinquante-six, soixante-dix-huit.**

Comprehension Practice 6

Vrai ou faux?

New words:

le technicien	*technician*
une pure perte de temps	*a pure waste of time*
bruyant	*noisy*
réparer	*to repair*
refuser	*to refuse*
laisser beacoup à désirer	*to leave much to be desired*

1 Tout le matériel livré à Mme Duval est défectueux.

2 L'un des traitements de texte est très bruyant.

3 Mr Jackson propose d'envoyer son technicien à Paris pour réparer l'imprimante.

4 Les machines envoyées par Mr Jackson sont équipées de prises.

5 Mr Jackson refuse de rivaliser avec les concurrents français.

6 La traduction en français du mode d'emploi laisse beaucoup à désirer.

7 La traduction du texte sera refaite par un membre du personnel de la société Excel-Equip.

8 La conversation au téléphone entre Mme Duval et Mr Jackson a été une pure perte de temps!

FLUENCY PRACTICE 28

This is an easy exercise. Which is the odd one out and why?

1 a) le chef du personnel
   b) la directrice des ventes
   c) l'ouvrier
   d) le directeur adjoint

2 a) le micro-ordinateur
   b) la prise de courant
   c) le télécopieur
   d) la calculatrice

3 a) partir
   b) arriver
   c) expédier
   d) aller

4 a) la Belgique
   b) l'Espagne
   c) le Royaume-Uni
   d) les États-Unis

5 a) le document
   b) le règlement
   c) le paiement
   d) le virement

FLUENCY PRACTICE 29

Give the French equivalent of:

1 Can I leave a message for him/her?
2 Do you know when he/she will be back?
3 What is it in connection with?
4 He's not available.
5 She's abroad.
6 Perhaps I can help you.

FLUENCY PRACTICE 30

New words:

le service de la comptabilité	*accounts department*
la Grande-Bretagne	*Britain*
l'Union soviétique	*Soviet Union*
la vidéo-conférence	*teleconference*
la direction	*management*
les revendications (*f.*) salariales	*salary claims*
les biens(*m.*) de consommation	*consumer goods*
informatiser	*to computerize*
tenir (*irreg.*)	*to hold*
satisfaire (*irreg.*)	*to satisfy*
plus de biens de consommation	*more consumer goods*

Translate the verb(s) in brackets:

1 L'entreprise (would computerize) le service de la comptabilité, si …
2 Nous (would be able to hold) une vidéo-conférence, si …
3 La direction (would be ready to) satisfaire les revendications salariales, si …
4 Les pays de la CEE (would export) plus de biens de consommation en Union soviétique, si...

FLUENCY PRACTICE 31

New words:

le/la collègue	*colleague*
la TVA	*VAT*
l'atelier (*m.*) de montage	*assembly shop*
les congés payés	*annual paid holidays*
verser un acompte	*to make a down payment*
diminuer	*to decrease*
quelquefois	*sometimes*

Answer the following two questions using **ne … jamais** ('never'), as in the example:

Vous prenez toujours vos cinq semaines de congés payés?	*Do you always take your five weeks' annual leave (paid holidays)?*
Non, je ne prends jamais mes cinq semaines de congés payés.	*No, I never take my five weeks' annual leave (paid holidays).*

1 La TVA diminue quelquefois?
2 Avez-vous visité l'atelier de montage?

Now reply using **ne ... rien** ('nothing')
3 Ont-ils fait le nécessaire?
4 Vous versez un acompte?

Now use **ne ... personne** ('no one')
5 Combien d'ouvriers avez-vous licenciés?

Now use **personne ne ...**
6 Votre collègue va vous aider?

FLUENCY PRACTICE 32

New words:

le bon de commande	*order form*
le jour	*day*
la taille	*size*
la robe d'été	*summer dress*
l'adresse (f.)	*address*
reprendre	*to take back*
parfait	*perfect*
sous les yeux	*in front of me (lit. 'under the eyes')*
Comment?	*Pardon?*
Quand?	*When?*

We want you to imagine that you've just received a consignment of dresses from Boutique Toutes-Tailles in Lyon. The problem is - you cancelled the order two weeks ago! You decide to telephone the company. Take part in the following conversation in French:

Toutes-Tailles:	**Allô, Toutes-Tailles. Bonjour.**
You:	*Good morning. Can I have extension 34 please?*
	...
Toutes-Tailles:	**Allô, Pierre Dupont.**
You:	*Good morning, Monsieur Dupont. This is Mike Smith speaking of Splendid Wear in Canterbury. You've sent me 50 Summer dresses but I've cancelled this order.*
Toutes-Tailles:	**Ah bon? Quand avez-vous annulé la commande?**

You:	*Three weeks ago.*
Toutes-Tailles:	Vous avez le numéro du bon de commande?
You:	*Yes, it's order form number 79.*
Toutes-Tailles:	Comment? Je vous entends mal. Pouvez-vous répéter le numéro, s'il vous plaît?
You:	79.
Toutes-Tailles:	Oui, j'ai le bon de commande sous les yeux ... . Mais la commande n'a pas été annulée!
You:	*But I assure you that I spoke to Mademoiselle Tétenlère three weeks ago.*
Toutes-Tailles:	Oui, oui, je vous crois, Monsieur Smith, mais Mademoiselle Tétenlère ne travaille plus ici. Ce n'est pas grave. Nous avons une livraison sur Londres jeudi prochain. Nous pourrons reprendre les marchandises ce jour-là.
You:	*That's perfect. Do you want the address of my company?*
Toutes-Tailles:	Non, non, l'adresse est sur le bon de commande.
You:	*Thank you very much. Goodbye.*

FLUENCY PRACTICE 33

Take the English translation of the conversation between Mme Duval and Mr Jackson and translate the paragraph beginning 'Really? We, of course, followed ...' back into French.

DICTIONARY PRACTICE 2

We want you to imagine that you work for British Telecom. Your head of department (who knows no French) has come across this French advertisement. He's wondering whether France Telecom has come up with some new and exciting service that he should know about. He's asked you to give him the gist of the advertisement in English. You'll need your dictionary. Check later with the Key.

Remember, your boss has only asked for the gist of the ad. - don't be too worried by any grammatical forms we haven't yet discussed!

The advertisement is on the following two pages.

AGENCE COMMERCIALE DE LA MANCHE

Offre
EXCEPTIONNELLE
Economisez
1 024 F. T.T.C.

Chère Madame, Cher Monsieur,

vous Connaissez

POINT PHONE!
Le téléphone en libre service!

Le **POINT PHONE** est un téléphone à pièces qui trouve sa place dans votre établissement, au service de votre clientèle.

Avec **POINT PHONE**, vos clients peuvent téléphoner sans occuper votre poste, sans que vous ayez à payer leur communication et sans vous déranger.

Rendez-leur ce service!

Jugez vous même

M.R., propriétaire d'un café-restaurant. "Je n'étais pas équipé de poste public, mais mes clients avaient souvent besoin de téléphoner; évidemment je ne pouvais pas refuser, mais c'est quand même moi qui payais leurs communications! J'ai vu une publicité sur le Point Phone, je me suis renseigné aux Télécom et depuis quelques mois, j'ai fait installer un Point Phone sur mon comptoir. Plus besoin de proposer mon poste privé, c'est vraiment pratique et utile quand on est dans le commerce et croyez-moi mes clients aussi l'apprécient."

En prenant le **POINT PHONE** dès maintenant, vous économiserez:

- Installation ligne   Point Phone : **310 F. T.T.C.**
- 3 premiers mois de location ligne   Point Phone : **714 F. T.T.C.**

soit une économie de plus de 1 000 F. T.T.C.

Pour les 9 mois suivants, votre abonnement mensuel sera de
210 F. T.T.C.

Profitez vite de cette offre valable un mois en utilisant le bon de commande
ci-joint ou en commandant directement par téléphone au

33 06 15 11

Mon Attaché Commercial prendra très prochainement rendez-vous
avec vous.

Persuadé que cette offre exceptionnelle vous intéressera, je vous dis
Chère Madame, Cher Monsieur, au revoir et à bientôt.

Le Directeur d'Agence,

J.P GANDET

The advertising campaign

> *In this unit you'll learn the subjunctive, how to put forward your suggestions ('Let's...') and ask people to do things, question actions and make decisions.*
>
> *France-Burotic feels it is time to organize an advertising campaign in order to boost sales and to launch the new portable word processor produced by Excel-Equip. Mme Duval consults an advertising agency.*

Mme Duval: Bonjour, Monsieur. Permettez-moi de me présenter … Madame Duval. J'ai rendez-vous avec Monsieur Lanonse à dix heures.

M. Lanonse: C'est moi-même. Bonjour, Madame. Je vous attendais justement. Passons dans mon bureau … Asseyez-vous donc, Madame.

Mme Duval: Voilà. Je suis la responsable de la publicité pour une société qui se spécialise dans la bureautique. Nous avons l'intention de lancer une campagne publicitaire pour promouvoir nos nouveaux produits et, en particulier, un tout nouvel article qui nous vient d'Angleterre … un traitement de texte portable. Nous avons déjà fait une étude de marché et nous voulons que la publicité vise une cible précise, c'est à dire les chefs d'entreprise de petite et moyenne taille qui débutent dans les affaires et s'installent dans la région parisienne.

M Lanonse: Dans ce cas, il est préférable que nous commencions par mettre des annonces dans les magazines d'actualité tels que l'Express et plus tard dans les magazines économiques comme, par exemple, l'Usine Nouvelle et l'Expansion, sans oublier la presse spécialisée en bureautique comme '01 Informatique'.

Mme Duval: Oui, je suis d'accord. Vous avez probablement raison. Quel style de publicité me recommandez-vous pour ces magazines?

M. Lanonse: Les statistiques prouvent que le public est davantage stimulé par un message visuel et amusant. C'est pourquoi nous utilisons souvent des dessins humoristiques, des bandes dessinées et des caricatures - tous accompagnés d'un slogan original.

Mme Duval: Un slogan original plein d'humour britannique, peut-être?

M. Lanonse: Et pourquoi pas? … Ce qui continue à avoir un impact sur le public, ce sont les affiches, placées dans le centre-ville, dans les couloirs du métro et la distribution de dépliants et de prospectus aux heures d'affluence dans le quartier des affaires.

Mme Duval: Oui, la publicité traditionnelle, quoi. Mais il faut qu'elle soit percutante. Il faut qu'elle attire l'attention des gens pressés. Et les spots publicitaires à la télévision, qu'est-ce que vous en pensez?

M Lanonse: Le petit écran reste, à mon avis, le support publicitaire le plus efficace. Il touche toutes les tranches de la société, sans exception … Si votre budget publicité n'est pas trop limité, vous pourriez considérer la dernière nouveauté - le vidéo mailing.

Mme Duval: Ah bon? En quoi consiste le vidéo mailing exactement?

M. Lanonse: Il consiste à envoyer un message publicitaire sur vidéo-cassette directement aux chefs d'entreprise.

Mme Duval: Ah oui, c'est une bonne excuse pour regarder son magnétoscope au bureau. Bien, tout cela est très intéressant. J'aimerais que vous m'envoyiez un devis me donnant le coût de chaque support publicitaire pour une période d'un mois ainsi que quelques maquettes d'affiches. J'en parlerai à la prochaine réunion du conseil d'administration. Nous prendrons alors une décision et je vous contacterai immédiatement.

M Lanonse: Parfait, Madame.

Mme Duval: Au revoir, Monsieur.

M Lanonse: Au revoir, Madame.

TRANSLATION

Mme Duval: Good morning. May I introduce myself … Madame Duval.
I've an appointment with Monsieur Lanonse at ten o'clock.

M Lanonse: That's me (*lit.* 'that's myself'). Good morning. I was (just)
expecting you. Let's go into my office … Do sit down.

Mme Duval: Right. I'm the person in charge of advertising for a
company which specializes in office automation. We
intend to launch an advertising campaign to promote our
new products and, in particular, a completely new article
that comes to us from England … a portable word
processor. We've already carried out a market survey
and we want the advertising to be directed at (*lit.* 'to aim
at') a specific target, that's to say the heads of small and
medium-sized firms who are starting up in business and
setting up in the Paris area.

M Lanonse: In that case, it's preferable that we begin by putting
advertisements in the current affairs magazines such as
l'Express and later in the economic magazines like, for
example, l'Usine Nouvelle and l'Expansion, not forgetting
the press specializing in office automation like '01
Informatique'.

Mme Duval: Yes, I agree. You're probably right. What style of
advertising do you recommend for these magazines?

M Lanonse: Statistics prove that the public is more stimulated by a
visual and amusing message. That's why we often use
cartoons, comic strips and caricatures, all accompanied
by an original catch-phrase.

Mme Duval: An original catch-phrase full of British humour, perhaps?

M Lanonse: And why not? … What is continuing to have an impact on
the public are posters, placed in the town centre, in the
corridors of the metro and the distribution of folders and
leaflets during the rush hour in the business quarter.

Mme Duval: Yes, traditional advertising, you mean (*lit.*'what'). But it
must be forceful. It must attract the attention of people in
a hurry. And what about TV commercials, what do you
think of them?

M Lanonse: Television (*lit.* 'the small screen') remains, in my opinion,
the most effective advertising medium. It reaches all
sections of society, without exception … If your publicity
budget isn't too limited, you might consider the latest
idea –video mailing.

Mme Duval:	Really? What does video mailing consist of, exactly?
M Lanonse:	It consists in sending an advertising message on video cassette directly to the heads of companies.
Mme Duval:	Oh yes, that's a good excuse for watching one's video recorder in the office. Fine, all that is very interesting. I'd like you to send me an estimate giving me the cost of each advertising medium for a period of one month, together with a few paste-ups of posters. I'll discuss it at the next board meeting. We'll take a decision then and I'll contact you immediately.
M Lanonse:	That's fine.
*Mme Duva*l:	Goodbye.
M. Lanonse:	Goodbye.

Checklist 7

Masculine nouns:

le/la responsable	*person in charge*
le chef d'entreprise	*head of company*
le style	*style*
le conseil d'administration	*board of directors*
le magazine d'actualité	*current affairs magazine*
le dessin humoristique	*cartoon*
le couloir	*corridor*
le dépliant	*folder*
le centre-ville	*town centre*
le quartier des affaires	*business quarter*
le spot publicitaire	*commercial*
le support publicitaire	*advertising medium*
le devis	*estimate, quotation*
le magnétoscope	*video recorder*
le coût	*cost*
l'écran	*screen*
le petit écran	*television*
les gens	*people*

Feminine nouns:

la campagne publicitaire	*advertising campaign*
la cible	*target*
la bande dessinée	*comic strip*
la maquette	*paste-up*
la presse	*press*
la taille	*size*
la tranche	*section, bracket*
l'étude de marché	*market survey*
l'annonce	*advertise-ment*
l'affiche	*poster*
les affaires	*business*

Adverbs:

souvent	*often*
justement	*just*
exactement	*exactly*
directement	*directly*

Adjectives:

moyen,-enne (*f.*)	*medium, average*

nouveau	*new*	aux heures	*during rush*
nouvel (*m. sing*, used before		d'affluence	*hour*
vowel and silent h)		ce qui	*what* (sub.)
nouveaux (*m.pl*)		ce que	*what* (obj.)
nouvelle (*f.sing.*)		plus tard	*later*
nouvelles (*f.pl*)		sans exception	*without*
précis	*precise,*		*exception*
	specific	je vous attendais	*I was*
spécialisé	*specialized*		*expecting*
percutant	*forceful*		*you*
plein	*full*		
pressé	*in a hurry*		
efficace	*effective*	**Verbs:**	
parfait	*perfect*		
intéressant	*interesting*	lancer	*to launch*
portable	*portable*	viser	*to aim at*
(portable is often used as an		débuter	*to begin*
alternative to portatif)		commencer	*to begin*
prochain	*next*	utiliser	*to use*
		attirer	*to attract*
		toucher	*to reach;*
Other words/expressions:			*to touch;*
			to cash
moi-même	*myself*	regarder	*to watch*
davantage	*more*	oublier	*to forget*
chaque	*each*	donner	*to give*
asseyez-vous donc	*do sit down*	prouver	*to prove*
dans ce cas	*in that case*	s'installer	*to set*
tel, tels (*m. pl.*), telle	*such as*		*oneself up*
(*f.*), telles (*f. pl.*) que			

Irregular verbs:

promouvoir *to promote*
present: not used
past: j'ai promu

permettre *to allow, permit*
present: je permets, il permet, nous permettons, vous permettez, ils
permettent
past: j'ai permis

venir *to come*
present: je viens, il vient, nous venons, vous venez, ils viennent
past: je suis venu
future: je viendrai

envoyer *to send*
present: j'envoie, il envoie, nous envoyons, vous envoyez, ils envoient
future: j'enverrai

CHECKNOTES

52 Making suggestions

To make a suggestion simply drop the **nous** of the present tense:

passons dans ...	*let's go into ...*
organisons une campagne publicitaire	*let's organize an advertising campaign*
faisons une étude de marché	*let's do a market survey*

We already know that pronouns are placed <u>before</u> the verb in French and we've had many examples of that in the conversations. But when we ask people to do things, we put the pronoun <u>after</u> the verb:

Le député?	*The member of parliament?*
Mais invitez-le.	*(But) invite him.*
Le contrat d'assurance?	*The insurance contract?*
Mais résiliez-le.	*Cancel it.*
La police d'assurance?	*The insurance policy?*
Mais tapez-la.	*Type it.*
Les documents?	*The documents?*
Mais télécopiez-les.	*Fax them.*
Asseyez-vous.	*Sit down.*
Admettons-le.	*Let's admit it.*

Oddly enough, however, the pronoun returns to its original place <u>before</u> the verb in the negative request:

La secrétaire?	*The secretary?*
Ne la renvoyez pas.	*Don't dismiss her.*
Les dépliants?	*The folders?*
Ne les distribuez pas.	*Don't distribute them.*

53 Questions

Où?	*Where?*
Quand?	*When?*
Comment	*How?*
Qui?	*Who, whom?*
Pourquoi?	*Why?*
Pour quelle raison?	*For what reason?*
Combien?	*How much/many?*
Quel/Quelle/Quels/Quelles ... ?	*Which/What ... ?*
De quelle façon ... ?	*In what way ... ?*

Examples:

Où est l'agence de publicité?
Where is the advertising agency?

Quand allez-vous lancer la campagne publicitaire?
When are you going to launch the advertising campaign?

Comment allez-vous convaincre les clients potentiels que vos prix sont compétitifs?
How are you going to convince potential clients that your prices are competitive?

Qui avez-vous nommé comme chef de la publicité?
Whom did you appoint as publicity manager?

Pourquoi ne faites-vous pas de réduction sur les fins de série?
Why don't you make a reduction on the discontinued lines?

Combien de voyageurs de commerce employez-vous?
How many sales representatives do you employ?

Quels moyens publicitaires avez-vous choisis?
Which advertising media have you chosen?

54 Prepositions + verbs

Study the following:

a) Avant de mettre l'annonce dans le journal, il faut consulter le rédacteur-concepteur.
Before putting the advertisement in the newspaper we must consult the copywriter.

b) On ne peut pas lancer ce nouveau produit sans faire une étude de marché.
One can't launch this new product without carrying out a market survey.

c) Le P.-D.G. a commencé par féliciter la force de vente.
The Managing Director began by congratulating the sales force.

You'll have noticed that, in English, verbs preceded by a preposition (to, without, before, after, for, by, etc.) end in -ing; in French the infinitive (or dictionary form) is used.

55 Expressions with avoir

In Checklist 3 we met **avoir raison** ('to be right') and **avoir tort** ('to be wrong'). Here are some more expressions which in English are used with 'to be' but which take **avoir** in French:

avoir faim	to be hungry
avoir soif	to be thirsty
avoir chaud	to be warm

avoir froid	to be cold
avoir sommeil	to be sleepy
avoir honte	to be ashamed
avoir peur	to be afraid
avoir (30) ans	to be (30) years old

Examples:

Nous essayons de toucher les cadres qui ont entre 25 et 35 ans.
We're trying to reach managers who are between 25 and 35 years old.

J'ai peur que vous ne soyez (see Checknote 60) déficitaire.
I'm afraid that you might show a deficit.

N'avez-vous pas honte de la mauvaise qualité des messages publicitaires à la radio?
Aren't you ashamed of the poor quality of the commercials on the radio?

56 Relative pronouns

qui (subject): who, which, that
que (object): whom, which, that

The following examples will show how these relative pronouns are used, but if you're having difficulty in deciding whether 'who/which/that' is the subject or the object, here's a rule to help you: (1) If in English the verb comes immediately after 'who/which/that', as in 'the car which has broken down', use **qui**. (2) If in English there's another word between 'who/which/that' and the verb, as in 'the car which I prefer', use **que**.

... les jeunes chefs d'entreprise qui débutent dans les affaires
... young company bosses who are starting up in business

... un nouvel article qui nous vient de Grande-Bretagne
... a new article which comes to us from Britain

... le premier candidat que je voudrais interviewer
... the first candidate whom I'd like to interview

... les machines que nous vous avons livrées
... the machines which we have delivered to you

You'll remember learning in Checknote 43 that the past participle (**contacté, copié commandé, vendu, choisi,** etc.) has to reflect the gender and number of the direct object pronouns used with it; the same principle applies to **que** ('who, which'):

le message que j'ai reçu ce matin	*the message which I received this morning*
la lettre que j'ai reçue hier	*the letter that I received yesterday*
les factures que nous avons envoyées	*the invoices we sent*

You'll have noticed from the last example that the relative pronoun is sometimes omitted in English but it must always be expressed in French.

57 Ce qui/ce que ('what')

The words **qui** and **que** can be preceded by **ce**, in which case they translate the English 'what' in sentences like the following:

> **Ce qui continue à avoir un impact sur le public, ce sont les affiches.**
> *What continues to have an impact on the public are posters.*

> **Vous devez trouver un bon slogan, voilà ce que je vous recommande.**
> *You must find a good catch-phrase, that's what I recommend.*

58 The present participle

The English ending -ing is often expressed by **-ant** in French (but see Checknote 54):

> **Envoyez-moi un devis me donnant les détails du coût des publicités à la télévision.**
> *Send me an estimate giving details of the cost of commercials on television.*

This **-ant** is added to the **nous**-form of the present tense of the verb after removing the **-ons**:

donner (*to give*)	nous donnons	**donnant**	*giving*
illustrer (*to illustrate*)	nous illustrons	**illustrant**	*illustrating*
décrire (*to describe*)	nous décrivons	**décrivant**	*describing*
vendre (*to sell*)	nous vendons	**vendant**	*selling*

There are three exceptions:

avoir (*to have*)	**ayant**	*having*
être (*to be*)	**étant**	*being*
savoir (*to know*)	**sachant**	*knowing*

The **-ant** form in French is often used with the word **en** to mean 'while', 'by' or 'in':

> **En travaillant dur et en planifiant bien votre carrière, vous pourriez faire partie un jour de la direction.**
> *By working hard and planning well, you could one day form part of the management.*

59 The subjunctive

Study the following:

a) vous êtes là à 10 heures — *you are here at 10 o'clock*
   BUT:
   je veux que vous soyez là à 10 heures — *I want you to be here at 10 o'clock*

b) le texte est facile à comprendre — *the text is easy to understand*
   BUT:
   il faut que le texte soit facile à comprendre — *the text must be easy to understand*

c) la traduction est claire — *the translation is clear*
   BUT:
   il est crucial que la traduction soit claire — *it is crucial that the translation be clear*

d) la machine est défectueuse — *the machine is faulty*
   BUT:
   c'est la seule machine qui soit défectueuse — *it's the only machine which is faulty*

e) notre service d'emballage et d'expédition fait le nécessaire — *our packing and dispatch department does everything necessary*
   BUT:
   je veillerai à ce que notre service d'emballage et d'expédition fasse le nécessaire — *I'll see to it that our packing and dispatch department does everything necessary*

Why the changes? Because in French (and many other languages) certain verbs and expressions are followed by the subjunctive mood and this often requires a change in the form of the verb that follows.

For the time being you really only need to remember that the subjunctive is used after:

a) a wish
b) a preference
c) a necessity
d) a suggestion
e) regret
f) **il est** (it is) + most adjectives (important, possible, normal, etc.)

The subjunctive is nearly always preceded by **que** ('that').

60 The formation of the subjunctive

Remove the **-ent** ending from the 3rd person plural (the 'they-form') of the present tense and add:

je	-e
il/elle	-e
nous	-ions
vous	-iez
ils/elles	-ent

In the right-hand column below you'll see a 'composite' present subjunctive tense made up from typical **-er**, **-ir** and **-re** verbs:

négocier	(to negotiate)	ils négocient	(que/qu')	je négocie
importer	(to import)	ils importent		il importe
embaucher	(to take on)	ils embauchent		elle embauche
garantir	(to guarantee)	ils garantissent		nous garantissions
investir	(to invest)	ils investissent		vous investissiez
répondre	(to reply)	ils répondent		ils répondent
vendre	(to sell)	ils vendent		elles vendent

There are also some irregular forms which we shall study later, but for the time being learn:

être (to be)	(que)	je sois, il soit, nous soyons, vous soyez, ils soient
faire (to do, make)		je fasse, il fasse, nous fassions, vous fassiez, ils fassent
pouvoir (to be able)		je puisse, il puisse, nous puissions, vous puissiez, ils puissent

Examples:

Je veux (voudrais) que le client négocie un emprunt avec sa banque.
I want (would like) the client to negotiate a loan with his bank.

Il faut que nous embauchions du personnel supplémentaire.
We must take on some additional staff.

Le Président suggère que la société investisse 18 milliards de francs à l'étranger.
The Chairman suggests that the company invest 18 billion francs abroad.
(N.B. un milliard = a thousand million)

Il est regrettable que je ne vende pas mes produits en Arabie saoudite.
It is regrettable that I don't sell my products in Saudi Arabia.

Il est peut-être normal que la France suspende temporairement les importations de viande de bœuf britannique à cause de la maladie de la 'vache folle' (l'encéphalite spongiforme bovine).
It's perhaps normal that France is temporarily suspending imports of

British beef because of 'mad cow' disease (bovine spongiform encephalopathy).

N.B. If the subject of the dependent verb is the same as that of the main verb, we use the infinitive, not the subjunctive. Compare:

Je veux téléphoner.	I want to telephone.
Je veux que vous téléphoniez.	I want you to telephone.

Comprehension Practice 7

Answer the questions, after noting the vocabulary and paying special attention to the accent changes in the verb suggérer.

New words:

le genre	kind
le/la publicitaire	advertising executive
fonctionner	to function
avoir besoin de	to need
suggérer	to suggest

present: je suggère, il suggère, nous suggérons, vous suggérez, ils suggèrent
past: j'ai suggéré
future: je suggérerai

1 Pour quelle raison Madame Duval contacte-t-elle une agence de publicité?

2 Quel est le nouvel article qu'elle veut lancer sur le marché français?

3 Quelle cible Madame Duval veut-elle viser dans cette campagne publicitaire?

4 Dans quel genre de magazines le publicitaire va-t-il mettre les annonces?

5 Quel style de publicité suggère-t-il?

6 En quoi consiste la publicité traditionnelle?

7 Comment fonctionne le principe du vidéo mailing?

8 De quoi Mme Duval a-t-elle besoin avant de pouvoir prendre une décision?

FLUENCY PRACTICE 34

New words:

le cadre	*executive*
la faillite	*bankruptcy*
faire faillite	*to go bankrupt*
les jeunes	*the young*
faire du zapping	*to switch repeatedly from one TV channel to another, to zap*
confirmer	*to confirm*
tous	*all*

Say in French:

1 I'd like you to send me a letter confirming the price and delivery period.
2 The company finished up by going bankrupt.
3 The young of today cannot watch TV without switching repeatedly from one channel to another.
4 The customer is always right.
5 The customer is never wrong.
6 The executives in this firm are all very young. They're between 23 and 30 years old.

FLUENCY PRACTICE 35

New words:

le cours	*course, class*
la référence	*reference*
l'informatique	*computing*
collaborer	*to collaborate*
suivre	*to attend, to follow*
perfectionner	*to improve, to perfect*
voyager	*to travel*
fournir	*to supply, to provide*
faire des heures supplémentaires	*to work overtime*

We want you to imagine that you have just been interviewed for a post in a company in France. The personnel manager is willing to offer you the position on certain conditions. Here are the conditions. What words did the interviewer use? Complete the following sentences:

a) Il faut que vous (être) disponible le 24 Août.
b) Il faut que vous (perfectionner) votre français.
c) J'aimerais que vous (suivre) un cours d'informatique.
d) Je voudrais que vous (voyager) à l'étranger.

e) Il est important que vous (pouvoir) collaborer avec vos collègues.
f) Il est nécessaire que vous (fournir) des références.
g) Il est possible que vous (faire) des heures supplémentaires.

FLUENCY PRACTICE 36

New words:

le courrier	*mail*
le prix de lancement	*introductory price*
la population cible	*target group*
l'échéance (*f.*)	*bill which is due*
gratuit	*free*
susceptible (de)	*likely (to)*
prévu	*due, planned*
faire face à	*to meet*
adresser	*to send*
par	*per*

Match the words in the first column with those in the second.

a) la population cible

b) l'échantillon gratuit

c) les publicitaires

d) le prix de lancement

e) nous vous adressons ci-joint la documentation

f) le client ne peut pas faire face à l'échéance

1) qui sera de 100 francs par article

2) que nous avons consultés

3) qui serait susceptible d'acheter nos produits

4) que j'ai reçu au courrier hier

5) qui est prévue pour le 15 Novembre

6) que vous avez demandée dans votre lettre du 10 Mai

FLUENCY PRACTICE 37

Translate back into French all the English examples in Checknote 53 in order to have a little more practice in asking questions.

DICTIONARY PRACTICE 3

This advertisement has been taken from **Ouest-France**, a newspaper which is on sale in the west of France. The car being advertised is rather special. Read the text with the help of your dictionary and answer the following questions in English. Here's the meaning of a colloquial expression you may not find in your dictionary: **comme c'est pas permis**, 'like you've never seen' (lit. 'like it's not permitted').

Questions

1 There's something unusual about this car, something that would probably not be allowed in Britain. What is it?
2 Why has the expression "comme c'est pas permis" been chosen for this advertisement?
3 What are the other three advantages of this car?
4 Has this type of car been a success so far?
5 With what other type of car is it being compared?
6 What brand of oil does Microcar recommend?

FLUENCY PRACTICE 38

If you feel confident enough (and you should after all the practice we've given you in using the telephone) why don't you ring the agent, le concessionnaire, in Valognes and ask the following questions (and any others that occur to you):

1 What's the price of the car?
2 What colours are available?
3 What's the delivery period?
4 Can the car be rented (to rent, hire = louer) for two weeks?

DICTIONARY PRACTICE 4

Did you know that you can now teach yourself management skills using computer software? Find out more by studying this French advertisement and then answer the questions in English. The advertisement is on the next page.

Questions

1 What is the French word for 'management'?
2 How long does this management course last?
3 What are the advantages of the course?
4 What is the French expression for the following:
    a) accounting
    b) break-even point
    c) working capital
    d) cash-flow plan
    e) forecast budget
5 Are there any opportunities for assessing the business skills you have acquired?
6 How will the software be sent to the purchaser?

LES LOGICIELS DÉFIGESTION

Un logiciel pour apprendre soi-même la gestion

Avec DÉFIGESTION, logiciel d'enseignement assisté par ordinateur, vous apprendrez vous-même les rudiments de la gestion de votre entreprise, agréablement, et à votre rythme (durée du cours: 5 heures en moyenne).

Configuration nécessaire : tous compatibles PC MS/DOS, 2 disquettes ou disque dur, 256 K RAM. Les 2 disquettes DÉFIGESTION et leur mode d'utilisation : 1 100 F TTC (927,48 F HT, déductibles des frais de votre entreprise).

Le logiciel DÉFIGESTION vous sera adressé sous pli recommandé, accompagné d'une facture acquittée.

DÉFIGESTION traite 5 chapitres principaux :

• La comptabilité;
• Comment établir un plan de trésorerie ;
• Le point mort, comment le calculer ;
• Comment construire un budget prévisionnel ;
• Comment estimer les besoins en fonds de roulement (BFR).
De nombreux exercices pratiques vous permettent de tester les connaissances que vous avez acquises.

DÉFIS, 33 rue Faidherbe, 75011 Paris
Tél.: (1) 43 70 04 04

The trade exhibition

> *Another past tense (the imperfect 'I was doing' or 'I used to --') is explained, together with the passive voice and some useful prepositional phrases. There's more dictionary practice and you'll learn how to add a touch of colour to your conversation.*
>
> *As part of their sales drive, France-Burotic decide to take a stand at the Salon IBB (Informatique-Bureautique-Bureau): Mme Duval rings Mr Jackson in London to ask if it would be possible for him to attend this trade exhibition too.*

Mme Duval: Allô, Monsieur Jackson? C'est Madame Duval à l'appareil. Je ne vous dérange pas, j'espère?

Mr Jackson: Non, non, pas du tout.

Mme Duval: Je vous téléphone à propos du Salon IBB qui aura lieu au Parc des Expositions à Paris du 14 au 19 février. Ce Salon est réservé aux professionnels la première journée et est ouvert au grand public les autres jours. Il rassemble environ 300 exposants et attire toujours de nombreux visiteurs. Je voulais vous demander s'il vous serait possible de représenter votre compagnie à cette Exposition. Ou bien est-ce qu'un de vos associés américains voudrait saisir cette occasion pour visiter Paris?

Mr Jackson: Je crois que mon collègue de New York assistera à ces dates-là à un congrès international en Floride, mais moi, je viendrai certainement. Avec plaisir. Ce sera aussi une occasion pour rencontrer la clientèle française. Vous dites que c'est du 14 au 19 février? Attendez, je vérifie sur mon agenda ... zut alors, j'ai un rendez-vous le quatorze ... ça ne fait rien, j'annulerai cette réunion. Je veux être présent le jour de l'inauguration.

Mme Duval: Parfait. Nous avons déjà réservé notre stand, car les meilleurs emplacements partent très rapidement, vous savez. J'ai loué un stand de 12m^2 (12 mètres carrés) pour 10 000 francs. Le mobilier nous sera fourni automatiquement et j'ai demandé qu'on nous installe quelques prises de courant supplémentaires. Bien sûr, les frais d'électricité et les primes d'assurance sont en plus.

Mr Jackson: Très bien. Mais où sommes-nous placés exactement dans le hall de l'Exposition?

Mme Duval: Nous sommes situés à côté du bureau d'accueil, à gauche du vestiaire et juste en face du bar et du self-service. C'est le stand 191, allée J.

Mr Jackson: En face du bar? Oh, à la bonne heure! Il faut toujours savoir joindre l'utile à l'agréable, n'est-ce pas, Madame? Au fait, pour l'aménagement du stand, aurez-vous besoin de documentation supplémentaire, … de photos, d'affiches?

Mme Duval: Si vous pouviez nous envoyer quelques affiches en couleurs de vos produits, nous vous en serions reconnaissants; elles ajouteront un cachet britannique.

Mr Jackson: Oui, oui. Je n'y manquerai pas. Comptez sur moi le 14 février. J'en profiterai pour jeter un coup d'œil sur les autres stands dans le but de faire un peu d'espionnage industriel …. Une dernière question, Madame, … où se trouve exactement le Parc des Expositions? Je ne veux surtout pas me perdre! Je ne connais pas bien Paris.

Mme Duval: Porte de Versailles. Prenez le métro et descendez à la station Porte de Versailles. C'est juste à côté.

Mr Jackson: Très bien.J'en ai pris note. Merci d'avoir téléphoné. Au revoir, Madame.

Mme Duval: Au revoir, Monsieur.

TRANSLATION

Mme Duval: Hello, Mr Jackson. This is Madame Duval speaking. I'm not disturbing you, I hope?

Mr Jackson: No,no, not at all.

Mme Duval: I'm 'phoning you in connection with the IBB Trade Exhibition which is going to take place at the Parc des Expositions in Paris from the 14th to the 19th February. This Exhibition is reserved for the trade the first day and is open to the general public on the other days. It brings together about 300 exhibitors and always attracts numerous visitors. I wanted to ask you if it would be possible for you to represent your company at this Exhibition. Or would one of your American partners like to take this opportunity to visit Paris?

Mr Jackson: I think my New York colleague will be attending an international convention in Florida on those dates, but I'll certainly come. With pleasure. It will also be an opportunity to meet the French customers. You say it's from the 14th to the 19th February? Hang on, I'll check (*lit.* 'I check') my diary ... damn, I've an appointment on the fourteenth ... it doesn't matter. I'll cancel this meeting. I want to be present on the opening day.

Mme Duval: Fine. We've already reserved our stand, because the best positions go very quickly, you know. I've hired a stand measuring 12 square metres for 10,000 francs. The furniture will be provided for us automatically and I've asked that they install for us a few additional power points. Of couse, electricity costs and insurance premiums are extra.

Mr Jackson: That's fine. But where are we positioned exactly in the Exhibition hall?

Mme Duval: We're situated next to the reception centre, to the left of the cloakroom and just opposite the bar and self-service restaurant. It's stand 191, aisle J.

Mr Jackson: Opposite the bar? Oh, splendid! One must always know how to combine business with pleasure (*lit.* 'join the useful to the pleasant'), isn't that so, Madame? Incidentally, for the preparation of the stand, will you need any additional literature ... photos, posters?

Mme Duval: If you could send us a few colour posters of your products, we'd be grateful. That'll add a British flavour.

Mr Jackson: Yes, yes, I won't forget (*lit.* 'I won't fail'). Count on me on the fourteenth February. I'll take the opportunity to have a quick look at (lit. 'to throw a glance on') the other stands with a view to carrying out a little industrial espionage. ....One last question ... where exactly is the Parc des Expositions? I certainly don't want to get lost (*lit.* 'I especially don't want to lose myself')! I don't know Paris well.

Mme Duval: Porte de Versailles. Take the metro and get out at Porte de Versailles station. It's just alongside.

Mr Jackson: Right. I've made a note. Thanks for 'phoning. Goodbye.

Mme Duval: Goodbye.

Checklist 8

Masculine nouns:

le salon	exhibition
le congrès	convention
le stand	stand
le mobilier	furniture
le hall	hall
le vestiaire	cloakroom
le self-service	self-service restaurant
l'exposant	exhibitor
l'associé, -e (f.)	partner
l'agenda	diary, notebook
l'emplacement	place
l'aménagement	fitting-out
l'espionnage industriel	industrial espionage

Feminine nouns:

la journée	day
Floride	Florida
la clientèle	clientele
la prime d'assurance	insurance premium
la photo	photo
la couleur	colour
la saveur	flavour
l'exposition	exhibition
l'occasion	opportunity
l'allée	aisle
les toilettes	toilets

Adjectives:

ouvert	open
fermé	closed
situé	situated
utile	useful
agréable	pleasant
reconnaissant	grateful
supplémentaire	additional
nombreux, -euse (f.)	numerous

Adverbs:

automatiquement	automatically

Where?

à côté de	beside
à gauche de	to the left of
à droite de	to the right of
en face de	opposite

Other words/expressions:

environ	about
toujours	always; still
ou bien	or
surtout	especially
autre	other
avoir lieu	to take place
je voulais	I wanted
avec plaisir	with pleasure
zut alors	damn
au fait	by the way
en plus	extra
à propos de	in connection with
ça ne fait rien	that doesn't matter
si vous pouviez	if you could
à la bonne heure	splendid
un peu (de)	a little
dans le but de	with a view to
jeter un coup d'œil sur	to glance at
n'est-ce pas	isn't it/aren't you?/don't they? etc.

Numbers:

quatre-vingts	80
quatre-vingt-un	81
quatre-vingt-deux	82
quatre-vingt-huit	88
quatre-vingt-dix	90
quatre-vingt-onze	91
quatre-vingt-dix-neuf	99

cent	100	demander	to ask
cent un	101	saisir	to seize
cent dix	110	assister	to attend
cent cinquante	150	rencontrer	to meet
deux cents	200	vérifier	to check
trois cents	300	annuler	to cancel
quatre cents	400	louer	to hire, rent
cinq cent vingt	520	installer	to install
six cent cinquante	650	manquer	to fail; to miss
		compter	to count

N.B.: Both **quatre-vingts** and **cents** drop the s when another number follows.

profiter de	to take advantage of
se trouver	to be situated
fournir	to supply, provide

Verbs:

déranger	to disturb	descendre	to go down, get off
réserver	to reserve		
rassembler	to gather	se perdre	to get lost

Irregular verbs:

partir *to leave*
present: je pars, il part,nous partons,vous partez, ils partent
past: je suis parti

savoir *to know (how to)*
   see Checklist 3

joindre *to join; to contact*
present: je joins, il joint, nous joignons. vous joignez, ils joignent
past: j'ai joint

connaître *to know*
present: je connais, il connaît, nous connaissons, vous connaissez,
   ils connaissent
past: j'ai connu

N.B. The verb **connaître** means 'to know' in the sense of 'being acquainted with' - with a place or person, for example. The verb **savoir** means to know a fact.

CHECKNOTES

61 The imperfect tense

We already know how to talk about the past in French:

J'ai loué un stand de 12m^2.	*I've rented a stand measuring 12m^2.*
Nous lui avons envoyé quelques affiches.	*We've sent him/her a few posters.*
M.Jackson s'est perdu dans le métro.	*Mr Jackson got lost in the Metro.*

This is called the perfect tense and is used in connection with a completed action in the past. But there's another tense that refers to the past - the imperfect. This tense is employed when we want to express 'was/were doing', (when something happened), or 'used to do' (i.e. habitual action); Here are two examples:

Je préparais le stand, lorsque le premier client est arrivé.
I was preparing the stand, when the first customer arrived.

L'Exposition fermait tous les soirs à 7 heures.
The exhibition used to close every evening at 7 o'clock.

To form the imperfect tense, remove the **-ons** ending from the **nous**-form of the present and add:

je	-ais
il/elle	-ait
nous	-ions
vous	-iez
ils/elles	-aient

Examples:

Autrefois ce Salon attirait de nombreux visiteurs.
Formerly this Exhibition used to attract numerous visitors.

Les démonstrations finissaient tous les jours à 18 heures.
The demonstrations used to finish every day at 6 p.m.

L'entreprise perdait de grosses sommes d'argent avant l'arrivée du nouveau P.-D.G.
The company was losing large sums of money before the arrival of the new Managing Director.

The English 'was/were' and 'had' are usually expressed by the imperfect of **être** and **avoir**:

j'étais	*I was, etc.*	j'avais	*I had, etc.*
il/elle était		il/elle avait	
nous étions		nous avions	

vous étiez   vous aviez
ils/elles étaient   ils/elles avaient

The imperfect is also used in conjunction with the conditional to translate such sentences as:

I would contact the organizers, if I had their telephone number on me.
Je contacterais les organisateurs, si j'avais leur numéro de téléphone sur moi.

We would place an order immediately, if you could deliver tomorrow.
Nous passerions commande tout de suite, si vous pouviez nous livrer demain.

If you had carried out the inventory correctly, we wouldn't be out of stock.
Si vous aviez fait l'inventaire correctement, nous ne serions pas en rupture de stock.

62 The passive voice

The passive is formed, as in English, with the verb **être** and the past participle:

Le mobilier nous sera fourni gratuitement.
The furniture will be provided for us free of charge.

Le Salon de l'automobile sera inauguré par le Ministre des Transports.
The Motor show will be opened by the Minister of Transport.

La tour Eiffel a été érigée pour l'Exposition universelle de 1889.
The Eiffel Tower was erected for the World Exhibition of 1889.

Note that the past participle agrees with the subject of the sentence.

You'll remember that, in Checknote 47, we mentioned that the indefinite pronoun **on** is often used in place of the passive. In the following example, note that **être en train de faire quelque chose** means 'to be in the process of doing something':

On est en train de renégocier les conditions de travail.
The working conditions are being renegotiated.

See Checknote 40 for additional examples of the use of the passive.

63 Prepositions/prepositional phrases

Study the following (many of these words have already been given in the examples throughout the Course):

sur	*on*	**après**	*after*
sous	*under*	**près de**	*near*
devant	*in front of*	**loin de**	*far from*
derrière	*behind*	**à côté de**	*next to*

avec	with	**à gauche de**	to the left of
sans	without	**à droite de**	to the right of
avant	before	**en face de**	opposite

Examples:

sur le bureau	on the desk
devant le bureau d'accueil	in front of the reception centre
avec un peu de chance	with a little luck
après la conférence internationale	after the international conference
avant l'ouverture de la filiale	before the opening of the subsidiary company
loin de l'ascenseur	far from the lift
à côté de la banque	next to the bank
en face du bar	opposite the bar
à gauche du vestiaire	to the left of the cloakroom
à droite des toilettes	to the right of the toilet(s)

64 The verb **manquer**

This verb often causes problems for speakers of English. It can mean:

a) to miss

Il a manqué l'avion.
He has missed the plane.

Vous ne devez pas manquer cette occasion.
You must not miss this opportunity.

Nous avons manqué une réunion importante.
We've missed an important meeting.

But when 'to miss' means 'to regret that someone is absent', the French construction is the opposite of the English. Study the following carefully:

Vous me manquez.
I miss you.

Le chef de la publicité est en déplacement; sa famille lui manque beaucoup.
The head of publicity is away on business; he misses his family a great deal.

b) to be lacking/to lack

Ce ne sont pas les créneaux qui manquent.
There's no lack of gaps in the market.

Nous manquons d'argent.
We're short of money.

c) to fail

Je ne manquerai pas de régler la facture.
I won't fail to pay the invoice.

Un bon chef d'entreprise ne manque jamais à sa parole.
A good company boss never fails to keep his word.

65 Proverbs

The right proverb or saying at the right time can add a touch of colour and authenticity to your speech. Earlier in this Unit, for example, we met:

Il faut toujours savoir joindre l'utile à l'agréable.
One must always know how to combine business with pleasure.

You might find it useful to learn these proverbs:

Mieux vaut tard que jamais.
Better late than never.

Il ne faut pas vendre la peau de l'ours avant de l'avoir tué.
Don't count your chickens before they're hatched (lit. 'One must not sell the skin of the bear before having killed it').

Point de nouvelles, bonnes nouvelles.
No news is good news.

Après la pluie, le beau temps.
Every cloud has a silver lining (lit. 'After the rain, the fine weather').

Il n'y a pas de fumée sans feu.
There's no smoke without fire.

Quand on parle du loup, on en voit la queue.
Speak of the devil and he will appear (lit. 'When one speaks of the wolf, one sees his tail').

114

Comprehension Practice 8

As usual, learn the new words and then answer the questions; vrai ou faux?

New words:

la location	hiring
la banque	bank
inclus	included
ravi	delighted
seulement	only
apprendre	to learn
s'intéresser (à)	to be interested (in)

1 Mme Duval téléphone à M. Jackson au mauvais moment.

2 Le Salon IBB est un salon spécialisé, réservé aux professionnels seulement.

3 Le Salon IBB attire de nombreux visiteurs.

4 M. Jackson viendra au Salon et en profitera pour faire connaissance avec les clients français.

5 Le jour de l'inauguration du Salon a lieu le 13 janvier.

6 Les frais d'électricité et les primes d'assurance sont inclus dans le prix de location du stand.

7 Le stand de France-Burotic est situé à côté de la banque.

8 M. Jackson est ravi d'apprendre que le stand se trouve en face du bar.

9 M. Jackson ne s'intéresse pas aux produits de ses concurrents.

10 Il faut descendre à la station de métro Porte de Versailles pour aller au Parc des Expositions.

FLUENCY PRACTICE 39

New words:

le compte	account
le four à micro-ondes	micro-wave oven
la liaison ferroviaire	rail link
la pièce	part
l'ouvrier non qualifié	unskilled worker
l'huissier	bailiff

les revendications syndicales	*union demands*
le SMIC (salaire minimum interprofessionnel de croissance)	*guaranteed minimum wage*
réparer	*to repair*
gagner	*to earn; to win*
retirer	*to withdraw*

Irregular verb:

construire *to build*
present: je construis, il construit, nous construisons, vous construisez,
  ils construisent
past: j'ai construit

Complete the following:

1 Je (*used to repair*) les pièces défectueuses.
2 Autrefois cet ouvrier non qualifié (*was only earning*) le SMIC.
3 Le chef d'entreprise (*always used to succeed in*) satisfaire les revendications syndicales.
4 Nous (*were getting off the*) train, quand nous avons vu de la publicité pour un nouveau four à micro-ondes.
5 (*Were you doing*) vos comptes, quand l'huissier est arrivé?
6 Ils (*were in the process of*) construire la liaison ferroviaire, lorsque le gouvernement a décidé de retirer son aide financière.

FLUENCY PRACTICE 40

New words:

le pouvoir d'achat	*purchasing power*
le distributeur automatique (de billets)	*automatic cash dispenser*
l'argent (*m.*) liquide	*ready cash*
se mettre en grève	*to go on strike*
prendre sa retraite	*to retire*
malade	*ill*

Answer the questions in the way seen in this example:

Qu'est-ce que vous feriez, si le P.-D.G. était malade?
What would you do if the managing director were ill?
[I would cancel the meeting.]

Si le P.-D.G. était malade, j'annulerais la réunion.
If the managing director were ill, I would cancel the meeting.

1 Qu'est-ce que vous feriez, si on ne vous fournissait pas le mobilier pour le stand?
   [I would contact the organizers]

2 Qu'est-ce que M. Jackson ferait, s'il se perdait dans Paris?
[He would take a taxi to the Exhibition]
3 Qu'est-ce que nous ferions, si nous manquions d'argent liquide?
[We would go to the cash dispenser]
4 Qu'est-ce que les employés feraient, si leur pouvoir d'achat
continuait à baisser?
[They would go on strike]
5 Qu'est-ce que je ferais, si je faisais encore faillite?
[You would retire]

FLUENCY PRACTICE 41

New words:

le percepteur	*tax collector*
le fournisseur	*supplier*
la lettre de rappel	*reminder letter*
l'impôt	*tax*
inquiet, -ète	*worried*
exigeant	*demanding*
depuis	*since*
j'attends depuis deux semaines	*I've been waiting for two weeks*
par-dessus le marché	*into the bargain*
le/la voilà	*here he/she is*
réclamer	*to ask for*
rentrer à la maison	*to return home*
hériter	*to inherit*
payer	*to pay*
baisser	*to go down*
pointer	*to clock in/out*
porter	*to wear*

acheter *to buy*
present: j'achète, il achète, nous achetons, vous achetez, ils achètent
past: j'ai acheté
future: j'achèterai

ouvrir *to open*
present: j'ouvre, il ouvre, nous ouvrons, vous ouvrez, ils ouvrent
past: j'ai ouvert

Find a French proverb that best describes each of the following
situations:

1 Selon les rumeurs, on va licencier vingt membres du personnel,
parce que le chiffre d'affaires de cette année a beaucoup
baissé. Mais ce n'est peut-être pas vrai...
2 Notre chef, il est vraiment exigeant. Il veut que nous pointions

tous les matins et tous les soirs, il veut que nous travaillions tous les samedis, il veut, en plus, que nous portions un uniforme, il veut que nous .... Attention, le voilà.

3 Le fournisseur a finalement été payé par le client après cinq lettres de rappel.

4 J'ai l'intention de lancer un nouveau produit sur le marché, j'ai l'intention d'ouvrir trois nouvelles filiales en France, j'ai l'intention d'exporter mes produits à l'étranger, et avec tout l'argent que je gagnerai, je m'achèterai un yacht, une cadillac, un château ....

5 Je suis inquiet, parce qu'il est possible que je reçoive une lettre du percepteur me réclamant des impôts supplémentaires. J'attends depuis deux semaines, mais ... toujours rien.

6 Il a manqué son train, il a donc manqué son avion, il a donc manqué son interview avec le directeur de la banque, il manquera donc d'argent et par-dessus le marché sa secrétaire lui manque. En rentrant à la maison, il apprend qu'il a hérité une fortune d'un oncle qu'il ne connaissait pas.

FLUENCY PRACTICE 42

Study this conversation between a potential customer and Mr Jackson at the trade exhibition and compare it carefully with the English translation which follows. Be ready to answer questions later on in French.

Mr Jackson: Vous désirez un renseignement, Madame?

Customer: Oui, Monsieur. Ce traitement de texte m'intéresse particulièrement à cause de sa petite taille. Est-il différent des traitements de texte habituels?

Mr Jackson: Oui, la grande différence, c'est qu'il est portatif, c'est à dire on peut l'emporter dans son attaché-case partout. On peut même travailler dans l'avion. Il est léger et marche à la fois sur pile et secteur.

Customer: Vraiment? Vous pouvez me faire une démonstration?

Mr Jackson: Avec plaisir, Madame. Avez-vous l'habitude d'utiliser un traitement de texte?

Customer: Oui ... c'est à dire ... non, pas vraiment.

Mr Jackson: Très bien. Regardez. Voici le clavier. Il contient toutes les touches nécessaires. L'écran est facile à lire. Le lecteur de disquettes est incorporé dans la machine. L'imprimante à marguerite est tout à fait silencieuse.

Customer: Donc on peut enregistrer les données dans la mémoire, là où on se trouve et on n'a plus qu'à imprimer le texte plus tard?

Mr Jackson: C'est exactement ça. C'est formidable, n'est-ce pas?

Customer: Mais est-ce que cette machine offre les mêmes avantages qu'un traitement de texte ordinaire?

Mr Jackson: Peut-être même plus. Malgré sa petite taille, ce traitement de texte offre les avantages suivants: - il identifie les fautes de frappe et les corrige automatiquement; - il a un dictionnaire électronique; - il contient une liste de synonymes.

Customer: Excellent. C'est exactement ce qu'il me faut -moi qui ai des problèmes en orthographe. Vraiment on n'arrête pas le progrès! Et maintenant, la question cruciale, quel en est le prix?

Mr Jackson: 6500 F, TTC. Mais nous offrons 10% de réduction, c'est le prix-expo, si vous passez votre commande tout de suite.

Customer: Quelle est la garantie?

Mr Jackson: Elle est d'un an.

Customer: Et les frais d'entretien, sont-ils élevés?

Mr Jackson: Mais non, pas du tout. Et de toutes façons, nous vous proposons une assurance pour cinq ans à un tarif très, très avantageux.

Customer: Merci, Monsieur. Vous m'avez convaincue. Je vais passer commande tout de suite!

TRANSLATION

Mr Jackson: Would you like some information, Madam?

Customer: Yes. This word processor particularly interests me because of its small size. Is it different from the usual word processors?

Mr Jackson:	Yes, the great difference is that it's portable, that's to say one can carry it in one's attaché-case everywhere. One can even work in the plane. It's light and works both on battery and mains electricity.
Customer:	Really? Can you give me a demonstration?
Mr Jackson:	Of course. With pleasure. Are you used to working with a word processor?
Customer:	Yes … that's to say … no, not really.
Mr Jackson:	Good. Have a look. This is the keyboard. It contains all the necessary keys. The screen is easy to read. The disk drive is incorporated in the machine and the daisywheel printer is quite silent.
Customer:	So, you can store the data in the memory wherever you happen to be and you simply print the text later?
Mr Jackson:	That's exactly it. It's wonderful, isn't it?
Customer:	But does the machine offer the same advantages as an ordinary word processor?
Mr Jackson:	Perhaps even more. In spite of its small size, this word processor offers the following advantages: - it identifies the typing errors and corrects them automatically; - it has an electronic dictionary; - it contains a list of synonyms.
Customer:	Excellent. That's exactly what I need - I, who have problems with spelling. Really, you can't stop progress! And now, the crucial question, what's the price of it?
Mr Jackson:	6500 francs, all taxes included. But we're offering 10% reduction, it's the Exhibition price, if you place your order right away.
Customer:	What's the guarantee?
Mr Jackson:	It's one year.
Customer:	And the maintenance costs, are they high?
Mr Jackson:	No, not at all. And, in any case, we offer you an insurance for five years at a very advantageous price.
Customer:	Thank you. You've convinced me. I'm going to place an order immediately.

And now, answer these questions to complete Fluency Practice 42:

New words:

le montant	*amount*
qu'est-ce qui	*what (subject of the sentence)*

attractif, -ive (f.) attractive
autre   other
rendre   (+adj.) to make

1 Qu'est-ce qui attire la cliente au stand de M. Jackson?
2 Qu'est-ce qui rend le traitement de texte attractif?
3 Quelles sont les quatre parties du traitement de texte mentionnées
   par M. Jackson?
4 Quels autres avantages impressionnent la cliente?
5 Quel est le prix que la cliente doit payer, si elle passe commande
   à l'Exposition?
   Donnez le montant exact.
6 Est-ce que les frais d'entretien posent un problème?

DICTIONARY PRACTICE 5

You work in the staff training department of a British firm. One of
your responsibilities is to develop foreign language courses within
the company, which use the latest teaching methods. You've
come across the following article in a French magazine, which
gives details of a forthcoming language exhibition -
EXPOLANGUES - in Paris. Clearly, a visit would be of great help to
you. Produce a summary of the article in English and present it to
your departmental head in the hope that s/he'll authorize a trip to
France! Check later with the key.

EXPOLANGUES

VOCABLE SUPPLEMENT EXPOLANGUES - 1er FEVRIER 1990

EDITO

EN ROUTE POUR EXPOLANGUES.
Parce que les langues vivantes sont "le meilleur moyen de s'entendre" ceux qui les aiment et les pratiquent avaient besoin d'un lieu de rencontre. Depuis 8 années consécutives, les amoureux des langues et des cultures du monde ont leur forum: EXPOLANGUES.

En 1990, le salon est plus moderne que jamais: intégrant toutes les nouvelles technologies, des méthodes les plus traditionnelles aux plus sophistiquées, quelque 250 intervenants et 40.000 visiteurs se retrouvent ici pour échanger, communiquer et avancer ensemble...

Depuis 10 ans, l'enseignement des langues s'est beaucoup développé en France, du fait de la modernisation des techniques, mais aussi d'une prise de conscience, plus particulièrement chez les jeunes. On apprend plus de langues, plus vite, et sans doute mieux. De ce mouvement, qui s'étend aujourd'hui même aux plus jeunes, Expolangues est sûrement le reflet, et peut-être même l'un des moteurs.

A l'aube du marché unique de 1992, la préoccupation linguistique est de plus en plus pressante dans toute la communauté des 12 (qui rappelons- le s'exprime d'une seule voix, mais en 9 langues différentes).

Alors, enseignement, traduction, traitement informatique du language, suivez-nous dans la grande aventure des langues et des cultures!

GUIDE PRATIQUE

Lieu: Parc des Expositions, Porte de Versailles, hall 5.
Dates: Du 15 au 19 février 1990. Journée professionnelle: mercredi 14 février.
Heures d'ouverture: Tous les jours de 10 h à 19 h. Nocturne vendredi 16 jusqu'à 22 h.
Moyens d'accès: Métro : Porte de Versailles - Place Balard. Bus: lignes 39, 42, 49, PC
Prix d'entrée: 35 F. Tarif réduit 20 F pour élèves, étudiants et enseignants.
Surface d'exposition: 8 000 m^2
Cinq salles de conférence: hall 5
Nombre d'exposants: 250
Catalogue: 25F

Président du salon: Jean-Pierre van Deth
Commissaire général: Jean-Pierre Jouët
Responsable commerciale: Christine Frichet
Communication: Henri Jobbé-Duval
Relations presse: Valérie Vésine
Organisation: OIP/CLC, 62, rue de Miromesnil, 75008 Paris
Tél: (1) 45.62.84.58
Télécopieur: (1) 45.63.89.82
Télex: 644 259 F
Infos minitel: 3616 code SALONS

Applying for a job in France

The course now covers more complex notions such as 'trap words', adjectives with double meanings and conjunctions. Further uses of the subjunctive are also given. It's all quite concentrated, but there are plenty of model sentences illustrating the points we briefly explain. And you have already made very good progress!

With all the opportunities that the Single European Market offers, Mr Jackson has been thinking for some time now about the possibility of living and working permanently in France. He's therefore very interested when he comes across an advertisement in a French newspaper that might well suit him. Here's the advertisement:

M A R K E T I S

Chiffre d'affaires: +320 millions de francs. Effectif: 150

Pionniers et leaders dans le domaine de la bureautique, nous recherchons

DIRECTEUR DES VENTES (H/F)
(poste basé à Cherbourg)

VOS MISSIONS:
a) Vous serez responsable du marrketing et du développement commercial.
b) Vous animerez notre équipe de 15 technico-commerciaux.
c) Vous consoliderez notre position sur le marché national.
d) Vous créerez de nouveaux débouchés à l'étranger.

VOUS OFFREZ:
a) Une formation supérieure (HEC, ESSEC ou équivalent).
b) 8 à 10 ans d'expérience réussie dans les ventes.
c) La maîtrise totale de l'anglais et une bonne connaissance d'une seconde langue étrangère.
d) Le sens de la créativité et des responsabilités.
e) Des qualités de leader, d'organisateur et de négociateur.

NOUS OFFRONS:
a) Une opportunité de carrière intéressante.
b) Une rémunération attractive: 400-500 KF/an + voiture de fonction.

Merci d'adresser votre dossier de candidature: CV + photo, lettre manuscrite et rémunération actuelle sous réf. 123/B à:

Madame A. Leblanc, Chef du personnel
SOCIETE MARKETIS
RUE DU 14 JUILLET
50100 CHERBOURG

TRANSLATION

M A R K E T I S

Turnover: +320 million francs. Workforce: 150

We are pioneers and leaders in the field of office automation and we are looking for a

SALES MANAGER (M/F)
(position based in Cherbourg)

YOUR DUTIES:
a) You will be responsible for marketing and sales development.
b) You will lead our team of 15 technical salespeople.
c) You will consolidate our position on the national market.
d) You will create new outlets abroad.

YOU OFFER:
a) A university-level education (HEC, ESSEC or equivalent).
b) 8 to 10 years' experience in sales.
c) A complete mastery of English and a good knowledge of a second foreign language.
d) A sense of creativity and responsibility.
e) The qualities of a leader, organizer and negotiator.

WE OFFER:
a) An opportunity for an interesting career.
b) An attractive salary: 400-500 KF a year + company car

Please send your application: CV, photo, handwritten letter and present salary, quoting ref. 123/B to

Madame A. Leblanc, Head of personnel
MARKETIS
RUE DU 14 JUILLET
50100 CHERBOURG

Having studied the advertisement, Mr Jackson decides to apply for the position. He prepares his CV (or résumé, as his American bosses at Excel-Equip, New York, would call it) and then - as requested - he writes this covering letter by hand:

Peter Jackson
19 Hugo Lane
ORPINGTON
Kent BR7 ABC
Angleterre

Société Marketis
rue du 14 Juillet
50100 CHERBOURG
France

Orpington, le 3 Juillet 1990

A l'attention de Madame Leblanc.

Madame,

Votre annonce parue dans "La Gazette de l'Ouest" du 18 Juin 1990 a retenu toute mon attention.

Actuellement Directeur des ventes dans la société Excel-Equip (Londres) depuis cinq ans, j'ai acquis une expérience diversifiée dans les domaines de la vente, de l'export et de l'informatique. Au cours de ces années, j'ai exercé des responsabilités de manager et d'animateur d'une équipe de vendeurs.

Je vis actuellement en Angleterre, mais souhaiterais trouver une situation professionnelle me permettant de m'établir définitivement en France. Étant de mère française, je suis parfaitement bilingue.

Vous trouverez ci-joint un curriculum vitae détaillant mon cursus universitaire ainsi que mon parcours professionnel. Je me tiens à votre disposition pour vous exposer plus amplement mes objectifs et mes ambitions au cours d'un prochain entretien.

En espérant que ma demande retiendra votre attention, je vous prie d'agréer, Madame, l'expression de mes sentiments dévoués.

Jackson

P.S. Mon salaire actuel est de £32.000.

TRANSLATION

(Note, in the original, the plain 'Madame' opening. and the flowery signing-off phrase in place of 'Yours sincerely'.)

For the attention of Madame Leblanc.

Dear Madame Leblanc,

I was very interested in your advertisement which appeared in "La Gazette de l'Ouest" of the 18th June 1990 (*lit.* 'Your advertisement ... held all my attention').

I have been the Sales Manager with Excel-Equip (London) for five years (*lit.*' At the moment Sales Manager with ... since five years') and I have gained wide experience in the areas of sales, exports and computing. During this period (*lit.* 'In the course of these years') I have been responsible for managing and motivating (*lit.* 'I have exercised the responsibilities of manager and coordinator of) a team of salespeople.

I am living at present in England, but I would like (*lit.* 'would wish') to find a position which would enable (*lit.* 'enabling') me to settle permanently in France. As I have a French mother (*lit.* 'Being of French mother'), I am completely bilingual.

Please find enclosed a curriculum vitae giving details of my university studies and my professional experience. I would be very pleased (*lit.* 'I hold myself at your disposal') to explain to you in greater detail what my aims and ambitions are at an interview in the near future.

Hoping that my application will be of interest to you,

Yours sincerely,

P.S. My present salary is £32,000.

CURRICULUM VITAE

Peter Jackson
19 Hugo Lane, Orpington, Kent BR7 ABC, Angleterre
Tél: (19 44) 81 1234567
Né: le 31 juillet 1960
Marié - 3 enfants
Nationalité: anglaise

FORMATION

1976: GCE 'O' levels (équivalence BEPC)
1978: GCE 'A' levels (équivalence Baccalauréat)
1981: BA (Hons) Economics (équivalence Licence en sciences
économiques), Université de Bristol

LANGUES

Anglais - Français: bilingue
Allemand: lu-parlé-écrit
Espagnol: notions

EXPERIENCE PROFESSIONNELLE

1981: Ets. Grandivitte
(Service Informatique)
stage de trois mois
1982-5: Brown International Engineering Ltd, Londres
(machines agricoles)
Assistant export
1985: Excel-Equip (London) Ltd, Londres
(bureautique)
Directeur des ventes

LOISIRS

Arts martiaux japonais (judo, karaté)
Parachutisme
Musique

OBJECTIFS

Utiliser mon expérience professionnelle passée, mes contacts
avec l'étranger et mes qualités relationnelles au profit du
développement commercial de Marketis.

Checklist 9

Masculine nouns:

le poste	post
le technico-commercial	technical salesman
le débouché	outlet
le domaine	field
le cursus universitaire	university studies
le parcours professionnel	track record
le stage	training period
le curriculum vitae	CV, résumé
le loisir	leisure
l'effectif	workforce
l'animateur	driving force
l'entretien	interview

Feminine nouns:

la candidature	application
la voiture de fonction	company car
la formation	education, training
la langue	language
la maîtrise	mastery
la connaissance	knowledge
la situation professionnelle	position, post
la mère	mother
la demande	request, application
la licence	degree
la disposition	disposal
l'équipe	team
les notions	elementary knowledge
les qualités relationnelles	ability to develop interpersonal relationships

Adjectives:

responsable (de)	responsible (for)
réussi	successful
supérieur	of university level
diversifié	varied
allemand	German
espagnol	Spanish
japonais	Japanese
bilingue	bilingual
agricole	agricultural
passé	past
prochain	next, impending
marié	married
étranger,-ère (f.)	foreign
actuel,-elle (f.)	present

Adverbs:

définitivement	permanently
parfaitement	perfectly
amplement	fully
actuellement	at present

Examinations:

BEPC = Brevet d'Études du Premier Cycle = GCE O-levels/GCSE
Baccalauréat = GCE A-levels

University-level business schools:

HEC = École des hautes études commerciales
ESSEC = École supérieure des sciences économiques et commerciales

Abbreviations:

Ets = Établissements
Ets Grandivitte   Grandivitte & Co.

Other words/expressions:

depuis	since
plus amplement	in greater detail
à l'étranger	abroad
retenir l'attention de quelqu'un	to hold someone's attention

Verbs:

rechercher	*to seek*	trouver	*to find*
animer	*to motivate, lead*	exposer	*to expound*
créer	*to create*	détailler	*to detail*
exercer	*to exercise*	utiliser	*to use*
souhaiter	*to wish*	s'établir	*to settle*

Irregular verbs:

offrir *to offer*
present: j'offre, il offre, nous offrons, vous offrez, ils offrent
past: j'ai offert

tenir *to hold*
  see venir, Checklist 7 (but past is: j'ai tenu)

acquérir *to acquire*
present: j'acquiers, il acquiert, nous acquérons, vous acquérez,
  ils acquièrent
past: j'ai acquis
future: j'acquerrai

vivre *to live*
present: je vis, il vit, nous vivons, vous vivez, ils vivent
past: j'ai vécu

lire *to read*
present: je lis, il lit, nous lisons, vous lisez, ils lisent
past: j'ai lu

écrire *to write*
present: j'écris, il écrit, nous écrivons, vous écrivez, ils écrivent
past: j'ai écrit

naître *to be born*
past: je suis né (*I was born*)

paraître *to appear*
present: je parais, il paraît, vous paraissez, nous paraissons,
  ils paraissent
past: j'ai paru

CHECKNOTES

66 Countries

You were introduced to a number of countries in Checknote 51; they were all feminine:

la Belgique	*Belgium*	L'Espagne	*Spain*
L'Angleterre	*England*	L'Allemagne	*Germany*
L'Italie	*Italy*		

Here are some more feminine countries:

la Grande-Bretagne	*Britain*	la Tchécoslovaquie	*Czechoslovakia*
la France	*France*	la Roumanie	*Romania*
La Finlande	*Finland*	la Grèce	*Greece*
la Norvège	*Norway*	la Turquie	*Turkey*
la Suède	*Sweden*	l'Irlande	*Ireland*
la Suisse	*Switzerland*	l'Autriche	*Austria*
la Yougoslavie	*Yugoslavia*		

And now for some masculine countries:

le Royaume-Uni	*United Kingdom*	le Brésil	*Brazil*
le Luxembourg	*Luxembourg*	le Mexique	*Mexico*
le Danemark	*Denmark*	le Japon	*Japan*
le Portugal	*Portugal*	le Canada	*Canada*

Some countries are plural:

les États-Unis	*The United States*
les Pays-Bas	*the Netherlands*

It's important to know whether a country is masculine, feminine or plural because this affects the preposition used with it:

en France (*f.*)	*in/to France*
au Portugal (*m.*)	*in/to Portugal*
aux Pays-Bas (*pl.*)	*in/to the Netherlands*

Examples:

Le Marché commun a son siège en Belgique.
The Common Market has its headquarters in Belgium.

La France exporte beaucoup de voitures au Royaume-Uni.
France exports lots of cars to the United Kingdom.

Nous devons augmenter nos ventes aux États-Unis.
We must increase our sales in the United States.

67 Position of adjectives

In the advertisement prepared by Marketis for a sales manager we met the following:

Vous créerez de nouveaux débouchés à l'étranger.
You will create new outlets abroad.

Vous serez responsable du développement commercial.
You will be responsible for sales development.

La maîtrise totale de l'anglais et une bonne connaissance d'une seconde langue étrangère.
Complete mastery of English and a good knowledge of a second foreign language.

You'll have noticed that in French the adjective is sometimes placed in front of the noun and sometimes after. In fact, most adjectives come after, but here's a list of those which normally precede the noun:

bon, bonne (*f.*)	*good*
mauvais	*bad*
petit	*small*
grand	*large*
joli	*pretty*
court	*short*
long, longue (*f.*)	*long*
nouveau (see Checklist 7)	*new*
jeune	*young*
vieux	*old*
vieil (*m.* sing. before vowel and silent h)	
vieux (*m. pl.*)	
vieille (*f.*)	
vieilles (*f. pl.*)	
beau	*fine, beautiful, handsome*
bel (*m. sing.* before vowel and silent h)	
beaux (*m. pl.*)	
belle (*f.*)	
belles (*f. pl.*)	

Just before we leave this point, we must mention that some adjectives have one meaning when they precede the noun and a different meaning when they follow. Study the following:

Ancien, ancienne (*f.*)

Before the noun = 'former'; after the noun = 'old', 'antique':

Mon ancien associé s'est maintenant installé à son compte.
My former partner has now set up his own business.

Mon comptable se passionne pour l'histoire ancienne.
My accountant is fascinated by ancient history.

Certain

Before the noun = 'certain', 'some'; after the noun = 'positive':

Certains employés sont prêts à faire des heures supplémentaires, mais pas tous.
Some employees are ready to work overtime, but not all.

Ça, c'est une chose certaine!
That's a certainty!

Cher, chère (f.)

Before the noun = 'dear' (a term of endearment); after the noun = 'expensive':

Cher Monsieur Jackson
Dear Mr Jackson

des biens de consommation chers
expensive consumer goods

Dernier, dernière (f.)

Before the noun = 'last'; after the noun = 'last' (i.e. just elapsed):

Leur dernière proposition était inacceptable.
Their last proposal was unacceptable.

la semaine dernière
last week

Différent

Before the noun = 'various'; after the noun = 'different':

Nous avons discuté de différents problèmes.
We discussed various problems.

Là, vous parlez d'un problème différent.
You're talking there about a different problem.

Même

Before the noun = 'same'; after the noun = 'even':

Ce sont toujours les mêmes dactylos qui arrivent en retard.
It's always the same typists who arrive late.

Les pilotes mêmes se sont mis en grève.
Even the pilots went on strike.

Pauvre

Before the noun = 'poor' (unfortunate); after the noun = 'poor' (without funds):

Ce pauvre employé de banque a échoué à son examen de comptabilité pour la deuxième fois.
This poor bank employee has failed his accountancy examination for the second time.

Avez-vous jamais rencontré un Japonais pauvre?
Have you ever met a poor Japanese?

Propre

Before the noun = 'own'; after the noun = 'clean';

Je me sers toujours de ma propre voiture pour les déplacements professionnels.
I always use my own car for business trips.

Voilà ce que j'appelle une voiture propre!
That's what I call a clean car!

68 Adverbs (2)

You'll remember from Checknote 27 that French adverbs are often formed by adding **-ment** (English -ly) to the feminine form of the adjective. In this Unit, for example, we've seen:

parfaitement	*perfectly*
amplement	*fully*
définitivement	*permanently*
actuellement	*at present*

Adverbs are often formed in this way – often, but NOT always. Adjectives ending in **-ant** and **-ent** become adverbs by changing **-nt** to **-mment**:

suffisant	**suffisamment**	*sufficiently*
constant	**constamment**	*constantly*
récent	**récemment**	*recently*
évident	**évidemment**	*obviously*

69 Possessive adjectives/pronouns

We are already familiar with the possessive adjectives:

mon cursus universitaire	*my university studies*
ma candidature	*my application*
mon expérience (*f.*)	*my experience*
mes contacts avec l'étranger	*my foreign contacts*
son profil professionnel	*his/her career profile*
sa voiture de fonction	*his/her company car*
son adresse (*f.*)	*his/her address*
ses objectifs	*his/her aims*
votre annonce	*your advertisement*
vos qualités de leader	*your qualities of leadership*
vos loisirs	*your free moments*
notre position sur le marché	*our position on the market*
nos équipes	*our teams*
leur chef du personnel	*their head of personnel*
leurs débouchés au Brésil	*their outlets in Brazil*

You'll also need to know the possessive pronouns:

Masc. sing./pl.   Fem. sing./pl

le mien	/ les miens	*mine*		la mienne / les miennes
le sien	/ les siens	*his/hers*		la sienne / les siennes
le nôtre	/ les nôtres	*ours*		la nôtre / les nôtres
le vôtre	/ les vôtres	*yours*		la vôtre / les vôtres
le leur	/ les leurs	*theirs*		la leur / les leurs

The above must agree with the noun they replace:

votre entretien et le mien	*your interview and mine*
ma commission et la vôtre	*my commission and yours*
nos points forts et les siens	*our strong points and his/hers*
vos points faibles et les nôtres	*your weak points and ours*
sa rémunération et la mienne	*his/her salary and mine*

70 Faux amis

We mentioned in Unit 1 that there are thousands of English and French words which have the same spelling and meaning and this is true but, nevertheless, you do have to be careful because there are traps awaiting the unwary. These traps are called **faux amis** - 'false friends'. **Faux amis** are French words which look as if they could have the same meaning as their English 'twin' but which, in fact, refer to something totally different. The French words **actuellement** and **éventuellement**, for example, do NOT mean 'actually' and 'eventually'.

Here is a list (it's far from being complete) of examples of **faux amis.**

	French	English

Masculine nouns:

le bachelier = *someone who has the baccalauréat*   *bachelor/(girl)* = le/la célibataire

le car = *coach* (*bus*)   *car* = la voiture

le pétrole = *oil*   *petrol, gasoline* = l'essence (*f.*)

le stage = *training period*   *stage* = la scène

le starter = *choke*   *starter* = le démarreur

l'agenda = *diary*   *agenda* = l'ordre du jour

l'éditeur = *publisher*   *editor* = le rédacteur, la rédactrice

l'avertissement = *warning*   *advertisement* = l'annonce

Feminine nouns:

la librairie = *bookshop*   *library* = la bibliothèque

la lecture = *reading*   *lecture* = la conférence

Adjectives:

large = *wide*   *large* = grand

sensible = *sensitive*   *sensible* = sensé

Adverbs:

actuellement = *at present*   *actually* = en fait

éventuellement = *if necessary, possibly*   *eventually* = finalement

Verbs:

assister à = *to attend; to assist*   *to assist* = aider, assister

attendre = *to wait* (*for*)   *to attend* = assister à

charger = *to load*   *to charge* = faire payer

demander = *to ask* (*for*)   *to demand* = exiger

prétendre = *to claim*   *to pretend* = faire semblant

71 Subjunctive (2)

In Checknote 59 we mentioned some of the situations in which you need to use the subjunctive, but that wasn't the complete story. It's also employed:

a) After certain conjunctions, among which are:

quoique	although	pourvu que	provided that
bien que	although	jusqu'à ce que	until
pour que	in order that	de peur que*	for fear that
afin que	in order that	à moins que*	unless
à condition que	on condition that	avant que*	before

*These require ne before the verb.

Examples:

Bien que vous ayez une maîtrise en gestion, vous n'avez pas suffisamment d'expérience professionnelle.
Although you have a master's degree in management, you don't have sufficient professional experience.

Avant que nous ne commencions l'entretien, le jury va se présenter.
Before we begin the interview, the members of the panel will introduce themselves.

Afin que les compagnies françaises puissent implanter des filiales aux États-Unis, les banques américaines offrent des modalités de financement intéressantes.
So that French companies can set up subsidiaries in the United States, the American banks are offering attractive financing terms.

b) after a superlative:

C'est le meilleur candidat que nous ayons interviewé ce matin.
This is the best applicant we've interviewed this morning.

c) after **seul**:

C'est la seule machine qui soit défectueuse.
This is the only machine that's faulty.

d) when there's uncertainty about the existence of someone or something:

Je cherche une secrétaire qui sache parler et le japonais et le chinois!
I'm looking for a secretary who can (knows how to) speak both Japanese and Chinese!

Before leaving the question of the subjunctive, you'll need to learn some more irregular forms, as they appear all the time:

avoir (*to have*) (**que/qu'**) j'aie, il ait, nous ayons, vous ayez, ils aient

aller (*to go*)   j'aille, il aille, nous allions, vous alliez, vous alliez, ils aillent

prendre (*to take*)   je prenne, il prenne, nous prenions, vous preniez, ils prennent

savoir (*to know*)	je sache, il sache, nous sachions, vous sachiez, ils sachent
venir (*to come*)	je vienne, il vienne, nous venions, vous veniez, ils viennent

72 Conjunctions

We mustn't give you the impression that ALL conjunctions are followed by the subjunctive. These are not:

Reason		Time	
parce que	*because*	**pendant que**	*while*
car	*for, because*	**maintenant que**	*now that*
puisque	*since*	**quand***	*when*
comme	*as*	**lorsque***	*when*
donc	*so, therefore*	**dès que***	*as soon as*
		aussitôt que	*as soon as*

Contrast

mais	*but*
tandis que	*whereas*

*These are followed by the future tense when the future is referred to.

Examples:

Comme je vous l'ai mentionné au téléphone ...
As I mentioned to you on the telephone ...

Puisque vous serez responsable du service après-vente ...
Since you will be responsible for the after-sales service ...

Pendant que vous vérifiez les chiffres, je ...
While you check the figures, I'll ...

... parce que vous avez beaucoup de contacts à l'étranger.
... because you have lots of contacts abroad.

Maintenant que vous parlez si bien français ...
Now that you speak French so well ...

Aussitôt que je recevrai votre lettre ...
As soon as I receive (will receive) your letter ...

Comprehension Practice 9

In this exercise we are giving you the answers to some questions. What were the questions?

New words:

l'emploi (*m.*)	*job, employment*
la date de naissance	*date of birth*
suivant	*following*
retenu	*engaged*
poser sa candidature à	*to apply for*

Here are the answers:

A) The Marketis advertisement

1 Les caractéristiques de la société Marketis sont les suivantes:
   a) elle réalise un chiffre d'affaires de 320 millions de francs
   b) elle emploie 150 personnes
   c) elle est le pionnier et le leader dans le domaine de la bureautique

2 C'est le poste de directeur des ventes qui est vacant.

3 Ce poste est basé à Cherbourg.

4 Le candidat retenu sera responsable du développement commercial, de l'animation de 15 technico-commerciaux, de la consolidation de Marketis en France et de la création de débouchés à l'étranger.

5 Parce qu'il offre une bonne rémunération, une voiture de fonction et une opportunité de carrière intéressante.

6 Si je décide de poser ma candidature à ce poste, il faudra que j'envoie un CV avec une photo et une lettre manuscrite.

B) Mr Jackson's CV

7 M.Jackson est né le 31 juillet 1960.

8 Non, il est marié et a trois enfants.

9 Non, ce n'est pas son premier emploi. Il a déjà tavaillé comme assistant export et directeur des ventes dans deux autres sociétés.

10 Oui, à mon avis, les loisirs de M. Jackson correspondent bien à sa personnalité dynamique, à son sens des contacts humains et à son intérêt pour les pays étrangers.

FLUENCY PRACTICE 43

New words:

le courrier   *mail*
la nouvelle   *news*
presque   *almost*

Choose a suitable adjective from the list below and place it in its correct position (before or after the noun?) in the text that follows. Make sure it agrees with the noun.

nécessaire   bon
insuffisant   vacant
petit   mauvais
actuel   jeune

1 La candidate pense qu'elle a les ... qualités ... pour le poste de responsable des achats.
2 Ce candidat est presque bilingue; il a une ... connaissance ... de l'anglais et du français.
3 Je n'ai pas posé ma candidature à cause de mon ... expérience ...
4 Le .... poste .... d'attaché de presse est déjà pris.
5 Pouvez-vous nous indiquer votre ... rémunération ...?
6 La mobilité est un élément essentiel pour ce nouveau poste, mais c'est un ... sacrifice ... à faire pour le salaire offert, n'est-ce pas?
7 La ... secrétaire ... qui a été récemment embauchée semble être très compétente.
8 Nous avons reçu une ... nouvelle ... au courrier de ce matin.

FLUENCY PRACTICE 44

New words:

la station-service   *service station*
chaque   *each*
emprunter   *to borrow*

Complete the following with a suitable word, but be wary of **faux amis!**

1 Je dois aller à la station-service acheter 100 francs d' ...
2 Vous voyagerez en voiture ou en ...?
3 Avez-vous l'intention d' ... à la réunion du conseil d'administration?
4 Attention! Ne le vexez pas, car il est très ...
5 Chaque semaine j'emprunte cinq livres à la ... municipale.

FLUENCY PRACTICE 45

New words:

le coût de la vie	*the cost of living*
le cadeau	*gift*
le chien	*dog*
l'ami, amie (f.)	*friend*
la maison	*house*
la campagne	*countryside*
l'école (f.)	*school*
élevé	*high*
pratiquer	*to practise*
réagir	*to react*
entendre	*to hear*

Mr Jackson is talking to a colleague about the reactions of his wife and children to the news that he plans to apply for a job in France. Put the verbs in brackets into the correct form (i.e. indicative or subjunctive mood):

Bien que ce poste de directeur des ventes (correspondre) parfaitement à mes objectifs, j'ai hésité à poser ma candidature, car je ne savais pas quelle serait la réaction de ma famille. Lorsque, finalement, je l'(avoir) annoncé à ma femme, elle a réagi favorablement:

a) à condition que les enfants (aller) dans une école internationale pour qu'ils (pouvoir) continuer à pratiquer l'anglais

b) pourvu que le salaire (être) supérieur à mon salaire actuel, puisque le coût de la vie (être) plus élevé en France

c) à condition que nous (acheter) une vieille maison à la campagne

J'ai donc décidé d'en parler aux enfants. Aussitôt qu'ils (avoir) entendu la nouvelle, ils ont imposé leurs propres conditions: 'Nous ne partirons pas à moins que vous ne nous (offrir) un cadeau à tous les trois, c'est à dire un poney, un chien et un hamster. C'est normal, parce que nous (aller) perdre tous nos amis et puisque nous (vivre) à la campagne, ce ne sera pas un problème!'

FLUENCY PRACTICE 46

One of the C.A.L.L. (Computer Assisted Language Learning) techniques often used now in teaching consists in the computer removing from a text every fourth or sixth or eighth, etc. word and asking the student to fill in the gaps. The computer gives clues and the correct answer immediately but, of course, you have the benefit of the key at the back of the book. We have decided to omit every eighth word. You're already familiar with the text of Peter Jackson's job-hunting letter to Madame Leblanc:

Madame,

Votre annonce parue dans "La Gazette de … (1)" du 18 Juin 1990 a retenu toute … (2) attention.

Actuellement Directeur des ventes dans la … (3) Excel-Equip (Londres) depuis cinq ans, j'ai … (4) une expérience diversifiée dans les domaines de … (5) vente, de l'export et de l'informatique.

Au … (6) de ces années, j'ai exercé des responsabilités de … (7) et d'animateur d'une équipe de vendeurs.

Je … (8) actuellement en Angleterre, mais souhaiterais trouver une … (9) professionnelle me permettant de m'établir définitivement en … (10). Étant de mère française, je suis parfaitement … (11)

Vous trouverez ci-joint un curriculum vitae … (12) mon cursus universitaire ainsi que mon parcours … (13).

Je me tiens à votre disposition pour … (14) exposer plus amplement mes objectifs et mes … (15) au cours d'un prochain entretien.

En espérant … (16) ma demande retiendra votre attention, je vous … (17) d'agréer, Madame, l'expression de mes sentiments dévoués.

DICTIONARY PRACTICE 6

Produce the English version of this French advertisement:

POLAROID EUROPEAN MARKETING HEADQUARTERS
recherche une

Secrétaire de direction parfaitement bilingue

Langue maternelle anglaise

Avec quelques années d'expérience au sein d'un Service Financier/Informatique, vous connaissez la sténo, la dactylo, le traitement de texte Multimate et la micro-informatique. Vous aimez les chiffres.

Salaire x 13.

Merci d'adresser lettre manuscrite en anglais, CV, photo et salaire à POLAROID Europe, Direction du Personnel, 4 rue J.P. Timbaud, 78391 Bois-d'Arcy Cedex.

MEDIA-SYSTEM

Polaroid

DICTIONARY PRACTICE 7

Study this ad. Then answer the following questions in French:

CABINET JURDIQUE INTERNATIONAL
Pour assurer l'accueil dans nos nouveaux locaux, situés dans le 8, nous recherchons

2 HOTESSES BILINGUES

1 de langue maternelle anglaise
1 de langue maternelle française

Votre profil : ces postes requièrent un réel sens de l'accueil et la maîtrise des contacts à haut niveau. Vous avez une excellente présentation et vous exprimez, avec la même aisance, en anglais et en français.

Votre mission : accueillir nos clients et autres visiteurs. Vous êtes également chargées d'appeler taxis et coursiers, de réceptionner le courrier et les billets d'avion.

Nous vous offrons : un travail en équipe, dans un environnement international en forte expansion. Un choix d'horaires de 8h30 à 17h30 ou de 10h à 19h. Une rémunération motivante.

Merci de nous téléphoner ou d'adresser votre candidature, sous réfé. 279DT à Françoise THOUVENIN, EUROSELECTION, 98 route de la Reine 92513 Boulogne cédex France. Tél.: (33-1) 47 12 51 51.

E
U
R
O
SELECTION

Questions:

1 De quel genre d'entreprise s'agit-il? (il s'agit de = it's a question of)
2 Quel est le profil requis pour les deux postes?
3 Quelles seront les responsabilités des deux hôtesses?
4 Quels avantages ce cabinet juridique offre-t-il à ses employés?

The interview

> *The familiar form of address (as opposed to the formal, which you've been using up to now) is an important element of this unit, together with more work on 'who', 'whom', 'which' and the ubiquitous verb 'faire'.*
>
> *Mr Jackson has been short-listed for the post of sales manager with Marketis and arrives at their head office in Caen for an interview with Mme Lepic, the managing director.*

Mr Jackson:	Bonjour, Madame. J'ai une entrevue à deux heures. Peux-tu me dire, -oh, pardon, pouvez-vous me dire où se trouve le bureau de Madame Lepic? ...

In the interview room

Mme Lepic:	Bonjour, Monsieur Jackson. Asseyez-vous, s'il vous plaît ... Nous avons regardé votre CV avec intérêt et nous aimerions maintenant vous poser des questions supplémentaires. Tout d'abord, pourquoi avez-vous décidé de poser votre candidature à un poste en France? Après tout, vous travaillez en Angleterre depuis longtemps.
Mr Jackson:	Il y a trois raisons principales: Premièrement, j'ai toujours voulu m'installer en France avec ma famille. Ma femme est d'origine française, comme moi d'ailleurs, et nos enfants sont entièrement bilingues. Deuxièmement, ce poste chez Marketis semble bien correspondre à mes objectifs professionnels ainsi qu'à mon expérience. Troisièmement, je suis particulièrement attiré par la dimension internationale de votre compagnie et par les contacts à l'étranger.
Mme Lepic:	Vous venez de mentionner le mot 'expérience', qu'est-ce que cette expérience vous a apporté tant sur le plan professionnel que sur le plan personnel?
Mr Jackson:	Eh bien, mon premier contact avec le monde du travail a été en France dans les Établissements

Grandivitte où j'ai fait un stage dans le Service Informatique. J'avais choisi l'informatique par intérêt personnel et aussi parce que je pensais que c'était un atout supplémentaire qui, dans mon cas, s'est avéré très utile par la suite. Puis je suis entré chez Brown International Engineering Ltd. Là, j'étais davantage impliqué dans le fonctionnement de l'entreprise. J'ai appris à travailler au sein d'une équipe et ma responsabilité principale consistait à nouer des contacts avec les clients étrangers. J'ai quitté Brown International Engineering de mon plein gré pour le poste que j'occupe à l'heure actuelle depuis cinq ans. À Excel-Equip j'ai élargi mes connaissances dans le domaine de la promotion des ventes. Je suis chargé d'animer une équipe de douze technico-commerciaux et cette année je dois dire que nous avons constaté une très nette progression des ventes, peut-être due au système de primes que j'ai mis sur pied. Sur le plan personnel, je me suis enrichi au contact de mes collègues qui m'ont aussi beaucoup apporté. Je pense que cette formation est une excellente base pour le poste que vous proposez.

Mme Lepic: Vous avez, sans doute, beaucoup de qualités et je suppose … peut-être quelques défauts? Pouvez-vous nous parler de vos points forts et de vos points faibles?

Mr Jackson: Mes points forts sont, je crois, mon désir de réussir, d'aller de l'avant, mais sans jamais prendre trop de risques. Je sais analyser une situation et choisir le moment propice pour agir, ce qui est important dans le monde des affaires. Je sais aussi déléguer mes reponsabilités et ne me crois pas irremplaçable. Je fais de mon mieux pour générer une bonne ambiance dans mon service. Par contre, on m'a parfois accusé d'être inflexible mais j'aime penser que cette soi-disant 'inflexibilité' a toujours été pour une bonne cause.

Mme Lepic: Dans votre lettre, vous avez fait mention de votre salaire actuel. Comme vous le savez, la rémunération offerte pour ce poste va de 400 000 F à 500 000 F. Quelles sont vos prétentions en matière de rémunération?

Mr Jackson:	C'est une question difficile. Disons que je suis prêt à négocier. Mais vous serait-il possible de clarifier certains points en ce qui concerne la rémunération? À part la voiture, existe-t-il d'autres avantages dont les employés peuvent bénéficier?
Mme Lepic:	Oui, tous nos employés peuvent souscrire une assurance-vie et participer aux bénéfices de la compagnie par un système d'intéressement. Nous trouvons que c'est un moyen efficace pour accroître la motivation et augmenter la productivité. En plus, nous offrons aussi les avantages d'un comité d'entreprise* très dynamique ainsi que des chèques-repas.
Mr Jackson:	La rémunération annuelle comporte, je vois, treize mois de salaire. À quel moment de l'année cette prime est-elle payée?
Mme Lepic:	En général, au mois de décembre, qui est payé double. Une dernière question … est-ce que vous seriez en mesure de faire face aux déplacements professionnels fréquents?
Mr Jackson:	Oui, certainement. J'aime toutes formes de voyages. Les voyages d'affaires ne me dérangent nullement et ne posent aucun problème. Ce sera une occasion pour tester mes connaissances linguistiques, lorsque j'irai à l'étranger.
Mme Lepic:	Si nous vous offrions ce poste, quelle serait votre date de disponibilité?
Mr Jackson:	Je dois normalement donner trois mois de préavis.
Mme Lepic:	Très bien. Avez-vous des questions à poser?
Mr Jackson:	Oui, deux petites questions. D'abord, quelle est la durée de la période d'essai? Ensuite, le principe des horaires variables, est-il en vigueur dans votre compagnie?
Mme Lepic:	La période d'essai est de trois mois et, en ce qui concerne les horaires mobiles, nous sommes en train d'étudier la question, c'est à l'état de projet.
Mr Jackson:	Parfait. Tout est clair.
Mme Lepic:	Nous avons déjà un échantillon de votre écriture pour le graphologue, mais nous voudrions

maintenant vous faire passer quelques tests psychologiques qui font partie de nos méthodes de sélection habituelles.

Mr Jackson: Maintenant? Tout de suite?

Mme Lepic: Oui … si vous n'y voyez pas d'inconvénient.

Mr Jackson: Non, non … aucun.

Mme Lepic: Merci, Monsieur Jackson. Nous contacterons tous les postulants par téléphone d'ici une semaine. Merci d'être venu. Bon voyage pour le retour. Je crois que la grève des compagnies maritimes et celle des aiguilleurs du ciel sont maintenant terminées.

Mr Jackson: Espérons-le. Merci beaucoup.

TRANSLATION

Mr Jackson: Good morning. I have an appointment at two o'clock. Can you (*familiar style*) tell me -oh, sorry, can you (*formal style*) tell me where Madame Lepic's office is? …

In the interview room

Mme Lepic: Good morning, Mr Jackson. Please sit down … We've looked at your CV with interest and we'd like to ask you some additional questions. First of all, why have you decided to apply for a job in France? After all, you've been working in England for a long time.

Mr Jackson: There are three main reasons:
Firstly, I've always wanted to settle in France with my family. My wife is of French origin, as indeed I am, (*lit.* 'like me, for that matter') and my children are completely bilingual. Secondly, this position with Marketis seems to correspond very well to my career objectives and also to my experience. Thirdly, I'm particularly attracted by the international dimension of your company and by the contacts abroad.

Mme Lepic: You've just mentioned the word 'experience', what has this experience brought you both on a professional and personal level?

Mr Jackson: Well, my first contact with the world of work was in France with Grandivitte and Company where I completed a period of training in the computer department. I chose (*lit.* 'I had chosen') computing out of personal interest because I thought it was an additional asset which, in my case, did prove eventually to be very useful. Then, I joined Brown International Engineering Ltd. There I was more involved in the running of the firm. I learned to work as a member of a team (*lit.* 'within a team') and my main responsibility consisted in building up contacts with foreign clients. I left Brown International Engineering of my own accord for the position I've now held for five years. At Excel-Equip I have widened my knowledge in the field of sales promotion. I'm responsible for motivating a team of twelve technical salespeople and this year I have to say that we've noticed a very marked increase in sales, perhaps as a result of the bonus system I've set up (*lit.* 'I've put on foot'). On a personal level, I've gained (*lit.* 'I've enriched myself') from my contacts with my colleagues who have also taught (*lit.* 'brought') me a great deal. I think this training is an excellent basis for the post you offer.

Mme Lepic: You no doubt have many qualities and I suppose … perhaps a few failings? Can you tell us something about (*lit.* 'speak to us of') your strong points and weak points?

Mr Jackson: My strong points are, I think, my desire to succeed, to go forward, but without ever taking too many risks. I know how to analyse a situation and to choose the right moment to act, which is important in the world of business. I also know how to delegate my responsibilities and I don't consider myself to be irreplaceable. I do my best to create a good atmosphere in my department. On the other hand, I have been accused on occasions of being inflexible, but I like to think that this so-called 'inflexibility' has always been in a good cause.

Mme Lepic: In your letter you mentioned your present salary. As you know, the salary offered for this position is between 400,000 and 500,000 francs. What are your requirements as regards salary?

Mr Jackson: That's a difficult question. Let's say that I'm prepared to negotiate. But would it be possible for you to clarify certain points as far as the salary is concerned? Apart from the company car, are there any other advantages that the employees can benefit from?

Mme Lepic: Yes, all our employees can take out life insurance and participate in the company's profits through a profit-sharing scheme. We find that this is an effective way of increasing motivation and productivity. In addition, we also offer the advantages of a very dynamic works committee* as well as luncheon vouchers.

Mr Jackson:	The annual salary includes, I see, thirteen months' pay. At what time of the year is this bonus paid?
Mme Lepic:	Generally, in December, when you receive two months' pay (*lit.* 'which is paid double'). One last question … would you be in a position to cope with the frequent business trips?
Mr Jackson:	Yes, certainly. I enjoy all forms of travel. Business trips don't worry (*lit.* 'disturb') me at all and present no problem. It'll be an opportunity to test my linguistic knowledge when I go abroad.
Mme Lepic:	If we were to offer you the post, when would you be available?
Mr Jackson:	Normally I have to give three months' notice.
Mme Lepic:	Fine. Have you any questions to ask?
Mr Jackson:	Yes, two minor questions. First, how long does the trial period last (lit.'what is the duration of …')? Next, is flexi-time in operation in your company?
Mme Lepic:	The trial period is three months and, as regards flexible hours, we're in the process of studying the question, it's in the planning stage.
Mr Jackson:	Excellent. That's all very clear. Thank you.
Mme Lepic:	We already have a sample of your handwriting, but we'd like you now to take a few psychological tests which are part of our usual methods of selection.
Mr Jackson:	Now? Right away?
Mme Lepic:	Yes … if you have no objections.
Mr Jackson:	No, no … none.
Mme Lepic:	Thank you, Mr Jackson. We'll be contacting all the applicants by telephone in a week's time. Thank you for coming. Have a good journey back. I believe that the shipping companies' strike and the air-traffic controllers' are now over.
Mr Jackson:	Let's hope so. Thank you very much.

* Le comité d'entreprise: This consists of representatives of staff and management. It has a consultative role and discusses such matters as staff training, working hours, the introduction of new technology and so on. The committee also plans the social activities of the company (organized holidays, Christmas parties, etc.) and often subsidizes the staff canteen.

Checklist 10

Masculine nouns:

le mot	word
le monde	world
le défaut	failing
le bénéfice	profit
le moyen	means, way
le comité d'entreprise	works committee
le chèque-repas	luncheon voucher
le préavis	(advance) notice
le postulant	applicant
le retour	return
l'atout	asset
l'intéressement	profit sharing
l'aiguilleur du ciel	air-traffic controller
les horaires variables/mobiles	flexible hours

Feminine nouns:

la prime	bonus
la raison	reason
la disponibilité	availability
la durée	duration
la période d'essai	trial period
la grève	strike
la compagnie maritime	shipping company
l'assurance-vie	life assurance
l'entrevue	interview
les prétentions	(salary) requirements

Adjectives:

fort	strong
faible	weak
propice	opportune
irremplaçable	irreplaceable
soi-disant (invariable)	so-called
chargé de	responsible for
principal, principaux (m. pl.)	main
net, nette (f.)	marked
habituel, -elle (f.)	usual
dû, due (f.) à	due to

Adverbs:

premièrement	firstly
deuxièmement	secondly
troisièmement	thirdly
entièrement	entirely
nullement	not at all
ensuite	afterwards
longtemps	a long time
parfois	on occasions
tout de suite	right away

Other words/expressions:

depuis	since
moi	me
puis	then
là	there; here
dont	see Checknote 78
celle	see Checknote 76
tout d'abord	first of all
d'ailleurs	for that matter; besides
peut-être	perhaps
sans doute	no doubt, probably
par contre	on the other hand
à part	apart from
en vigueur	in operation
tant … que	both … and
par la suite	eventually
au sein de	within
en matière de	as regards
faire face à	to cope with
faire partie de	to form part of
d'ici une semaine	in a week's time
mettre sur pied	to set up
sur le plan professionnel	professionally
être en mesure de	to be in a position to

à l'état de projet	in the planning stage
de mon plein gré	of my own accord
si vous n'y voyez pas d'inconvénient	if you have no objection

Numbers:

sept cents	700
sept cent soixante	760
huit cents	800
huit cent quatre -vingt-dix	890
neuf cents	900
mille	1000
deux mille	2000
cinq mille	5000
neuf mille	9000
un million	1,000,000

Verbs:

payer	to pay (see essayer, Checklist 5)
regarder	to look at
poser	to put, to pose
impliquer	to involve
nouer	to form
quitter	to leave
constater	to notice
déléguer	to delegate
générer	to generate
négocier	to negotiate
clarifier	to clarify
bénéficier	to benefit
trouver	to find
passer	to sit (examination)
terminer	to end
s'avérer	to prove to be
élargir	to widen
agir	to act
s'enrichir	to enrich oneself

Irregular verbs:

souscrire *to take out* (*insurance*): see écrire, Checklist 9

accroître *to increase*
present: j'accrois, il accroît, nous accroissons, vous accroissez, ils accroissent
past: j'ai accru

CHECKNOTES

73 The familiar form

It was a slip of the tongue when Mr Jackson said to the receptionist 'Peux-tu me dire ...' because **tu** (you) is only used when addressing members of the family, close friends, children and animals; **tu** is also used among young people probably up to the age of 23 or 24 from the very first meeting, when they belong to the same milieu (school, university, work, etc.). In addition, an adult will normally say **tu** to a teenager, even when they don't know each other well, although of course the teenager will reply with **vous**.

Many French language courses teach this familiar form right from lesson 1, but we have preferred to wait until the **vous**-form was firmly established in your mind before introducing another way of saying 'you'. It would certainly surprise French people if you addressed them as **tu**, when they were expecting the more formal **vous**. It would certainly create a bad impression during an interview for a job!

The whole question of whether to use **tu** or **vous** remains a nebulous area and so much depends on the personality of the French people concerned. Some are pleased to use the familiar form at the first opportunity, others find it extremely difficult to employ **tu** to anyone other than their family and close friends. Our advice to the English-speaking businessman or businesswoman is to keep to the **vous**-form until your French contact asks '**On se tutoie**?' ('Shall we use **tu**?')

To help you prepare for that occasion, here are the various forms you'll need:

FORMAL

FAMILIAR

Speaking to one person: **vous**
Speaking to more than one: **vous**

Speaking to one person: **tu**
Speaking to more than one: **vous**

-er verbs:

pres: vous importez	tu importes	*you import*
perf: vous avez exporté	tu as exporté	*you exported*
fut: vous téléphonerez	tu téléphoneras	*you will telephone*
cond: vous commanderiez	tu commanderais	*you would order*
impf: vous organisiez	tu organisais	*you used to organise*
subj: que vous fabriquiez	que tu fabriques	*(translation varies)*

-ir verbs:

pres: vous investissez	tu investis	*you invest*
perf: vous avez réagi	tu as réagi	*you reacted*
fut: vous réussirez	tu réussiras	*you will succeed*
cond: vous finiriez	tu finirais	*you would finish*
impf: vous choisissiez	tu choisissais	*you used to choose*
subj: que vous enrichissiez	que tu enrichisses	*(translation varies)*

-re verbs:

pres: vous vendez	tu vends	*you sell*
perf: vous avez attendu	tu as attendu	*you waited*
fut: vous perdrez	tu perdras	*you will lose*
cond: vous répondriez	tu répondrais	*you would reply*
impf: vous rendiez	tu rendais	*you used to give back*
subj: que vous descendiez	que tu descendes	*(translation varies)*

Irregular verbs:

	FORMAL	FAMILIAR	
	present:	*present:*	
faire	vous faites	tu fais	*you do, make*
pouvoir	vous pouvez	tu peux	*you can*
savoir	vous savez	tu sais	*you know*
vouloir	vous voulez	tu veux	*you want*
recevoir	vous recevez	tu reçois	*you receive*
mettre	vous mettez	tu mets	*you put*
prendre	vous prenez	tu prends	*you take*
résoudre	vous résolvez	tu résous	*you solve*
croire	vous croyez	tu crois	*you believe*
dire	vous dites	tu dis	*you say*
suivre	vous suivez	tu suis	*you follow*
connaître	vous connaissez	tu connais	*you know*
voir	vous voyez	tu vois	*you see*
venir	vous venez	tu viens	*you come*
partir	vous partez	tu pars	*you leave*
offrir	vous offrez	tu offres	*you offer*

We mustn't, of course, forget the two most important verbs of all:

être	vous êtes	tu es	*you are*
avoir	vous avez	tu as	*you have*

Possessive adjectives:

FORMAL	FAMILIAR	
votre bureau (*m.*)	ton bureau	*your office*
votre voiture (*f.*) de fonction	ta voiture de fonction	*your company car*
vos objectifs (*pl.*) professionnels	tes objectifs professionnels	*your career objectives*

Possessive pronouns:

FORMAL	FAMILIAR	
le vôtre (*m. sing.*)	le tien	*yours*
la vôtre (*f. sing.*)	la tienne	*yours*
les vôtres (*m. pl.*)	les tiens	*yours*
les vôtres (*f. pl.*)	les tiennes	*yours*

Direct/indirect object pronouns:

FORMAL	FAMILIAR	
je vous rencontrerai devant la Chambre de Commerce	je te rencontrerai devant la Chambre de Commerce	*I'll meet you in front of the Chamber of Commerce*
je vous attendais	je t'attendais	*I was expecting you*
je vous répondrai demain	je te répondrai demain	*I'll reply to you tomorrow*

74 Venir de ('to have just...'), depuis ('since')

Make a note of the very useful expression **venir de** ('to have just ...'):

Je viens de mettre sur pied un système de primes.
I've just set up a system of bonuses.

Nous venons de regarder votre CV.
We've just been looking at your CV.

Elle venait de payer sa cotisation à la retraite.
She had just paid her pension (retirement) contribution.

depuis ('since'):

You'll have noticed from this Unit's dialogue that English and French tenses do not always correspond. For example, the English past tense is sometimes translated by the French present:

Je travaille en Angleterre depuis longtemps.
I've been working in England a long time.
    (*lit.*'I work in England since a long time')

Il exerce cette profession depuis cinq ans.
He's been practising this profession for five years.

In other words, when an action begun in the past is still continuing in the present, then the French consider the present tense to be more logical.

75 Faire

The verb that has the largest number of pages devoted to it in an English dictionary is 'to get'. The verb which takes up most space in a French dictionary is **faire**, which can mean:

a) to do:

Je fais souvent des heures supplémentaires.
I often do overtime.

Avez-vous fait un stage?
Have you done a period of training?

b) to make:

> L'entreprise a fait cette année des bénéfices importants.
> *The company this year has made large profits.*

> L'offre qu'ils ont faite est inacceptable.
> *The offer they have made is unacceptable.*

c) to give:

> Voulez-vous faire une conférence sur les tests psychologiques?
> *Will you give a lecture on psychological tests?*

> Je serai, malheureusement, obligé de faire un discours le jour où je prendrai ma retraite.
> *Unfortunately, I'll have to give a speech on the day I retire.*
> (*lit.*'… the day <u>where</u> …')

d) to take:

> Puis-je compter sur vous pour faire toutes les démarches nécessaires?
> *May I count on you to take all the necessary steps?*

> N.B **Puis-je** …? is a more formal alternative to **Est-ce que je peux** …? and means 'May I …?'

> Il faut que nous fassions l'inventaire rapidement, sinon nous risquons d'être en rupture de stock.
> *We must take an inventory quickly, otherwise we risk being out of stock.*

e) to have (something done):

> Non, je ne l'ai pas fait congédier.
> *No, I haven't had him sacked.*

> Il m'a fait muter à l'étranger.
> *He had me transferred abroad.*

> C'est l'ancien Directeur qui a fait construire les nouveaux locaux de la banque.
> *It's the previous Director who had the new premises for the bank built.*

f) **faire** is used in connection with the weather:

> Il a fait si mauvais que l'avion a été retardé de deux heures.
> *It was such bad weather that the plane was delayed by two hours.*

76 The one, those

Study the following:

celui (*m.*)   *the one*
ceux (*m. pl.*) *those*
celle (*f.*)   *the one*
celles (*f. pl.*) *those*

We use these words when we want to avoid repeating the same noun, for example:

> La dernière question, c'est celle qui concerne les déplacements professionnels.
> *The last question is the one that concerns the business trips.*
>
> Quel panneau d'affichage vous a amusé le plus?
> *Which advertisement hoarding amused you the most?*
>
> Celui qui vante les mérites de la crème antirides.
> *The one which extols the virtues of the anti-wrinkle cream.*

Note also the more specific 'this one (here)', 'that one (there)' and their plural forms, both masculine and feminine:

(m.)		(f.)	
celui-ci	*this one*	**celle-ci**	*this one*
celui-là	*that one*	**celle-là**	*that one*
ceux-ci	*these*	**celles-ci**	*these*
ceux-là	*those*	**celles-là**	*those*

> Cet échantillon-ci ou celui-là? *This sample or that one?*
> Ces questions-ci ou celles-là? *These questions or those?*

77 Quantities

Study the following:

beaucoup d'expérience	*a great deal of experience*
beaucoup de stagiaires	*many trainees*
trop d'indépendance financière	*too much financial independence*
trop de risques	*too many risks*
tant d'avantages en nature	*so many fringe benefits*
peu de prestations sociales	*few social security benefits*
assez de personnel	*sufficient staff*

You'll have noticed that when a noun follows -

beaucoup	*much, many*
trop	*too much, too many*
tant	*so much, so many*
peu	*little, few*
assez	*enough*

- they are linked to the noun by **de (d')**

78 Relative pronouns (2)

You learned in Checknote 56 that 'whom' in sentences like 'The candidate whom we interviewed this morning' is translated by **que**. However, after a preposition 'whom' is expressed as **qui**:

Où est la sténodactylo à qui vous avez confié le dossier?
Where is the shorthand typist to whom you entrusted the file?

After a preposition 'which' translates as:

lequel (*m.*)
lesquels (*m. pl.*)
laquelle (*f.*)
lesquelles (*f. pl.*)

The above words combine with **à** and **de** in the usual way:

le voyage au cours duquel j'ai rencontré votre femme pour la première fois
the journey in the course of which I met your wife for the first time

l'indemnité de licenciement à laquelle il s'attendait
the redundancy payment he was expecting

les primes de rendement auxquelles nous avons droit
the productivity bonuses to which we are entitled

The word **dont** is often used in place of **de qui**, **duquel**, **de laquelle**, **desquels** and **desquelles**:

Existe-t-il d'autres avantages dont les employés peuvent bénéficier?
Are there other advantages from which the employees can benefit?

Voici le jeune informaticien dont je vous ai parlé.
This is the young computer expert I spoke to you about
(lit.'... of whom I spoke to you').

We also use **dont** to translate 'whose', but sometimes the word order in French is a little unexpected:

le candidat dont j'ai perdu le dossier   *the applicant whose file I've lost*

'Whose' as a question is **À qui ... ?**

À qui est cette agrafeuse?   *Whose is this stapler?*

79 Some

As you know, 'some' is expressed as **du, de la, de l', des**:

J'ai du travail à faire.	*I have some work to do.*
Nous aimerions vous poser des questions.	*We'd like to ask you some questions.*

But when a plural noun is preceded by an adjective, the **des** becomes **de**:

de bons employés	*some good employees*
de nouveaux débouchés	*some new outlets*
d'autres avantages	*some other advantages*

Comprehension Practice 10

Vrai ou faux?

New words:

la perte de temps	*waste of time*
les avantages (m.) en nature	*fringe benefits*
trouver	*to find*
passer	*to spend (time),*
	to take (examination)
se tromper	*to make a mistake*
en grève	*on strike*

N.B. **tutoyer** *to use the* '**tu**' *form*
present: je tutoie, il tutoie, nous tutoyons, vous tutoyez, ils tutoient
past: j'ai tutoyé
future: je tutoierai

1 M. Jackson s'est trompé en tutoyant la réceptionniste.

2 Les membres du jury de Marketis n'ont pas trouvé le CV de M. Jackson particulièrement intéressant.

3 M. Jackson est très attiré par les activités internationales de Marketis.

4 M. Jackson pense que l'informatique est une pure perte de temps.

5 M. Jackson a quitté Brown International Engineering Ltd de sa propre initiative.

6 Du point de vue professionnel et personnel M. Jackson pense que les années qu'il a passées à Excel-Equip lui ont été bénéfiques.

7 La Société Marketis offre certains avantages (en nature, financiers) à ses employés.

8 Les déplacements d'affaires risquent de poser un problème à M. Jackson.

9 M. Jackson a trois questions supplémentaires à poser au jury.

10 Les horaires mobiles fonctionnent parfaitement bien chez Marketis.

11 M. Jackson ne peut pas rester pour passer les tests psychologiques.

12 Les avions et les ferries ne sont probablement plus en grève.

FLUENCY PRACTICE 47

New words:

le salaire brut	gross salary
le salaire net	net salary
sûrement	certainly
réfléchir sur	to reflect on

The following is a conversation between two close colleagues in connection with a forthcoming interview. Change the vous/votre/vos-forms into the corresponding familiar forms.

A J'ai regardé votre CV avec intérêt. Pourquoi avez-vous décidé de poser votre candidature à ce poste-là? Vous venez de mentionner le mot 'expérience', mais de quelle expérience est-ce que vous parlez? À l'entrevue, on vous demandera sûrement de parler de vos points forts et de vos points faibles. Dans votre lettre, vous avez déclaré votre salaire actuel, mais est-ce votre salaire brut?

B Oui, ce sont toutes des remarques intéressantes et j'y réfléchirai avant l'entrevue.

FLUENCY PRACTICE 48

New words:

l'employeur (m.)	employer
tôt	soon
encore	still, yet
c'est bien à savoir	that's good to know
être habitué à	to be used to
tirer des conclusions	to draw conclusions
se mettre d'accord sur	to agree on
en plus de	in addition to

Irregular verb:

introduire to introduce
present: j'introduis, il introduit, n. introduisons,.v introduisez,
  ils introduisent
past: j'ai introduit

Study again the main text of this Unit and then play the role of Mr Jackson in the following interview:

Mme Lepic: Bonjour Monsieur Jackson. Asseyez-vous. Nous venons de regarder votre CV et nous aimerions maintenant vous poser quelques questions.

	Pourquoi avez-vous posé votre candidature à ce poste de Directeur des Ventes?
Mr Jackson:	*Well, I believe that this position corresponds exactly to my career objectives and to my past experience. In addition, I'm particularly attracted by the international dimension of your company.*
Mme Lepic:	Vous avez mentionné votre expérience professionnelle. Pouvez-vous nous dire ce que cette expérience vous a apporté?
Mr Jackson:	*I've certainly acquired the necessary experience to build up contacts with foreign clients. I've widened my knowledge in the field of sales promotion and I'm now used to leading a team of twelve salespeople.*
Mme Lepic:	Une question un peu plus personnelle maintenant. Vous avez sans aucun doute des qualités, mais avez-vous aussi des défauts?
Mr Jackson:	*Well, yes, no-one's perfect. I have, I think, many qualities but I have also been accused, on occasions, of being inflexible. Personally, I think that this so-called 'inflexibility' has always been in a good cause.*
Mme Lepic:	Vous avez fait mention de votre salaire actuel, quelles sont exactement vos prétentions en matière de rémunération pour ce poste?
Mr Jackson:	*That's a difficult question and I'm ready to negotiate. But may I ask whether there are any other advantages in addition to the company car?*
Mme Lepic:	Oui, les employés peuvent souscrire une assurance-vie, par exemple, et aussi participer aux bénéfices de l'entreprise par le système d'intéressement.
Mr Jackson:	*That's good to know. Thank you. I'm sure we'll be able to agree on a salary.*
Mme Lepic:	Si nous vous offrions le poste, quelle serait votre date de disponibilité?
Mr Jackson:	*Well, normally, I have to give three months' notice to my present employer.*
Mme Lepic:	Cela me paraît normal. Bien, avez-vous des questions à nous poser?

| Mr Jackson: | Just one. *Is flexi-time in operation in your company?* |
| Mme Lepic: | Oui, nous venons juste de l'introduire et pour le moment, le système fonctionne bien. Mais il est encore trop tôt pour tirer des conclusions définitives. |

FLUENCY PRACTICE 49

New words:

le sous-directeur	*assistant manager*
le critère	*criterion*
la résidence secondaire	*second home*
lors de	*during*
chercher	*to look for*
utiliser	*to use*
garder	*to keep*

Irregular verb:

disparaître *to disappear*
see paraître, Checklist 9

Complete the following:

1 (I've just been promoted) au poste de sous-directeur.
2 (We've just agreed on) le salaire.
3 (I've been looking for) un poste en Allemagne depuis longtemps.
4 Depuis combien de temps (have you been using) les tests psychologiques et la graphologie dans vos méthodes de sélection?
5 Le jury (got the candidate to come back) pour une deuxième entrevue.
6 Beaucoup d'Anglais (are having a second home built for themselves) en France.
7 Mes critères de sélection sont (those) qui sont le plus souvent utilisés lors des entrevues.
8 Avez-vous l'intention d'accepter cette offre-ci ou (that one)?
9 J'apprécie beaucoup les collègues (with whom) je vais collaborer.
10 Le dossier (in which) je gardais mes documents confidentiels a disparu du classeur.

Buying a house in France

> There's a little more grammar, but the emphasis is on extending your comprehension, vocabulary and oral fluency through role-play.
>
> Mr Jackson has now heard from Marketis that his application for the post of sales manager has been successful. He therefore decides that he would like to buy a family house in France and goes along with his wife to discuss the matter with a French notary, Mme Gervais.

Mr Jackson:	Bonjour, Madame.
Mme Gervais:	Bonjour, Monsieur.
Mr Jackson:	Nous sommes un peu en avance.
Mme Gervais:	Non, pas du tout. Asseyez-vous. Je m'occupe de vous tout de suite ...
Mr Jackson:	Voilà, je suis Anglais et je viens d'obtenir un poste dans une compagnie à Cherbourg. Je cherche donc à acheter une maison dans la région pour moi et ma famille.
Mme Gervais:	Parfait. Avez-vous déjà une idée sur le genre de propriété que vous désirez, sur l'emplacement et surtout sur le prix?
Mr Jackson:	Oui, nous y avons déjà réfléchi et contrairement à la rumeur qui court ici en Normandie, à savoir que les Anglais sont souvent indécis, ma femme, elle, sait exactement ce qu'elle veut (remarquez, elle n'est qu'à moitié Anglaise!). Nous cherchons donc une maison ancienne, en pierre, avec quatre chambres, un garage et un peu de terrain autour, indépendante, et surtout qui soit habitable immédiatement. Vous comprenez, je ne suis pas bricoleur et ne le deviendrai probablement jamais. Bien sûr, nous nous attendons à ce qu'il y ait des aménagements à faire, mais le moins possible pour le moment.

Mme Gervais: Quelle est votre gamme de prix?

Mr Jackson: Entre 300.000 et 400.000F.

Mme Gervais: Nous avons quelques propriétés qui correspondent plus ou moins à votre description et qui sont dans vos prix. Regardez, voici des photos avec les détails de chaque maison et des environs proches.

Mr Jackson: Oui, celle-ci a beaucoup de charme, regarde chérie … celle-là aussi est jolie, le cadre est magnifique … mais la façade est plus ordinaire.

One hour later

Mr Jackson: Nous avons fait notre choix … celle-ci en pierre, à 350.000F, puis, celle qui a une véranda et le grand jardin à 370.000F, et celle qui a des dépendances et un champ derrière à 400.000F. Serait-il possible d'aller les visiter toutes les trois le même jour? Ces maisons sont-elles habitées en ce moment?

Mme Gervais: Oui, deux d'entre elles le sont, mais pas la troisième. Je vais prendre rendez-vous avec les propriétaires et je vous contacterai. J'ai vos coordonnées. C'est bien votre adresse et votre numéro de téléphone?

Mr Jackson: Oui, c'est bien ca. Nous sommes chez des amis qui habitent la région. Nous restons chez eux deux semaines.

A week later Mr and Mrs Jackson have visited the three houses for sale and are now back at the notary's office.

Mr Jackson: Après mûre réflexion, nous avons choisi cette maison-ci en vieilles pierres à 350.000F. Bien sûr, il aura quelques aménagements à faire, mais elle est habitable et elle a surtout un tel cachet! Est-il possible de faire une offre de 320.000F?

Mme Gervais: Vous pouvez toujours essayer. Je vais faire la proposition d'achat au vendeur et s'il accepte votre offre, je vous enverrai un compromis de vente. Je vous demanderais de me le retourner le plus rapidement possible avec les documents nécessaires, c'est à dire certificat de naissance et certificat de mariage et, bien sûr, un acompte de 10% du prix d'achat. De quelle manière envisagez-vous de financer votre acquisition? Disposez-vous des fonds nécessaires ou avez-vous l'intention de contracter un emprunt à la banque?

Mr Jackson: Nous avons l'intention de faire un emprunt bancaire.

Mme. Gervais: Dans ce cas, puisque vous aurez recours à un crédit bancaire, le compromis de vente sera conclu sous 'condition suspensive' de l'obtention de ce financement, c'est à dire que si vous n'obtenez pas le prêt, le compromis sera nul et non avenu et l'acompte que vous aurez versé vous sera restitué dans sa totalité.

Mr Jackson: Que se passerait-il si nous étions obligés de nous retirer pour une raison personnelle ou autre?

Mme Gervais: Dans ce cas-là, vous perdriez votre acompte de 10% qui serait versé à titre de compensation au vendeur qui, théoriquement, pourrait demander des dommages-intérêts supplémentaires.

Mr Jackson: Une autre question importante. Quel est normalement le laps de temps entre la signature du compromis et celle de l'acte de vente définitif?

Mme Gervais: Comme il y a emprunt, il faut compter approximativement deux mois. Cela dépend, bien sûr, en grande partie de la rapidité des transactions bancaires. Sans emprunt, le délai est de l'ordre de quatre à cinq semaines.

Mr Jackson: Pour en revenir à la question du règlement, donc, si j'ai bien compris, nous versons 10% à la signature du compromis et le solde, quand doit-il être payé?

Mme Gervais: Le solde doit être viré directement sur le compte du notaire pour le jour de la signature de l'acte de vente.

Mr Jackson: J'ai entendu dire que les frais d'achat sont plus élevés en France qu'ils ne le sont en Angleterre.

Quel est le montant approximatif de ces frais pour une maison comme celle que nous avons l'intention d'acheter?

Mme Gervais: Eh bien, les frais seront de l'ordre de 15% du prix d'achat. Ils comprennent à la fois les honoraires du notaire, les droits d'enregistrement et toutes les taxes relatives à l'achat. En plus, vous aurez aussi les frais de négociations, puisque vous avez trouvé votre maison par notre intermédiaire.

Mr Jackson: Et les impôts locaux, existent-ils?

Mme Gervais: Oui, il y en a deux qui sont payables à la commune: la taxe foncière, dont le taux varie d'une commune à l'autre et qui est payée par le propriétaire, et la taxe d'habitation qui est la responsabilité de la personne qui occupe la propriété.

Mr Jackson: Très bien. Je pense avoir tous les renseignements nécessaires pour le moment. Je vous retournerai le compromis dès que je l'aurai reçu et rempli, avec mon chèque, pour que vous puissiez préparer l'acte de vente au plus vite. J'espère qu'il n'y aura pas de problèmes inattendus comme, par exemple, la construction d'une route à proximité. Et maintenant il ne me reste plus qu'à faire les démarches nécessaires pour mon emprunt bancaire. Merci beaucoup, Madame.

Mme Gervais: N'hésitez pas à me contacter si vous avez des questions à éclaircir. Au revoir, Monsieur.

Mr Jackson: Au revoir, Madame.

TRANSLATION

Mr Jackson: Good morning.

Mme Gervais: Good morning.

Mr Jackson: We're a little early.

Mme Gervais: No, not at all. Do sit down. I'll be right with you …

Mr Jackson: Well, I'm English and I've just obtained a post with a company in Cherbourg. I'm trying therefore to buy a house in this area for me and my family.

Mme Gervais:	Fine. Do you already have an idea of the type of property you want, its location and, of course (*lit.* 'especially'), the price?
Mr Jackson:	Yes, we've already given it some thought and, contrary to the rumour that's circulating here in Normandy, namely that the English are often indecisive, my wife knows exactly what she wants (mind you, she is only half English!). So, we're looking for an old house, made of stone, with four bedrooms, a garage and a little land around it, detached, and which is above all inhabitable immediately. You see, I'm not much of a 'do-it-yourself' enthusiast and probably never will be (*lit.* 'and probably will never become it'). Of course, we expect some improvements to be necessary, but as few as possible for the time being.
Mme Gervais:	What is your price range?
Mr Jackson:	Between 300,000 and 400,000F.
Mme Gervais:	We do have a few properties which correspond more or less to your description and which are in your price range. Look, here are some photos with the details of each house and the immediate surrounding area.
Mr Jackson:	Yes, this one has a lot of charm, look darling ... That one's pretty too, the setting is wonderful ... but the front is more ordinary.

One hour later

Mr Jackson:	Right, we've made our choice ... This one in stone at 350,000F, then the one which has a verandah and the large garden at 370,000F, and the one with the outbuildings and a field behind at 400,000F. Would it be possible to go and visit all three the same day? Are these houses being lived in at the moment?
Mme Gervais:	Yes, two of them are, but not the third one. I'll make an appointment with the owners and contact you. I have your details. Is this your correct address and 'phone number?
Mr Jackson:	Yes, that's right. We're staying with friends who live in the area. We'll be with them for two weeks.

A week later

Mr Jackson:	After careful thought, we've chosen this house in old stone at 350,000F. Of course, there'll be a few improvements to carry out, but it is inhabitable and it has such character! Is it possible to make an offer of 320,000F?

Mme Gervais:	You can always try. I'll pass your offer on to the vendor and, if he accepts it, I'll send you a Sale Agreement. I would ask you to return it to me as quickly as possible with the necessary documents, that's to say birth certificate and marriage certificate and, of course, a deposit of 10% of the purchase price. In what way do you envisage financing your purchase? Do you have the necessary funds available or do you intend to contract a bank loan?
Mr Jackson:	We intend to take out a bank loan.
Mme Gervais:	In that case, since you'll be needing a bank loan, the Sale Agreement will be prepared with (*lit.* 'will be concluded under') a 'let-out' clause linked to the obtaining of this finance, that's to say that, if you don't obtain the loan, the Agreement will be null and void, and the deposit you will have paid will be returned to you in its entirety.
Mr Jackson:	What would happen if we had to withdraw for a personal reason or some other reason?
Mme Gervais:	In that case you would lose your deposit of 10% which would then be paid by way of compensation to the vendor who, theoretically, could ask for additional damages.
Mr Jackson:	Another important question. What is the normal time lapse between the signing of the Agreement and that of the Deed of Sale?
Mme Gervais:	As a loan is required, one must reckon approximately two months. It depends, of course, to a large extent on the speed of the bank transactions. Without a loan, the time lapse is in the order of four to five weeks.
Mr Jackson:	To get back to the question of payment then, if I've understood correctly, we put down 10% on the signing of the Agreement and the balance is paid when?
Mme Gervais:	The balance must be transferred directly to the notary's account by the day on which the Deed of Sale is signed.
Mr Jackson:	I've heard it said that the expenses in connection with the purchase are higher in France than they are in England. What's the approximate amount of these expenses for a house like the one we intend to buy?
Mme Gervais:	Well, the expenses will be in the order of 15% of the purchase price. They include the notary's fees, the registration charges as well as all the taxes connected

	with the purchase. In addition, you'll also have the negotiation fees, since you found your house through us.
Mr Jackson:	And do local taxes exist?
Mme Gervais:	Yes, there are two kinds of tax payable to the district council: 'property tax', the amount of which varies from one council to another and which is paid by the owner, and 'dwelling tax' which is the responsibility of the person who occupies the property.
Mr Jackson:	Fine. I think I have all the information I need for the time being. I'll return the Agreement to you as soon as I've received it and completed it, with my cheque, so that you can prepare the Deed of Sale as quickly as possible. I hope there'll be no unexpected problems like, for example, the construction of a road close by. And now I only have to take the necessary steps to obtain the bank loan. Thank you very much.
Mme Gervais:	Don't hesitate to contact me if you have any points that need clarification. Goodbye, Mr Jackson.
Mr Jackson:	Goodbye, Madame Gervais.

Checklist 11

Masculine nouns:

le terrain	*land*
le vendeur	*vendor*
le financement	*financing*
le règlement	*payment*
le solde	*balance*
le compte	*account*
le notaire	*notary*
le montant	*amount*
le taux	*rate*
le chèque	*cheque*
le bricoleur	*handyman*
le mari	*husband*
le cadre	*setting*
le choix	*choice*
le jardin	*garden*
le champ	*field*
le/la propriétaire	*owner*
le certificat de naissance	*birth certificate*
le certificat de mariage	*marriage certificate*
le laps de temps	*time lapse*
le prêt	*loan*
le compromis de vente	*sale agreement*
l'acte de vente	*deed of sale*
l'achat	*purchase*
l'acompte	*deposit*
l'aménagement	*renovation work*
l'emprunt	*borrowing*
l'emplacement	*location*
les fonds	*funds*
les dommages - intérêts	*damages*
les honoraires	*fee(s)*
les droits d'enregistrement	*registration fees*
les impôts locaux	*local taxes*
les environs	*surrounding area*
les renseignements nécessaires	*necessary information*
les frais	*expenses*
les coordonnées	*address and phone number*

Feminine nouns:

la propriété	*property*
la proposition	*proposal*
la signature	*signing, signature*
la taxe foncière	*property tax*
la taxe d'habitation	*dwelling tax*
la cour	*courtyard*
la route	*road*
la commune	*district council*
la rumeur	*rumour*
la femme	*wife, woman*
la pierre	*stone*
la gamme	*range*
la photo	*photo*
la compensation	*compensation*
la condition suspensive	*condition precedent*
l'acquisition	*purchase*
l'obtention	*obtaining*
les transactions	*transactions*
les négociations	*negotiations*
les dépendances	*outbuildings*

Adjectives:

indécis	*indecisive*
indépendant	*detached*
bancaire	*banking*
élevé	*high*
payable	*payable*
inattendu	*unexpected*
joli	*pretty*
personnel, -elle *(f.)*	*personal*
approximatif, -ive *(f.)*	*approximate*
relatif, -ive *(f.)* à	*relating to*
local, locaux *(m. pl.)*	*local*

Adverbs:

contrairement à	*contrary to*
théoriquement	*theoretically*

normalement	normally	après mûre réflexion	after careful thought
approximative-ment	approximately		

Verbs:

surtout	above all, especially
autour	around

remarquer	to notice
habiter	to live
envisager	to envisage
financer	to finance

Other words/expressions:

verser	to pay
restituer	to return
compter	to count, reckon

puis	then
derrière	behind
en avance	early
à savoir	namely
à moitié	half
chez eux	at their place
pour moi	for me
dès que	as soon as
C'est bien le/la …?	Is this the right …?
avoir recours à	to have recourse to
à titre de	by way of
à proximité	close by
à la fois	as well, at the same time
par notre intermédiaire	through us
nul et non avenu	null and void
j'ai entendu dire que …	I've heard it said that …

virer	to transfer
varier	to vary
hésiter	to hesitate
chercher (à acheter)	to try (to buy)
disposer de	to have available
se passer	to happen
se retirer	to withdraw
s'occuper de	to attend to
remplir	to fill up
éclaircir	to clarify
perdre	to lose
dépendre de	to depend on
s'attendre à ce que + subj.	to expect

Irregular verbs:

obtenir to obtain
see venir, Checklist 7 (but past is: j'ai obtenu)

devenir to become
see venir, Checklist 7

courir to run
present: je cours, il court, nous courons, vous courez, ils courent
past: j'ai couru
future: je courrai

conclure to conclude
present: je conclus, il conclut, nous concluons, vous concluez, ils concluent
past: j'ai conclu

CHECKNOTES

80 Disjunctive pronouns

We have already studied the various forms of the direct and indirect object pronouns in French, but there's another class of pronouns that you have to be familiar with.

Consider the following:

Je m'occupe d'eux tout de suite.
I'll attend to them right away.

Vous cherchez une maison pour lui ou pour elle?
Are you looking for a house for him or for her?

L'architecte est plus qualifié que moi.
The architect is more qualified than I am.

Qui est-ce qui a rédigé l'acte de vente, lui ou moi?
Who drew up the deed of sale, him or me?

C'est vous qui vendez le château sur la colline?
Is it you who's selling the château on the hill?

You'll have seen that disjunctive pronouns, as they're called, are used when they:

a) follow a preposition
b) form part of a comparison
c) stand alone
d) follow the verb être

Here's a complete list of these new forms:

moi	*I, me*	**nous**	*we, us*
toi	*you (fam.)*	**vous**	*you*
lui	*he, him*	**eux**	*they, them (m.)*
elle	*she, her*	**elles**	*they, them (f.)*

Note also the following:

moi-même	*myself*	**nous-mêmes**	*ourselves*
toi-même	*yourself (fam.)*	**vous-mêmes**	*yourself/yourselves*
lui-même	*himself*	**eux-mêmes**	*themselves (m.)*
elle-même	*herself*	**elles-mêmes**	*themselves (f.)*

81 The future perfect

You'll remember from Checknote 72 that you must use the future tense in French after **quand, lorsque, dès que** and **aussitôt que**, when the future is referred to:

Quand M.Jackson vivra en France, il sera soumis au système fiscal français.
When Mr Jackson lives in France, he'll be subject to the French tax system.

In the same way, the French use the future perfect when speaking of a completed action in the future:

Je vous retournerai le compromis dès que (or aussitôt que) je l'aurai reçu.
I'll return the agreement to you as soon as I've received it.

82 Negative prefixes

French doesn't differ very much from English in the way it makes a word negative:

in-/im-:

acceptable	*acceptable*	inacceptable	*unacceptable*
possible	*possible*	impossible	*impossible*

il-:

logique	*logical*	illogique	*illogical*
légal	*legal*	illégal	*illegal*

dés-:

avantage	*advantage*	désavantage	*disadvantage*
agréable	*pleasant*	désagréable	*unpleasant*

mé-:

content	*pleased*	mécontent	*displeased*
dire	*to say*	médire de	*to speak ill of*

mal-:

heureusement	*fortunately*	malheureusement	*unfortunately*
chance	*luck*	malchance	*misfortune*

83 The superfluous ne

During his conversation with the French notary Mr Jackson said, 'J'ai entendu dire que les frais d'achat sont plus élevés en France qu'ils ne le sont en Angleterre', and you may well have wondered why there's a **ne** and a **le** in this sentence. The answer is that the French insert a superfluous **ne** before a verb following an affirmative comparative, and often a **le** too:

L'appartement est plus cher que je ne le croyais.
The apartment is more expensive than I thought.

Comprehension Practice 11

As usual, note the new vocabulary and then answer the questions.

New words:

les travaux *(m.pl)*	*building work*
une fois	*once*
vouloir dire	*to mean*
changer d'avis	*to change one's mind*
d'après	*according to*

1 Quelle est la première question importante que le notaire pose à M. Jackson, lorsqu'il parle de son intention d'acheter une propriété?

2 Quelle est la rumeur qui court en Normandie sur les Anglais qui sont à la recherche d'une maison?

3 Les Jackson ont-ils une idée sur le genre de maison qu'ils désirent?

4 M.Jackson fera-t-il les travaux lui-même?

5 Quel prix les Jackson sont-ils prêts à mettre?

6 À quel moment Mme Gervais enverra-t-elle le compromis de vente?

7 Quels autres documents M. Jackson devra-t-il expédier au notaire avec le compromis de vente?

8 Comment les Jackson vont-ils financer l'achat de leur propriété?

9 Que veut dire la phrase 'le compromis de vente sera conclu sous condition suspensive de l'obtention du financement'?

10 Qu'est-ce qui se passerait, s'il changeait d'avis et décidait de retirer son offre après avoir signé le compromis?

11 Une fois l'acompte des 10% payé, comment se fait le règlement final?

12 De quoi sont composés les frais d'achat?

13 Quelle est la différence entre les deux impôts locaux mentionnés par le notaire?

14 D'après M.Jackson, quel genre de problème inattendu risque de se présenter?

FLUENCY PRACTICE 50

New words:

le goût	*taste*
l'agent (*m.*) immobilier	*estate agent*
l'acquéreur (*m.*)	*buyer*
la note	*bill*
la mensualité	*monthly payment*
divers	*various*
sérieux, -euse (*f.*)	*serious*
mieux	*better*
comme d'habitude	*as usual*
emprunter (à)	*to borrow (from)*
renseigner	*to inform*

Complete the following using disjunctive pronouns:

1 L'architecte? Nous avons rendez-vous (at his place) demain après-midi à trois heures.

2 Les agents immobiliers? L'important (for them), c'est de trouver des acquéreurs sérieux.

3 Qui vous a dit que vous pouviez emprunter à la banque 80% du prix de la maison? (You did!)

4 L'architecte qui fait les plans pour la rénovation de la maison est mieux renseigné (than we are) sur le goût des Anglais.

5 Non, chérie, les mensualités sont trop élevées. Après tout, qui paiera la taxe d'habitation, la taxe foncière, les notes de gaz et d'électricité, les assurances contre les risques divers, etc …? (I will, of course, as usual!)

FLUENCY PRACTICE 51

Which is the odd one out?

a) la rémunération
b) les honoraires
c) l'acompte
d) le salaire
e) la prime
f) le treizième mois

FLUENCY PRACTICE 52

New words:

les frais de déplacement	*travelling expenses*
les frais de scolarité	*school fees*
les frais d'entretien	*maintenance costs*
les faux frais	*incidental expenses*
les frais médicaux	*medical expenses*
le manoir	*manor*
le siècle	*century*
le trimestre	*term*
le budget-vacances	*holiday budget*
l'hôpital (m.)	*hospital*
la mutuelle	*private insurance*
la dépense	*expense*
l'école (f.)	*school*
privé	*private*
énorme	*enormous*
imprévu	*unexpected*
en vente	*for sale*
heureusement	*fortunately*
on a beau planifier	*however much one plans*
coûter	*to cost*

N.B. appeler *to call*
present: j'appelle, il appelle, nous appelons, vous appelez, ils appellent
past: j'ai appelé
future: j'appellerai

Irregular verb:

couvrir *to cover*
present: je couvre, il couvre, nous couvrons, vous couvrez, ils couvrent
past: j'ai couvert

In French there are a number of useful expressions using the word **frais** (expenses). Fill in the gaps in the following sentences choosing the most appropriate expression from the list above.

1 Lorsque je suis allé en France pour me présenter à l'entrevue, tous les frais de ...... m'ont été remboursés.

2 Le manoir qui est en vente date du 19ème siècle, il a beaucoup de style et un parc énorme mais les frais ...... coûtent trop cher au propriétaire.

3 Mes enfants vont maintenant tous les deux dans une école privée en Angleterre et chaque trimestre je dois payer des frais de ...... importants.

4 Après son accident de voiture, il est resté six mois à l'hôpital, heureusement il avait une mutuelle qui a couvert une partie des frais ……

5 On a beau planifier son budget-vacances, il y a toujours les petites dépenses imprévues. C'est ce que nous appelons les …… frais.

FLUENCY PRACTICE 53

New words:

le toit de chaume	thatched roof	libre	free
le (la) voisin (-ine, f.)	neighbour	environ	about
le village	village	moyen (-enne, f.)	average
la vitrine	shop window	la maison me	I like the house
la taille	size	plaît beaucoup	very much
la campagne	country(side)	(…pleases me)	
la partie	party	ça fait	that comes to
proche	close	plus	plus
isolé	isolated	considérer	to consider
loin	far	hériter	to inherit
âgé	elderly	s'engager	to commit
		oneself	

Irregular verbs:

conduire to drive
present: je conduis, il conduit, nous conduisons, vous conduisez, ils conduisent
past: j'ai conduit

valoir to be worth, to cost
present: je vaux, il vaut, nous valons, vous valez, ils valent
past: j'ai valu
future: je vaudrai

plaire to please
present: je plais, il plaît, nous plaisons, vous plaisez, ils plaisent
past: j'ai plu

Study again the conversation at the start of this unit, and then play the role of Mr Smith in the following dialogue with a French notaire.

Mr Smith:	Good morning. I'd like some additional information on a house I've seen in your window.
Mme Gervais:	Oui, asseyez-vous, Monsieur. Quelle maison vous intéresse en particulier?
Mr Smith:	The one that has the thatched roof, the garden in front and the field behind. How much is it?

Mme Gervais:	Elle vaut 360.000F. Elle est de taille moyenne, habitable, mais il y aura sans doute quelques travaux à faire.
Mr Smith:	*Are there any close neighbours?*
Mme Gervais:	Non, la maison est totalement isolée dans la campagne.
Mr Smith:	*Where's the nearest village?*
Mme Gervais:	À deux kilomètres seulement, ce n'est pas loin.
Mr Smith:	*Is the house occupied?*
Mme Gervais:	Non, pas en ce moment. Les propriétaires sont âgés et sont partis vivre avec leurs enfants.
Mr Smith:	*Is it possible to visit it today?*
Mme Gervais:	Attendez un instant … Michel! Es-tu libre cet après-midi? Oui? Oui, mon collègue va vous y conduire cet après-midi.

Three hours later

Mr Smith:	*I like the house very much. It would be a second home. I'd like to make an offer of 320.000F.*
Mme Gervais:	Je vais passer cette proposition d'achat aux vendeurs. Si elle est acceptée, je vous enverrai un compromis de vente.
Mr Smith:	*Un compromis de vente? What's that exactly?*
Mme Gervais:	C'est un avant-contrat par lequel les deux parties s'engagent, l'un à vendre, l'autre à acheter. Comment allez-vous financer cette acquisition?
Mr Smith:	*With money that I've inherited from my parents in England.*
Mme Gervais:	Donc vous ne faites pas d'emprunt bancaire?
Mr Smith:	*No, I'll have my funds transferred to France. Is there an initial payment to make?*
Mme Gervais:	Oui. Lorsque vous renverrez le compromis de vente avec tous les documents nécessaires - certificat de naissance, certificat de mariage - vous verserez 10% du prix d'achat au notaire, c'est à dire à moi.

Mr Smith:	*And when do I have to pay the balance?*
Mme Gervais:	Le jour où l'acte de vente sera signé. Le solde doit être versé directement sur le compte du notaire.
Mr Smith:	*How long should one reckon between the signing of the Agreement and that of the Deed of Sale?*
Mme Gervais:	Puisqu'il n'y a pas d'emprunt, environ quatre à cinq semaines.
Mr Smith:	*What would happen if I withdrew?*
Mme Gervais:	Vous perdriez vos 10% au profit des vendeurs.
Mr Smith:	*In addition to the price of the house, what are the other expenses to be considered?*
Mme Gervais:	Les frais d'achat qui seront de l'ordre de 15% du prix de la maison que vous voulez acheter. Ces frais comprennent les honoraires du notaire, les droits d'enregistrement et toutes les taxes. Vous aurez aussi à ajouter les frais de négociations.
Mr Smith:	*I see. So it'll be 320.000 plus 48.000. That comes to 368.000F in all.*
Mme Gervais:	Oui, si votre offre de 320.000F est acceptée. Je vous contacterai dès que j'aurai la réponse des vendeurs.
Mr Smith:	*Thank you very much. Goodbye.*
Mme Gervais:	Au revoir, Monsieur.

ADDITIONAL PRACTICE

The following is an authentic letter received from a French notaire regarding the purchase of a property in Normandy by a Mr Sands. Only the personal details have been changed. You should be able to understand the main points with the help of a dictionary.

Charles LEJUSTE

NOTAIRE

PROMENADE DES ANGLAIS
50100 CHERBOURG

Tel. 33 12 34 56

Monsieur Donald SANDS
Country Lane
ORPINGTON
Kent
Angleterre

V/REF:

Cherbourg, le 21 Août 1990

N/REF: CL/AB
Vente de Propriété
DUPONT/SANDS

Cher Monsieur,

      J'ai le plaisir de vous informer que votre proposition de prix pour l'achat de la propriété de BRICQUEBEC, 1 rue des Remparts, a été acceptée par les vendeurs.

      En conséquence, je vous adresse sous ce pli le compromis de vente (ou avant-contrat) en langue Française et Anglaise, préliminaire à la régularisation de l'acte de vente définitif.

      Vous voudrez bien me retourner ce document aussi rapidement que possible après l'avoir daté et signé de la façon suivante:
- vos initiales au bas de chaque page,
- votre signature à la fin du document, précédée de la mention manuscrite "lu et approuvé" puis de la mention qu'il vous faudra recopier à votre choix en Anglais ou en Français, relative à la loi du 13 Juillet 1979 et énoncée en bas de la dernière page.

      Comme je vous l'avais expliqué précédemment, cette dernière mention est justifiée par le fait que vous disposez des fonds nécessaires à l'acquisition, sans avoir besoin de recourir à la condition suspensive d'obtention d'un prêt, dont le refus éventuel rendrait le financement de l'achat impossible et le compromis nul et sans effet.

      Je vous serais très reconnaissant de bien vouloir m'adresser avec le compromis dûment régularisé par vos soins :
- vos certificats de naissance,
- et un certificat de mariage.
- et un acompte de 10% du prix de vente, soit 100.000 Frs, en utilisant le code étranger d'accès au compte bancaire de l'Étude :
      ABCDEF-ABC2 AB CD EF 123 - Agence CHERBOURG
      no 1234567

Dès réception de ces pièces, je vous adresserai le reçu de votre paiement, je recueillerai les signatures des vendeurs et procéderai sans plus tarder, tant à la rédaction du contrat de vente, qu'à la vérification des divers documents indispensables à la bonne sécurité de la transaction, à savoir :
- contrôle du titre de propriété des vendeurs,
- demande d'un extrait du cadastre de la propriété,
- demande d'un état hypothécaire négatif, certifiant que la propriété à vendre est libre d'hypothèques ou autres droits réels immobiliers (tels que droits de passage, usufruit, etc ...)

Je vous ferai parvenir la copie du contrat de vente afin de vous permettre d'en examiner les clauses et conditions avant la date de la signature que nous fixerons d'un commun accord.

Si vous souhaitez faire procéder à la traduction du contrat il me sera possible d'y pourvoir par l'intermédiaire d'un interprète agréé dont la rémunération s'élève approximativement à 3.000 Francs.

Vous aurez à me régler à la signature de l'acte, une somme de : 1.020.000 Francs se décomposant comme suit :
- prix d'acquisition ....1.000.000 Francs
- frais d'acte de vente (tout compris) ....120.000 Francs
                    Total..........1.120.000 Francs
Sous déduction de votre acompte de ....100.000 Francs
Solde à payer ....1.020.000 Francs

Je demeure bien entendu à votre entière disposition pour tous renseignements et précisions complémentaires.

Veuillez agréer, Cher Monsieur, l'assurance de mes sentiments les meilleurs et bien dévoués.

C. Lejuste

Additional Information

One of the French banks which have offices in London and which are able to offer financial help to British people interested in buying property in France is Crédit Agricole. Here is an extract from a brochure the bank has produced in this connection.

PURCHASING A FRENCH PROPERTY

MORTGAGE À LA FRANÇAISE

THE LEGAL PROCEDURE

Having found the house you like and agreed a price with the vendor, you now need to formally record the agreement by signing a conditional contract. This first stage is very important and can be done in various ways, however, there are certain forms of agreement which should be avoided.

RECOMMENDED FORMS
OF CONDITIONAL CONTRACT

It is best to choose either the Promise of Sale - *promesse de vente* - or the Sale Agreement - *compromis de vente* - which can be drafted and witnessed by a notary - *notaire* - *par acte authentique* - or more simply by a third party such as the estate agent - *sous seing privé* -. It is always advisable to use a notary who can, from the outset, collect all the necessary documents required to draft the Deed of Sale - *acte de vente* -.

THE NOTARY - *LE NOTAIRE* -

The notary is a "public official" whose main duty is to ensure that all deeds signed under his responsibility have authentic, absolute and incontestable value. You are free to choose your own notary.

THE SALE AGREEMENT - *LE COMPROMIS DE VENTE*

The Sale Agreement is the most commonly used form of conditional contract in France and it is the type we would recommend you to choose. This is a reciprocal agreement on signature of which the two parties concerned are immediately committed. The vendor is committed to selling to the purchaser for the agreed price and the purchaser is committed to buying from the vendor. The main clauses contained in the Sale Agreement are as follows:

• Description and definition of the property;
• Vendor's title to the property;
• The price and method of payment with or without recourse to a loan;
• The completion date (signature of the Deed of Sale in the presence of the notary);
• Deposit paid described as either - *dédit* - or - *acompte* -, usually 10% of the purchase price.

If a bank loan is required, the Sale Agreement will include the condition precedent -*condition suspensive* - of obtaining a loan. If your loan application is refused, the Sale Agreement will be considered null and void and you will be able to reclaim your deposit.

If you do not intend to use a loan to finance the purchase, you will be required to write in the Sale Agreement that you acknowledge having been informed that in the event of you requesting a loan at a future date, you will be unable to take advantage of the terms of the consumer protection law of 13 July 1979 (*Loi Scrivener*) regarding conditions precedent.

Once the conditions precedent have been fulfilled and one of the parties wishes to withdraw from the agreement, the vocabulary used to describe the deposit is of great importance. If the deposit has been referred to as a - *dédit* - then the purchaser may withdraw from the agreement, but will forfeit the deposit. In return, if the vendor wishes to withdraw, he may do so but must pay the purchaser an amount equal to double the deposit originally put down.

If the deposit has been defined by the term - *acompte* -, neither the purchaser nor the vendor may withdraw from the agreement. The sale may also be legally enforced.

THE PROMISE OF SALE - *LA PROMESSE DE VENTE* -

With this type of contract, the vendor commits himself to selling to the purchaser but allows the purchaser an option to buy with a cooling off period of usually 3 months. In return for the vendor's promise to sell to no other buyer during the agreed period, the purchaser pays a deposit to the notary of approximately 10% of the purchase price, known as the *- indemnité d'immoblisation -*.

If the purchaser does not take up the option to buy within the specified time the deposit will be forfeited. The clauses contained in this contract are the same as those found in the Sale Agreement with regard to the condition precedent of obtaining loan finance.

FORMS OF AGREEMENT TO BE AVOIDED

THE EXCHANGE OF LETTERS
- L'ÉCHANGE DE LETTRES -

This is too dangerous as often many important considerations are overlooked and the purchaser runs the risk of experiencing problems at a later stage.

THE OFFER OF SALE
- L'OFFRE DE VENTE

You should not settle for a simple offer of sale signed by the vendor, as this may be withdrawn at any time before you have formally accepted it.

THE OFFER OF PURCHASE
- L'OFFRE D'ACHAT.

This form of agreement does not commit your vendor to sell, though you the purchaser are irrevocably committed to buying the property once the vendor has accepted your offer. Frequently the buyer's decision has been taken too hastily before having had sufficient time to give the matter serious consideration.

Asking a French bank manager for a mortgage

In this final Unit we'll tidy up a few loose ends such as irregular comparisons and help you colour your dialogue with some more idiomatic expressions. You'll also learn about opening a French bank account.

Mr Jackson has been informed by the notary that his offer of 320,000F for the property in Normandy has been accepted by the owner, so he goes along to a French bank to ask for a home loan.

Mr Jackson: Pardon, Mademoiselle. Je suis venu me renseigner sur la possibilité d'obtenir un prêt immobilier. Je n'ai malheureusement pas de rendez-vous. J'ai déjà un compte chez vous. Je m'appelle Monsieur Jackson.

Mr Jackson is shown into the manager's office

Mme Lefranc: Bonjour, Monsieur. Entrez donc. Asseyez-vous.

Mr Jackson: Je vous remercie de me recevoir sans rendez-vous. Voilà, je suis Anglais et je viens d'être nommé directeur des ventes dans une entreprise française qui est basée ici à Cherbourg. Je cherche maintenant à acheter une propriété dans la région. J'ai eu la chance de tomber sur une maison ancienne qui me convient parfaitement et je voudrais savoir si je pourrais solliciter un prêt pour financer cette acquisition.

Mme Lefranc: Oui. Quel est le prix d'achat de cette maison?

Mr Jackson: Nous nous sommes mis d'accord sur 320.000F. Quel est le prêt maximum qui pourrait m'être accordé?

Mme Lefranc: En principe, la banque peut financer jusqu'à 80% de votre dépense totale, mais vous devez faire un apport personnel de 20%. Puis-je vous demander quel est votre salaire annuel et si vous avez d'autres revenus?

Mr Jackson: Je suis directeur des ventes depuis cinq ans dans la même compagnie en Angleterre et je touche un salaire annuel de 32.000 livres. J'ai maintenant obtenu un poste similaire en France pour un salaire de 410.000F, sans inclure les différentes primes. Je prendrai mes nouvelles fonctions le premier janvier.

Mme Lefranc: Très bien, Monsieur. Je dois d'abord attirer votre attention sur le fait que la politique de la banque est de s'assurer que tous les paiements que vous aurez à faire concernant le prêt immobilier sur votre résidence, les primes d'assurance et tout autre engagement financier ne dépassent pas un tiers de vos revenus disponibles sinon, et l'expérience le prouve, les emprunteurs courent le risque de ne plus pouvoir faire face à leurs échéances.

Mr Jackson: Oui, je comprends parfaitement. C'est, malheureusement, un problème que les Anglais connaissent trop bien, car il y a eu tant de fluctuations du taux d'intérêt sur les prêts immobiliers … et toujours dans le même sens! À propos, quel est le taux d'intérêt actuel?

Mme Lefranc: Nous vous proposons un taux fixe de 10,55% qui restera inchangé durant toute la période de votre emprunt, ainsi vous pouvez planifier votre budget. D'autre part, il existe aussi la possibilité d'un prêt à taux variable à 9,85%. En ce qui concerne la durée du prêt, nous choisirons celle qui conviendra le mieux à votre situation et elle peut varier de cinq à quinze ans.

Mr Jackson: Bien sûr, je préférerais un prêt sur une période d'au moins quinze ans pour éviter des mensualités trop élevées. Au fait, les remboursements, comment se font-ils exactement?

Mme Lefranc: Ils sont automatiquement débités de votre compte en banque. Il va sans dire que, pour garantir votre prêt, votre maison sera hypothéquée et, si vous ne pouviez plus faire face à vos échéances, la banque aurait le droit de mettre votre bien immobilier en vente. Il est d'usage d'avoir quelqu'un qui puisse servir de caution pour cet emprunt. En plus, vous serez obligé de souscrire une assurance-vie ainsi qu'une assurance habitation contre les risques d'incendie, d'inondation, d'ouragan, etc.

184

Mr Jackson:	Ce n'est pas une mauvaise chose. Mieux vaut prévenir que guérir. Une autre question, y a-t-il des frais annexes à prendre en considération?
Mme Lefranc:	Oui, il y a les frais d'hypothèque qui varient selon le montant de l'emprunt, par exemple, si vous empruntez 320.000F, les frais seront environ de 6.000F. Puis vous avez les frais de dossier dont le montant est calculé sur la base de 1,5% du capital emprunté, mais qui ne dépasse pas 10.000F.
Mr Jackson:	Parfait. Je n'ai plus qu'à emporter les formulaires nécessaires et vous les renvoyer dûment remplis et signés.
Mme Lefranc:	C'est ça. Voici les formulaires. Vous aurez à fournir vos trois derniers bulletins de salaire, une photocopie des cinq premières pages du passeport, un certificat de naissance et un certificat de mariage, des références bancaires et une copie du compromis de vente.
Mr Jackson:	Je vous remercie beaucoup. Au revoir, Madame.
Mme Lefranc:	Au revoir, Monsieur. À votre service.

TRANSLATION

Mr Jackson:	Excuse me. I've come to get some information about the possibility of obtaining a mortgage. Unfortunately, I don't have an appointment. I already have an account with you. My name is Mr Jackson.

Mr Jackson is shown into the manager's office

Mme Lefranc:	Good morning. Do come in. Take a seat.
Mr Jackson:	Thank you for seeing me without an appointment. The position is that I'm English and I've just been appointed sales manager with a French company based here in Cherbourg. I'm now trying to buy a property in the area. I've been lucky enough to come across an old house which suits me perfectly and I'd like to know whether I could request a loan to finance this purchase.
Mme Lefranc:	Yes. What's the purchase price of the house?
Mr Jackson:	We've agreed on 320.000F. What is the maximum loan that could be granted to me?

Mme Lefranc:	As a rule, the bank can finance up to 80% of your total costs, but you must make a personal contribution of 20%. May I ask what your annual salary is and whether you have any other income?
Mr Jackson:	I've been the sales manager for five years with the same company in England and I receive an annual salary of £32,000. I've now obtained a similar post in France with a salary of 410,000F, excluding the various bonuses. I start my new duties on the 1st January.
Mme Lefranc:	That's fine. I must, first, draw your attention to the fact that the bank's policy is to make sure that all the payments you'll have to make in connection with the mortgage on your home, the insurance premiums and any other financial commitment do not exceed one third of your disposable income, otherwise, and experience proves this, borrowers run the risk of not being able to meet their liabilities.
Mr Jackson:	Yes, I understand perfectly. Unfortunately, that's a problem that the British know only too well, because there have been so many fluctuations in the mortgage interest rate … and always in the same direction! By the way, what is the current rate of interest?
Mme Lefranc:	We offer a fixed rate of 10.55% which will remain unchanged for the whole period of the loan and, in this way, you can plan your budget. On the other hand, the possibility exists of a loan with a variable interest rate of 9.85%. As far as the term of the mortgage is concerned, we'll choose the period which is best suited to your situation and this can vary from five to fifteen years.
Mr Jackson:	Naturally, I'd prefer a loan over a period of at least fifteen years in order to avoid high monthly payments. Incidentally, how are the repayments arranged exactly?
Mme Lefranc:	They're automatically debited from your bank account. It goes without saying that, in order to guarantee your loan, your house will be mortgaged and, if you were no longer able to meet your repayments, the bank would have the right to put your property on sale. It's also normal practice to have someone who can stand as guarantor for the sum borrowed. In addition, you'll have to take out a life insurance as well as an insurance on the property against the risks of fire, flood, hurricane, etc.
Mr Jackson:	That's not a bad thing. Prevention is better than cure. One other question, are there any additional expenses that have to be taken into consideration?

Mme Lefranc:	Yes, there's the mortgage fee which varies according to the amount of the loan; for example, if you borrow 320,000F, the fee would be about 6,000F. Then you have the arrangement fee, the amount of which is calculated on the basis of 1.5% of the capital borrowed but which does not exceed 10.000F.
Mr Jackson:	Excellent. All I have to do now is to take away the necessary forms and send them back to you duly completed and signed.
Mme Lefranc:	That's correct. Here are the forms. You'll have to provide your last three salary-slips, a photocopy of the first five pages of your passport, a birth certificate and a marriage certificate, bank references and a copy of the sale agreement.
Mr Jackson:	Thank you very much. Goodbye, Madame Lefranc.
Mme Lefranc:	Goodbye, Mr Jackson. We're at your service.

Checklist 12

Masculine nouns:

le prêt immobilier	mortgage
le taux d'intérêt	interest rate
le remboursement	repayment, refund
le bulletin de salaire	salary slip
le formulaire	form
le tiers	third
le droit	right
le sens	direction
l'apport	contribution
l'engagement	commitment
l'incendie	fire
l'ouragan	hurricane
l'emprunteur	borrower
les revenus	income

Feminine nouns:

la dépense	expenditure
la mensualité	monthly payment
la caution	guarantor, guarantee
la livre	pound
la politique	policy
la durée	duration
l'échéance	bill
l'hypothèque	mortgage
l'assurance habitation	property insurance
l'inondation	flood
les fonctions	duties
les références bancaires	bank references

Adjectives:

disponible	disposable, available
inchangé	unchanged
annexe	supplementary, related
financier, -ière (f.)	financial

Other words/expressions:

sinon	otherwise
durant	during

ainsi	in this way	**Verbs:**	
environ	about	nommer	to appoint
dûment	duly	solliciter	to request
contre	against	dépasser	to exceed
entrez donc	do come in	planifier	to plan
à propos	by the way	éviter	to avoid
au fait	by the way	signer	to sign
au moins	at least	emporter	to take away
en vente	on/for sale	tomber sur	to come across
en principe	as a rule	se renseigner	to enquire
se mettre d'accord	to agree	remplir	to fill up
il est d'usage	it's normal practice	fournir	to provide
mieux vaut prévenir que guérir	prevention is better than cure		

N.B. hypothéquer *to mortgage*
present: j'hypothèque, il hypothèque, nous hypothéquons, vous hypothéquez, ils hypothèquent
past: j'ai hypothéqué
future: j'hypothéquerai

Irregular verbs:

servir *to serve*
present: je sers, il sert, nous servons, vous servez, ils servent
past: j'ai servi

convenir *to suit*
(see venir Checklist 7, but convenir forms past with avoir)

renvoyer *to send back*
(see envoyer, Checklist 7)

inclure *to include*
(see conclure Checklist 11, but past participle is inclus)

CHECKNOTES

84 Irregular comparisons

We've already discussed the way in which comparisons are made in French (see Checknote 26), but there are some important irregular forms that must be known. Study the following:

bon, *good*   **meilleur**, *better*   le (la) **meilleur(e)**, *the best*
mauvais, *bad*   **pire**, *worse*   le (la) **pire**, *the worst*

bien, *well*	mieux, *better*	le mieux, *the best*
peu, *little*	moins, *less*	le moins, *the least*
beaucoup, *much*	plus, *more*	le plus, *the most*

Examples:

C'est un bon placement.	*This is a good investment.*
C'est un meilleur placement.	*This is a better investment.*
C'est le meilleur placement.	*This is the best investment.*

Ma situation financière est mauvaise.	*My financial situation is bad.*
Ma situation financière est pire que je ne croyais.	*My financial situation is worse than I thought.*
Ma situation financière est la pire que j'aie connue depuis longtemps.	*My financial situation is the worst I've known for a long time.*

N.B. The regular forms **plus mauvais**, **le plus mauvais** are also often used.

La dactylo travaille bien.	*The typist works well.*
La sténodactylo travaille mieux.	*The shorthand typist works better.*
La sécretaire de direction travaille le mieux de toutes!	*The private secretary works best of all!*

85 Prepositions

It's probably true to say that, whatever language you happen to be studying, it's the prepositions that create most problems – and French is no exception. Very often you'll be surprised by the correct preposition to use or, indeed, by the absence of any preposition. Study the following examples taken from this Unit's conversation:

se renseigner **sur**	*to enquire about*
tomber **sur**	*to come across*
attirer l'attention de quelqu'un **sur** le fait que ...	*to draw someone's attention to the fact that ...*
remercier quelqu'un **de**	*to thank someone for*
faire face **à**	*to cope with*

Je suis venu me renseigner sur la possibilité d'ouvrir un compte bancaire.
I've come to enquire about the possibility of opening a bank account.

Il m'a remercié de lui avoir envoyé les formulaires nécessaires.
He thanked me for sending him/her the necessary forms.

Je dois attirer votre attention sur le fait que vous avez émis un chèque sans provision.
I must draw your attention to the fact that you have issued a cheque without having sufficient funds.

The preposition used with the following verbs will surprise you:

emprunter **à**	*to borrow from*
acheter **à**	*to buy from*
voler **à**	*to steal from*
se passer **de**	*to do without*
se servir **de**	*to use*
se souvenir **de**	*to remember*
dépendre **de**	*to depend on*
excuser **de**	*to forgive for*
féliciter **de**	*to congratulate on*

Examples:

Vous pouvez toujours emprunter à la banque.
You can always borrow from the bank.

Je ne peux pas me passer de ma carte de crédit.
I can't do without my credit card.

Savez-vous vous servir du distributeur de billets?
Do you know how to use the automatic cash (teller) machine?

Tout dépendera des mensualités que j'aurai à payer.
Everything will depend on the monthly payments I'll have to make.

Excusez-moi de vous déranger, Monsieur le Directeur.
Forgive me for disturbing you, Director.

Je vous félicite d'avoir conclu le marché.
I congratulate you on having concluded the deal.

Sometimes a preposition is required in French when none is needed in English.

demander **à** quelqu'un	*to ask someone*
ressembler **à** quelqu'un	*to resemble someone*
obéir **à** quelqu'un	*to obey someone*
dire **à** quelqu'un	*to tell someone*
permettre **à** quelqu'un	*to allow someone*

Examples:

Voulez-vous demander à Mlle Leclerc de lui envoyer un relevé de compte?
Will you ask Miss Leclerc to send him/her a bank statement?

Je trouve qu'ils ressemblent un peu aux bandits qui ont organisé le hold-up de la banque.
I find that they resemble a little the robbers who organized the hold-up at the bank.

Sometimes the reverse is the case and a preposition is needed in English but not in French:

approuver	*to approve of*
chercher	*to look for*
demander	*to ask for*
payer	*to pay for*
attendre	*to wait for*
écouter	*to listen to*
regarder	*to look at*

Examples:

J'approuve le principe du prélèvement automatique, parce que
c'est plus rapide et plus pratique.
*I approve of the principle of direct debiting, because it's faster and
more practical.*

Et qui paiera tous les soins médicaux?
And who will pay for all the medical care?

Qui est-ce que vous attendez? J'attends la caissière.
Who(m) are you waiting for? I'm waiting for the cashier.

86 Idiomatic expressions

We said in Checknote 65 that the occasional proverb or saying
can add a touch of colour to your speech. Here are some
idiomatic expressions that the French use a great deal in
conversation. But please note that the expressions in the following
list marked *(fam.)* are rather colloquial.

passer une nuit blanche	*to spend a sleepless night*
coûter les yeux de la tête	*to cost an arm and a leg*
rouler sur l'or	*to be rolling in money*
envoyer promener quelqu'un *(fam.)*	*to send someone packing*
donner un pot-de-vin à quelqu'un	*to give a bribe to someone*
l'échapper belle	*to have a narrow escape*
se vendre comme des petits pains	*to sell like hot cakes*
mettre de l'eau dans son vin	*to be less demanding*
faire marcher quelqu'un *(fam.)*	*to pull someone's leg*
dormir comme une souche *(fam.)*	*to sleep like a log*
le revers de la médaille	*the other side of the coin*
le système D *(fam.)*	*(unscrupulous?) resourcefulness*

Examples:

Les Français ont la réputation de pouvoir se sortir de toutes les situations
difficiles, grâce à leur fameux système D.
*The French have the reputation of being able to get out of all difficult
situations thanks to their well-known 'resourcefulness'.*

Mes collègues passent leur temps à me faire marcher. Heureusement,
je sais accepter la plaisanterie.

My colleagues spend their time pulling my leg. Fortunately, I can take a joke.

Il est vrai que nos deux salaires, nos actions et nos investissements nous apportent des revenus importants, mais le revers de la médaille, c'est que nous devons payer l'impôt sur les grandes fortunes.
It's true that our two salaries, our shares and our investments bring us a large income, but the other side of the coin is that we have to pay wealth tax.

87 The position of object pronouns appearing together

By now, you should be able to use the direct and indirect pronouns quite confidently and you should be quite clear about their place in the French sentence. One point that we haven't yet discussed, however, is the position of these pronouns when they appear together. Study the following:

Je n'ai plus qu'à emporter les formulaires et vous les renvoyer dûment remplis et signés.
All I have to do now is to take away the forms and send them back to you duly completed and signed.

Je vais vous la chercher tout de suite.
I'll fetch it for you right away.

Le chéquier? On le lui a donné hier.
The cheque book? They gave it to him yesterday.

You'll have noticed that sometimes the indirect pronoun precedes the direct and, sometimes, the reverse is the case. Eventually, you'll know instinctively which order to put them in but, for the time being, learn this short table by heart:

me le	vous le	nous le	le lui	le leur
me la	vous la	nous la	la lui	la leur
me les	vous les	nous les	les lui	les leur
m'en	vous en	nous en	lui en	leur en

Comprehension Practice 12

Vrai ou faux?

New words:

l'assurance (f.) multirisques	*comprehensive insurance*
au cas où ...	*in case*
avoir recours contre	*to have recourse against*
avant d'accorder	*before granting*
ouvrir	*to open* (see Fluency Practice 41)

1 M. Jackson va à la banque pour ouvrir un compte.

2 La banque ne peut financer que 20% du prix d'achat de la maison de M.Jackson.

3 M.Jackson prendra ses nouvelles fonctions chez Marketis le 1er janvier.

4 Avant d'accorder un prêt à M.Jackson, la banque doit s'assurer qu'il pourra faire face à tous ses engagements financiers.

5 La banque propose à M.Jackson un prêt à taux fixe dont les remboursements resteront constants pendant toute la durée de son emprunt.

6 M.Jackson devra payer ses mensualités par chèque.

7 Au cas où M.Jackson ne pourrait plus faire face à ses mensualités, la banque n'aurait aucun recours contre lui.

8 M.Jackson sera obligé de souscrire une assurance-vie ainsi qu'une assurance multirisques-habitation.

9 M.Jackson n'a pas de frais supplémentaires à payer à la banque pour l'obtention de son prêt.

10 Pour obtenir son prêt M.Jackson devra fournir une photocopie des cinq premières pages de son passeport, un certificat de naissance et de mariage, une copie du compromis de vente et une lettre de référence de son employeur actuel.

FLUENCY PRACTICE 54

New words:

le marché des changes	*foreign exchange market*
l'analyse (f.) de sang	*blood test*
fort	*strong*
défavorable	*unfavourable*

gros, grosse (f.)	*large*
en bonne santé	*in good health*
jusqu'à présent	*until now*
grâce à	*thanks to*
révéler	*to reveal* (see espérer Checklist 4)
indiquer	*to indicate*

There are a number of important expressions containing the word **taux** (rate):

le taux d'intérêt	*interest rate*
le taux de natalité	*birth rate*
le taux de mortalité	*death rate*
le taux de change	*exchange rate*
le taux de prêt	*lending rate*
le taux de cholestérol	*cholesterol level*

Complete the following:

1 Lorsque j'ai changé mes francs français, le taux de … m'a été défavorable, car la livre sterling est forte en ce moment.

2 Jusqu'à présent j'ai toujours fait mes gros achats à crédit, mais le taux … est maintenant si élevé que je préfère payer par chèque.

3 Elle n'était pas en bonne santé depuis longtemps, le médecin lui a fait faire une analyse de sang qui a révélé un taux de … trop élevé.

4 Si une banque française vous accorde un prêt en livres sterling, le taux … sera variable, car il dépendra du taux de la livre sur le marché des changes à Paris.

5 La famille française moyenne n'a que deux enfants, ce qui indique un déclin du taux de … en France.

6 Grâce aux progès de la médicine moderne, le taux de … infantile a nettement diminué.

FLUENCY PRACTICE 55

New words:.

le liquide	*ready cash*
le chèque sans provision	*bad cheque*
la réclame	*advertisement, advertising*
la police d'assurance	*insurance policy*
l'indemnité (f.)	*benefit, compensation*
par la poste	*through the mail*
un tas de	*lots of*
oser	*to dare*
avoir besoin de	*to need*

Irregular verb:

émettre *to write out, issue*
present: j'émets, il émet, nous émettons, vous émettez, ils émettent
past: j'ai émis

Complete the following, making sure you use the right preposition (if any):

1 Nous avons entièrement remboursé l'argent que *(we borrowed from the bank)* pour les coûts de rénovation de notre appartement.

2 La décision du comité en ce qui concerne mon emprunt bancaire *(will depend on)* mes revenus annuels *(and on the)* charges auxquelles je dois faire face.

3 Je reçois un tas de publicités par la poste et ce matin *(I came across)* une réclame pour une nouvelle assurance dont les cotisations semblent raisonnables et les indemnités élevées. Je n'ose pas y croire.

4 Lorsque je voyage à l'étranger *(I always use)* ma carte bancaire internationale, ainsi je n'ai pas besoin d'avoir trop de liquide sur moi.

5 Le client *(never used to look at)* son relevé bancaire et il a finalement émis plusieurs chèques sans provision.

FLUENCY PRACTICE 56

New words:

le téléphone sans fil	*cordless telephone*
le bilan	*balance sheet*
le syndicat	*union*
le stock est épuisé	*we are out of stock*
florissant	*flourishing*
étonnant	*surprising*
franchement	*frankly*
au bord de	*on the edge of*
avoir l'air fatigué	*to look tired*
arriver à	*to manage to*

Complete the following, choosing the most appropriate expression from those listed in Checknote 86:

1 Cette année, notre bilan est déficitaire. Franchement, la modernisation et l'automatisation de l'entreprise nous ont …

2 Je voudrais acheter un téléphone sans fil comme celui que vous aviez en promotion à 1.000F il y a quelques mois. Je regrette,

Madame, le stock est épuisé et nous attendons la prochaine livraison d'un jour à l'autre. Ces téléphones en ce moment … et nous n'arrivons pas à faire face à la demande.

3 J'étais sur le point d'investir une bonne partie de mes capitaux dans cette entreprise, lorsqu'elle était si florissante. Je l'ai …, car je viens d'apprendre qu'elle est au bord de la faillite.

4 C'est la troisième fois que les ouvriers demandent une augmentation de salaire cette année. Ils doivent penser que je …

5 Bonjour Michel, ça va? Tu as l'air fatigué.
Ce n'est pas étonnant, avec tous les problèmes que j'ai avec les syndicats en ce moment, j'ai …

FLUENCY PRACTICE 57

Role playing

New words:

le compte joint	joint account
le relevé d'identité bancaire	bank account identity document
la fin	end
la carte bancaire	banker's card
la note de gaz/d'électricité	gas/electricity bill
les devises (f.)	currency
gratuit	free of charge
fréquemment	frequently
souvent	often
ainsi que	together with
pour affaires	on business
et … et	both … and
tous les combien	how often
(placed at the end of the question)	
en même temps	at the same time
aider	to help
aller chercher	to fetch
virer	to transfer
verser sur	to pay into
délivrer	to issue
retirer	to withdraw
régler	to settle
il suffit de	it is sufficient to

A young English executive who will be working in France for a year is enquiring at a French bank about the possibility of opening an account. Play the part of the (lady) customer in the following conversation:

Customer: *Good morning. I'm going to spend a year here in France and I'd like to obtain some information about the services offered by your bank.*

Clerk: Oui, bien sûr. Comment puis-je vous aider, Madame?

Customer: *I'd like to open a joint account for myself and my husband. Can you let me have the necessary form?*

Clerk: Oui, attendez un petit instant. Je vais vous le chercher tout de suite … Voici le formulaire à remplir et à signer. Vous devrez aussi présenter vos deux passeports et votre compte sera ouvert immédiatement. Votre chéquier vous sera envoyé à votre domicile dans deux semaines environ.

Customer: *Fine. How often will we receive bank statements and will they be sent to us automatically?*

Clerk: Le relevé de compte est envoyé à la fin de chaque mois et plus souvent si vous le demandez. Avez-vous l'intention de faire virer votre salaire sur votre compte?

Customer: *Yes, my company will be paying my salary into my account, together with any additional bonuses. Will it be possible for me to obtain a banker's card?*

Clerk: Oui, certainement. Nous pouvons vous délivrer une carte bancaire qui vous permettra de retirer de l'argent dans les distributeurs automatiques ou de régler vos dépenses chez les commerçants.

Customer: *I frequently travel abroad on business and I'd like to have a card I can use both in France and abroad.*

Clerk: Dans ce cas-là, je vous recommande notre carte bancaire internationale. Elle vous permettra d'obtenir des devises à l'étranger. En plus, avec cette carte, vous bénéficierez aussi d'une assurance médicale gratuite et d'une assurance accident-voyage.

Customer: *I'd also like to arrange to have my gas and electricity bills paid directly by the bank.*

Clerk: Oui, sans problème. La banque peut se charger de vos prélèvements automatiques. Il suffit d'envoyer à l'EDF-GDF, c'est à dire Électricité de France et Gaz de France, un relevé d'identité bancaire, un RIB, qui donne tous les détails concernant votre compte et, en même temps, d'autoriser la banque à débiter l'argent.

Customer   *That's fine. Thank you very much. I'll send the form back to you as quickly as possible.*

Clerk   Très bien. À votre service, Madame.

Fluency Practice 57 brings us to the end of Hugo's "French for Business". There's a little more additional information for you to look at on the next few pages; reading this will reinforce your learning, so don't dismiss it as 'just a commercial for another credit card and insurance'! We hope that you have enjoyed the course and we feel certain that you can now 'talk business' in French quite confidently. We would like to take this opportunity of wishing you **bon courage** in your future studies and **bonne chance** in your/ business ventures!

Vous orienter sur la carte Maîtresse, c'est notre sens du conseil.

Carte Eurocard MasterCard

Eurocard MasterCard: la Carte Maîtresse.
Pour des avantages d'exception, en France comme à l'étranger.

Au Crédit Agricole, nous avons la Carte de la tranquillité, de votre tranquillité: retraits d'argent, paiement différé de vos achats, assistance et assurances garanties ... Avec la Carte Eurocard MasterCard, en France comme à l'étranger, vous vous simplifiez vraiment la vie.

• **Vous n'êtes jamais à court de liquide.** Oubliés les horaires d'ouverture des banques! Vous retirez de l'argent où et quand vous le voulez, auprès de n'importe quel distributeur. La Carte Eurocard MasterCard, c'est la liberté.

• **Vous réglez plus facilement vos achats et réservations.** Effectuer des achats, passer commande par correspondance ou par Minitel, réserver votre place de train, d'avion ou votre chambre d'hôtel, louer une voiture sans avoir à sortir son chèque ou à régler en liquide ... voilà qui a de quoi vous simplifier la vie de tous les jours. La Carte Eurocard MasterCard, c'est la simplicité.

Vous tirez avantage du paiement différé. Vous réglez plus tard ce que vous achetez aujourd'hui même. Vous profitez d'un véritable délai de paiement de 8 à 40 jours suivant la date de votre achat. C'est intéressant.

• **Vous profitez des mêmes avantages dans le monde entier.** Vous voyagez? La Carte Eurocard MasterCard vous suit partout où vous allez. Avec les mêmes avantages: retraits de devises auprès de plus de 350 000 guichets répartis dans 160 pays, paiement différé chez plus de 5,8 millions de commerçants à travers le monde, mêmes garanties de sécurité en cas de perte ou de vol ... Avec Eurocard MasterCard, vous profitez de la puissance d'un réseau mondial.
Alors, voyagez mieux avec votre Carte Eurocard MasterCard!

• **Vous bénéficiez d'une assistance médicale gratuite, d'une assurance accident/voyage et d'une garantie perte ou vol.** Avec la Carte Eurocard MasterCard, partez en France ou à l'étranger en toute tranquillité. Vous n'avez pas à souscrire un autre contrat d'assistance. Vous bénéficiez pour vous et votre famille d'une assistance médicale/rapatriement gratuite.

Ce n'est pas tout. La Carte Eurocard MasterCard a tout prévu pour vous assurer, ainsi qu'à vos proches, une triple sécurité:
- une assurance-décès/invalidité permanente garantissant le versement d'un capital jusqu'à 300 000 F, si vous avez un accident lors d'un voyage réglé avec votre Carte,
- une assurance vous couvrant, sous certaines conditions, en cas de vol ou de perte,
- une assurance libérant votre famille de toutes vos dépenses Eurocard MasterCard, en cas de décès.

La Carte Eurocard MasterCard du Crédit Agricole: pour une vie plus sereine, demandez-la à votre conseiller. Dès aujourd'hui.

Carte Eurocard MasterCard:
Profitez de ses 5 avantages.

1. Vous vous simplifiez la vie.

Vous n'avez plus à sortir votre chéquier ni à porter du liquide sur vous. Achats, réservations, commandes, locations ... tout devient plus facile.

2. Vous retirez de l'argent, en France, 7 jours sur 7, 24 h sur 24.

Oubliées les heures d'ouverture de votre agence puisque vous pouvez retirer de l'argent à tout moment dans tous les distributeurs automatiques de billets portant le panonceau CB.

3. A l'étranger, vous retirez des devises au fur et à mesure de vos besoins.

Inutile de prendre trop de liquide sur vous, votre Carte vous permet de retirer de l'argent dans toutes les banques affiliées au réseau MasterCard et au réseau Eurochèque.

4. Vous payez plus tard ce que vous achetez aujourd'hui.

Votre Carte vous procure automatiquement un délai de paiement de 8 à 40 jours.

5. Vous bénéficiez d'une assistance médicale gratuite et d'une assurance accident/voyage.

Vous réglez votre voyage avec votre Eurocard MasterCard? Vous êtes protégé automatiquement, vous et votre famille, pendant tous vos déplacements.

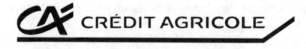

CRÉDIT AGRICOLE

Le bon sens en action

MULTIPREVOIR
Accident
CA

RECEVEZ 6.000 F D'INDEMNITÉS PAR MOIS EN CAS D'ACCIDENT

En cas d'accident, avez-vous pensé à tous les frais que peut entraîner une hospitalisation? Forfait hospitalier, supplément pour chambre individuelle, frais de déplacement pour les visites de votre famille, frais de garde de vos enfants, sans compter une éventuelle diminution de vos revenus! Que vous soyez victime d'un accident sur la route, chez vous, au travail, en vacances, même à l'étranger, MULTIPRÉVOIR Accident vous couvre. Pas de visite médicale préalable. Dès le cinquième jour de votre hospitalisation, et **pendant 6 mois** si nécessaire, le Crédit Agricole vous versera **200 F par jour**. Soit 6.000 F par mois, nets d'impôt. De plus, vous pourrez cumuler ces indemnités avec les remboursements de la Sécurité Sociale ou de tout autre contrat d'assurance.

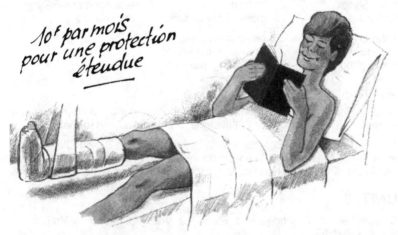

10 f par mois pour une protection étendue

Pour vos proches, un capital pouvant atteindre 250.000 F

Parce qu'en cas d'accident, il faut parfois envisager le pire, le Crédit Agricole aiderait aussi votre famille si vous veniez à disparaître. Il verserait en effet à vos ayants droit, immédiatement, un capital égal à trois fois le solde moyen de votre compte sur les douze derniers mois. Avec un **minimum de 25.000 F** et un maximum de **250.000 F**. De quoi

KEY TO EXERCISES

UNIT 1

Comprehension Practice 1:   1 Vrai.   2 Faux.   3 Faux.   4 Faux.
5 Vrai. 6 Vrai.

Fluency Practice 1:   1 Voici Mary Green, le chef du personnel.   2 Voici
Peter Brown, le directeur de la publicité.   3 Voici Rosalind et Amanda,
les deux secrétaires.   4 Voici Barbara White, l'analyste en études de
marché.   5 Je suis le président-directeur général.   6 Mary Green est le
chef du personnel.   7 David Smith est le directeur des ventes.
8 Rosalind et Amanda sont les deux secrétaires.   9 Je suis le président-
directeur général.

Fluency Practice 2:   1 Il a dix calculatrices.   2 Elle a huit micro-
ordinateurs.   3 Elles ont six traitements de texte.   4 J'ai quatre
télécopieurs.

Fluency Practice 3:

bah*ng*k	see-nyah-tür	kah-tah-log
kray-dee	ko*ng*-pah-nyee	bro-shür
ko*ng*-trah	feerm	a*ng*-por-tah-see-o*ng*
ah-zhah*ng*	ro-boh	eks-por-tah-see-o*ng*
foto-ko-pye*rz*	mahr-shah*ng*-deez	kah-lee-tay
ko*ng*-pay-tee-teef	pro-dük-sy*ong*	
a*ng*-dü-stree	dee-stree-bü-sy*ong*	
klee-yah*ng*	gah-rah*ng*-tee	
shek	fee-nah*ng*ss	
a*ng*-zhay-nye*rr*	see-nyay	

Fluency Practice 4:   1 organisons.   2 commandent.   3 importez.
4 vend.   5 a téléphoné.   6 j'ai signé.   7 a vendu.   8 ont attendu.

Fluency Practice 5:   Bonjour, Madame. Je suis John Brown. J'ai rendez-
vous avec Monsieur Martin à trois heures. /Oui, voici ma carte. /Je suis le
président-directeur général de la société Brown Engineering Ltd. /Merci.

UNIT 2

Comprehension Practice 2:   1 Faux.   2 Vrai.   3 Faux.   4 Vrai.
5 Vrai. 6 Faux.

Fluency Practice 6:   1 Pourriez-vous téléphoner à Monsieur Jackson à
Londres?   2 Pourriez-vous préparer l'ordre du jour pour la réunion?
3 Pourriez-vous organiser une réunion avec les cadres?   4 Pourriez-
vous m'apporter un café?

Fluency Practice 7:   1 est arrivée.   2 est parti.   3 sont allés.   4 est
revenu.

Fluency Practice 8:   1 a l'intention d'importer.   2 est heureux d'aider.
3 Il est impossible d'annuler.   4 avons le plaisir de vous informer.

Fluency Practice 11: arrivé; heures; parlé; fabrique; matériel; calculatrices; ... écrire électroniques; télécopieurs; exporter.

UNIT 3

Comprehension Practice 3: 1 Oui, elle est en pleine expansion. 2 Non, elle a une bonne réputation. 3 Oui, ils sont bien implantés sur le marché britannique. 4 Non, il n'augmente pas en ce moment. 5 À cause de l'inflation et des difficultés économiques du pays. 6 Oui, il est temps de commencer à exporter à l'étranger. 7 Les Français sont nos voisins les plus proches. 8 Non, elle vend des produits de fabrication française. 9 Oui, elle est prête à intégrer la technologie britannique à sa gamme de produits. 10 Oui, le fax, le marketing, le management, le business.

Fluency Practice 12: Nous nous spécialisons dans: a) la fabrication de machines à écrire électroniques. b) la bureautique. c) la technologie de pointe. d) la formation du personnel.

Fluency Practice 13: 1 Oui, nous nous reportons à notre dernière lettre. 2 Oui, elle s'occupe de toute la correspondance espagnole. 3 Oui, nous nous sommes documentés sur le service après-vente de nos concurrents. 4 Oui, elle s'élève à 5.000 francs.

Fluency Practice 14: a/g; b/e; c/h; d/f;

Fluency Practice 15: 1 Non, nos concurrents ne sont pas bien implantés sur le marché espagnol. 2 Non, vous n'avez pas raison. 3 Non, ils n'ont pas répondu à notre lettre. 4 Non, le prix n'est pas plus important que la date de livraison. 5 Non, nous ne nous spécialisons pas dans l'informatique. 6 Non, le client n'a pas accepté nos conditions de paiement.

Fluency Practice 18: 1 Il faut augmenter le prix. 2 Il faut répondre au télex. 3 Il faut parler de la possibilité d'une fusion entre nos deux sociétés. 4 Il faut faire l'inventaire. 5 Il faut finir le rapport.

UNIT 4

Comprehension Practice 4: 1 Le 3 Avril. 2 Il lui accordera une commission de 25%. 3 Il comprendra tous les frais de publicité et la participation à toute foire commerciale éventuelle. 4 Non, elle se fera par camion. 5 Il est de trois à quatre semaines. 6 Excel-Equip paie les frais de transport. 7 Le paiement des factures sera effectué par virement bancaire tous les deux mois. 8 Il mettra immédiatement à la disposition de Madame Duval un technicien bilingue qui pourra organiser un cours de formation.

Fluency Practice 19: 1 Non, je téléphonerai demain. 2 Non, je verserai des arrhes demain. 3 Non, nous parlerons du contrat demain. 4 Non, il fixera le rendez-vous demain. 5 Non, elle organisera la conférence de presse demain. 6 Non, vous programmerez les robots demain. 7 Non, ils livreront les machines demain. 8 Non, elles commanderont les marchandises demain. 9 Non, je finirai de classer les documents demain.   10 Non, nous réussirons probablement à contacter le directeur adjoint demain.   11 Non, il vendra le dernier Dictaphone demain.   12 Non, elles répondront au télex demain.

Fluency Practice 20:   Translation of the letter from Pierre Martin to John Brown: For the attention of Mr. John Brown: Dear Sir, Further to your letter dated 20th May regarding the article which appeared in La Normandie Verte of the 20th December 1989, we are pleased to give you, free of charge, our permission to reproduce this.

We would ask you to be good enough to ensure that all the usual references appear at the end of the text and to send us, in addition, two copies of the book on publication.

Thanking you (in advance), Yours faithfully …

Fluency Practice 21(A):   The attached is from Ets Martin, St. Lô. They have received the two faulty desk lamps, type AB and confirm that there is a fault and are looking into it. They are taking back the lamps and will credit our account.

21(B): 1 notre représentant.   2 retourner.   3 une lampe de bureau.
4 donner entière satisfaction.   5 examiner.   6 nous devons.
7 admettre.   8 il y a.   9 en effet.   10 un défaut.   11 les marchandises.
12 assurer.   13 la première fois.   14 un problème.   15 un article.
16 préciser.   17 intervenir.   18 sur ce point.   19 l'atelier.   20 bien entendu.   21 reprendre.   22 nous créditerons votre compte.   23 en conséquence.

Fluency Practice 22:   j.   d/a.   g/b.   f/i.   c.   e/h.

UNIT 5

Comprehension Practice 5:   1 Parce que le bureau est fermé.
2 Monsieur Jackson doit rappeler Madame Duval mercredi entre 8 heures et midi.   3 Parce que la ligne est mauvaise.   4 Non, ce ne sont pas des problèmes insurmontables.   5 Il veut donner toutes les chances de succès à leur future collaboration.   6 L'emballage inadéquat.
7 Non, il n'y a aucun dommage apparent.   8 Parce que deux ou trois caisses ont été abîmées.   9 Il va s'adresser à son service d'emballage et d'expédition.   10 Nous ne savons pas. Nous devons attendre la leçon 6.

Fluency Practice 24:   a) dix.   b) vingt.   c) trente.   d) quarante.
e) cinquante.   f) soixante.   g) soixante-dix.   h) quatre-vingts.
i) vingt-six.   j) trente-trois.   k) quarante et un.   l) cinquante-sept.
m) soixante-quatre.   n) soixante et onze.   o) soixante-douze.
p) soixante-dix-neuf.

Fluency Practice 25:   1 Je vous appelle de Londres.   2 Est-ce que je peux avoir le poste soixante-dix-neuf, s'il vous plaît?   3 Je n'ai peut-être pas le bon numéro/je me suis peut-être trompé de numéro.   4 Je pense que vous vous êtes trompé de numéro.   5 Je vous entends mal.

6 La ligne est mauvaise.   7 Excusez-moi de vous faire attendre.
8 Ça ne répond pas.   9 Préférez-vous rappeler plus tard?   10 Pourriez-vous me passer sa secrétaire, s'il vous plaît?

Fluency Practice 26:   (1 Oui, je l'ai contacté ce matin.)   2 Oui, je l'ai consultée ce matin.   3 Oui, je l'ai licencié ce matin.   4 Oui, je les ai imprimés ce matin.   5 Oui, je l'ai reçue ce matin.   6 Oui, je vous ai vu (vue) à la télévision ce matin.

Fluency Practice 27:   SMITH ess em ee tay ahsh;   BROWN bay air oh doobl-vay en;   JOHNSON zhee oh ahsh en ess oh en;   HARPER ahsh ah air pay er air;   BOURNEMOUTH bay oh ü air en er em oh ü tay ahsh;   NORWICH en oh air doobl-vay ee say ahsh;   CARLISLE say ah air el ee ess el er;   EDINBURGH er day ee en bay ü air zhay ahsh;   NEW YORK en er doobl-vay ee-grek oh air kah;   MIAMI em ee ah em ee;   SYDNEY ess ee-grek day en er ee-grek;   TORONTO tay oh air oh en tay oh.

Dictionary Practice 1:   1 Many of them are still burying their heads in the sand.   2 The purpose of the seminar is to persuade British businessmen to take their heads out of the sand and to make them realize that 1992 is not far away.   3 They will not be ready to face the French, Italian and German competition on British territory.   4 Trade between the various EEC countries will be made easier.   5 The language barrier, which is also a psychological barrier.   6 The price of land is really cheap and foreign businesses are being offered special concessions.   7 In order to boost a stagnant economy and to generate work for the unemployed.

UNIT 6

Comprehension Practice 6:   1 Faux.   2 Vrai.   3 Faux.   4 Faux. 5 Faux.   6 Vrai.   7 Faux.   8 Faux.

Fluency Practice 28: 1 c) because a, b, d are managerial posts. 2 b) because a, c, d are machines. 3 c) because this verb is conjugated with avoir whereas the other three are conjugated with être. 4 d) because the United States is not a member of the EEC. 5 a) because b, c, d are connected with payment.

Fluency Practice 29:   1 Est-ce que je peux lui laisser un message? 2 Savez-vous quand il/elle sera de retour?   3 C'est à quel sujet? 4 Il n'est pas disponible.   5 Elle est à l'étranger.   6 Je peux peut-être vous aider.

Fluency Practice 30:   1 informatiserait.   2 pourrions tenir.   3 serait prête à.   4 exporteraient.

Fluency Practice 31:   1 Non, la TVA ne diminue jamais.   2 Non, je n'ai jamais visité l'atelier de montage.   3 Non, ils n'ont rien fait.   4 Non, je ne verse rien.   5 Je n'ai licencié personne.   6 Non, personne ne va m'aider.

Fluency Practice 32:
- Bonjour, Madame. Est-ce que je peux avoir le poste 34, s'il vous plaît?
- Bonjour, Monsieur Dupont. Mike Smith à l'appareil, de Splendid Wear à Canterbury. Vous m'avez envoyé 50 robes d'été, mais j'ai annulé cette commande.
- il y a trois semaines.
- Oui, c'est le bon de commande 79.
- 79.
- Mais je vous assure que j'ai parlé à Mademoiselle Tétenlère il y a trois semaines.
- Parfait. Voulez-vous l'adresse de ma compagnie?
- Merci beaucoup. Au revoir.

Dictionary Practice 2:   This is a special offer for a pay-phone for your customers which can be installed on your premises. The advert quotes the example of the owner of a restaurant whose customers always used his private telephone and *he* paid for the calls! Eventually he had a Point Phone installed and now both he and his customers are happy. This special offer includes a reduction of 1024F on the usual price.

UNIT 7

Comprehension Practice 7:   1 Pour promouvoir ses nouveaux produits. 2 Un nouveau traitement de texte qui vient d'Angleterre.   3 Les chefs d'entreprise de petite et moyenne taille qui débutent dans les affaires et s'établissent dans la région parisienne.   4 Dans les magazines d'actualité et économiques ainsi que dans la presse spécialisée en bureautique.   5 Il suggère des dessins humoristiques, des bandes dessinées et des caricatures, tous avec un slogan original.   6 Elle consiste à mettre des affiches dans le centre-ville, dans les couloirs du métro et à distribuer des dépliants et des prospectus.   7 On envoie un message publicitaire sur vidéo-cassette directement aux chefs d'entreprise.   8 Elle a besoin d'un devis et de quelques maquettes d'affiches.

Fluency Practice 34:   1 J'aimerais que vous m'envoyiez une lettre confirmant le prix et le délai de livraison.   2 La compagnie a fini par faire faillite.   3 Les jeunes d'aujourd'hui ne peuvent pas regarder la télévision sans faire du zapping.   4 Le client a toujours raison.   5 Le client n'a jamais tort.   6 Les cadres de cette entreprise sont tous très jeunes. Ils ont entre 23 et 30 ans.

Fluency Practice 35:   a) soyez   b) perfectionniez   c) suiviez d) voyagiez   e) puissiez   f) fournissiez   g) fassiez

Fluency Practice 36:   a/3;   b/4;   c/2;   d/1;   e/6;   f/5.

Dictionary Practice 3:   1 You don't need a driving licence to drive this car (we should add, however, that it has a low-powered engine). 2 There is a play on words here as 'permis' means both 'licence' and 'permitted'.   3 It's reliable, economical and elegant.   4 Yes.   5 With small saloon cars.   6 Motul.

Fluency Practice 38:   1 Quel est le prix de la voiture?   2 Quelles sont les différentes couleurs?   3 Quel est le délai de livraison?   4 Peut-on louer la voiture pour deux semaines?

Dictionary Practice 4:   1 'Management' in French is la gestion.
2 5 hours on average.   3 You will learn the basics of management by yourself, pleasantly and at your own pace.   4 a) la comptabilité   b) le point mort   c) les fonds de roulement   d) le plan de trésorerie   e) le budget prévisionnel   5 Yes, numerous practical exercises enable you to test your knowledge.   6 By registered post, together with a receipted invoice.

UNIT 8

Comprehension Practice 8:   1 Faux.   2 Faux.   3 Vrai.   4 Vrai.
5 Faux.   6 Faux.   7 Faux.   8 Vrai.   9 Faux.   10 Vrai.

Fluency Practice 39:   1 réparais.   2 ne gagnait que.   3 réussissait toujours à.   4 descendions du.   5 Faisiez-vous.   6 étaient en train de.

Fluency Practice 40:   1 Si on ne me fournissait pas le mobilier pour le stand, je contacterais les organisateurs.   2 S'il se perdait dans Paris, il prendrait un taxi pour aller à l'Exposition.   3 Si nous manquions d'argent liquide, nous irions au distributeur automatique.   4 Si leur pouvoir d'achat continuait à baisser, ils se mettraient en grève.   5 Si vous faisiez encore faillite, vous prendriez votre retraite.

Fluency Practice 41:   1 Il n'y a pas de fumée sans feu.   2 Quand on parle du loup, on en voit la queue.   3 Mieux vaut tard que jamais.   4 Il ne faut pas vendre la peau de l'ours avant de l'avoir tué.   5 Point de nouvelles, bonnes nouvelles.   6 Après la pluie, le beau temps.

Fluency Practice 42:   1 Un traitement de texte portable.   2 Il est petit, il est léger et il marche à la fois sur pile et sur secteur.   3 Le clavier, l'écran, le lecteur de disquettes et l'imprimante.   4 Il corrige les fautes de frappe automatiquement, il a un dictionnaire électronique et contient une liste de synonymes.   5 5850 F.   6 Non, car il y a une assurance pour cinq ans à un tarif très avantageux.

Dictionary Practice 5:
EXPOLANGUES: For the last 8 years linguists and all those interested in the languages and cultures of the world have had a meeting place - Expolangues. The 1990 Show will be more modern than ever and the latest methods and technology will be on display. 250 contributors and 40,000 visitors will be able to exchange views. Language teaching has greatly improved in the last 10 years as a result of more modern techniques and an awareness of the importance of languages among young people. Expolangues has played its part in this development. The language problem will be even more acute in the Single Market of 1992, a Market which speaks with one voice in 9 different languages! So, come to Expolangues for information on language learning, translation and language computer programs.

208

UNIT 9

Comprehension Practice 9:   1 Quelles sont les caractéristiques de la
société Marketis?   2 Quel poste est vacant?   3 Où est-ce que ce
poste est basé?   4 Quelles seront les responsabilités du candidat
retenu?   5 Pourquoi est-ce que ce poste est attractif?   6 Si vous
décidez de poser votre candidature à ce poste, quelle documentation
faudra-t-il que vous envoyiez?   7 Quelle est la date de naissance de
Monsieur Jackson?   8 Est-il célibataire?   9 Ce poste chez Marketis,
est-ce que c'est son premier emploi?   10 À votre avis, les loisirs de
Monsieur Jackson correspondent-ils à sa personnalité?

Fluency Practice 43:   1 les qualités nécessaires.   2 une bonne
connaissance.   3 mon expérience insuffisante.   4 le poste vacant.
5 votre rémunération actuelle.   6 un petit sacrifice.   7 la jeune
secrétaire.   8 une mauvaise nouvelle.

Fluency Practice 44:   1 essence   2 car   3 assister   4 sensible
5 bibliothèque

Fluency Practice 45:   corresponde; ai; aillent; puissent; soit;
est; achetions; ont; offriez; allons; vivrons.

Fluency Practice 46:   1 l'Ouest   2 mon   3 société   4 acquis   5 la
6 cours   7 manager   8 vis   9 situation   10 France   11 bilingue
12 détaillant   13 professionnel   14 vous   15 ambitions   16 que
17 prie.
Dictionary Practice 6:

POLAROID EUROPEAN MARKETING HEADQUARTERS
is looking for a

completely bilingual Private Secretary

English mother tongue

You have had several years experience in a Finance/Computer
Department. You know shorthand, you can type and you are familiar with
the Multimate word processor and micro-computing. You like figures.
13 months'salary.

Please send handwritten letter in English, CV, photo and details of salary
to POLAROID Europe, Personnel Department, 4 rue J.P. Timbaud …

POLAROID

Dictionary Practice 7:   1 Il s'agit d'un cabinet juridique international.   2
Les qualités exigées pour ce poste sont un réel sens de l'accueil, la
maîtrise des contacts, une excellente présentation et la même aisance en
anglais et en français.   3 Elles auront la responsabilité d'accueillir les
clients et les visiteurs, d'appeler les taxis et les coursiers, de réceptionner
le courrier et les billets d'avion.   4 Les avantages offerts sont un
environnement international en expansion, un choix d'horaire et une
émunération motivante.

UNIT 10

Comprehension Practice 10:   1 Vrai.   2 Faux.   3 Vrai.   4 Faux.
5 Vrai.   6 Vrai.   7 Vrai.   8 Faux.   9 Faux.   10 Faux.   11 Faux.
12 Vrai.

Fluency Practice 47:   ton CV; as-tu décidé; ta candidature; Tu viens de
mentionner; ... tu parles?; on te demandera; tes points forts; tes points
faibles; Dans ta lettre, tu as déclaré ton salaire actuel, ...ton salaire brut?

Fluency Practice 48:
- Eh bien, je pense que ce poste correspond exactement à mes objectifs
  professionnels et à mon expérience passée. En plus, je suis
  particulièrement attiré par la dimension internationale de votre
  compagnie.
- J'ai certainement acquis l'expérience nécessaire pour nouer des
  contacts avec les clients étrangers. J'ai élargi ma connaissance dans
  le domaine de la promotion des ventes et je suis maintenant habitué à
  animer une équipe de douze vendeurs.
- Eh bien, oui, personne n'est parfait! J'ai, je pense, beaucoup de
  qualités mais on m'a aussi parfois accusé d'être inflexible.
  Personnellement, je pense que cette soi-disant inflexibilité a toujours
  été pour une bonne cause.
- C'est une question difficile et je suis prêt à négocier. Mais puis-je
  demander s'il y a d'autres avantages en plus de la voiture de fonction?
- C'est bien à savoir. Merci. Je suis sûr que nous pourrons nous mettre
  d'accord sur un salaire.
- Eh bien, normalement, je dois donner trois mois de préavis à mon
  employeur actuel.
- Juste une. Les horaires mobiles sont-ils en vigueur dans votre
  compagnie?

Fluency Practice 49:   1 Je viens d'être promu.   2 Nous venons de
nous mettre d'accord sur.   3 Je cherche.   4 utilisez-vous.   5 a fait
revenir le candidat.   6 se font construire une résidence secondaire.
7 ceux.   8 celle-là.   9 avec qui.   10 dans lequel.

UNIT 11

Comprehension Practice 11:   1 'Avez-vous déjà une idée sur le genre de
propriété que vous désirez, sur l'emplacement et surtout sur le prix?'.
2 La rumeur qui court, c'est que les Anglais sont souvent indécis.
3 Oui, ils désirent une maison ancienne, en pierre, avec quatre chambres,
un garage, un peu de terrain, indépendante et habitable tout de suite.
4 Non, car il n'est pas bricoleur et ne le deviendra probablement jamais.
5 Les Jackson sont prêts à mettre entre 300.000 et 400.000F.   6 Elle
enverra le compromis de vente lorsque le vendeur aura accepté l'offre de
Monsieur Jackson.   7 Il devra lui expédier un certificat de naissance et
un certificat de mariage.   8 Ils vont faire un emprunt à la banque.
9 Cette phrase signifie que si l'acheteur n'obtient pas son prêt, le
compromis sera nul et non avenu et l'acompte versé sera restitué dans sa
totalité.   10 Il perdrait son acompte de 10% qui serait versé à titre de

compensation au vendeur. 11 Le solde sera viré sur le compte du notaire le jour de la signature de l'acte. 12 Les frais d'achat sont composés des honoraires du notaire, des droits d'enregistrement et des taxes relatives à l'achat. 13 La taxe foncière est payée par le propriétaire et la taxe d'habitation par la personne qui occupe la propriété. 14 La construction d'une route à proximité.

Fluency Practice 50: 1 chez lui. 2 pour eux. 3 C'est vous! 4 que nous. 5 Moi, bien sûr, comme d'habitude!

Fluency Practice 51: c (deposit) because a,b,d,e,f, are forms of payment for services rendered.

Fluency Practice 52: 1 les frais de déplacement. 2 les frais d'entretien. 3 des frais de scolarité. 4 des frais médicaux. 5 les faux frais.

Fluency Practice 53:
- Bonjour Madame. Je voudrais des renseignements supplémentaires sur une maison que j'ai vue dans votre vitrine.
- Celle qui a un toit de chaume, le jardin devant et le champ derrière. Combien vaut-elle?
- Y a-t-il des voisins proches?
- Où est le village le plus proche?
- La maison est-elle habitée?
- Est-il possible de la visiter aujourd'hui?
- La maison me plaît beaucoup. Ce serait une résidence secondaire. J'aimerais faire une offre de 320.000F.
- Un compromis de vente? Qu'est-ce que c'est exactement?
- Avec de l'argent que j'ai hérité de mes parents en Angleterre.
- Non, je ferai transférer mes fonds en France. Y a-t-il un acompte à verser?
- Et quand est-ce que je dois payer le solde?
- Combien de temps faut-il compter entre la signature du compromis et celle de l'acte de vente?
- Qu'est-ce qui se passerait, si je me retirais?
- En plus du prix de la maison, quels sont les autres frais à considérer?
- Je vois. Donc ça fera 320.000 plus 48.000. Ça fait 368.000F en tout.
- Merci beaucoup. Au revoir, Madame.

UNIT 12

Comprehension Practice 12: 1 Faux. 2 Faux. 3 Vrai. 4 Vrai. 5 Vrai. 6 Faux. 7 Faux. 8 Vrai. 9 Faux. 10 Faux.

Fluency Practice 54: 1 le taux de change. 2 le taux d'intérêt. 3 un taux de cholestérol. 4 le taux de prêt. 5 taux de natalité. 6 le taux de mortalité.

Fluency Practice 55: 1 nous avons emprunté à la banque. 2 dépendra de … et des … 3 je suis tombé sur. 4 je me sers toujours de. 5 ne regardait jamais.

Fluency Practice 56: 1 … coûté les yeux de la tête. 2 … se vendent

comme des petits pains.   3 … échappé belle.   4 … roule sur l'or.   5
… passé une nuit blanche.

Fluency Practice 57:
- Bonjour, Monsieur. Je vais passer une année ici en France et j'aimerais
  obtenir des renseignements sur les services offerts par votre banque.
- J'aimerais ouvrir un compte joint pour moi et mon mari. Pouvez-vous
  me donner le formulaire nécessaire?
- Bien. Les relevés de compte, nous les recevrons tous les combien et
  est-ce qu'ils nous seront envoyés automatiquement?
- Oui, ma compagnie versera mon salaire sur mon compte ainsi que
  toutes les primes supplémentaires. Est-ce qu'il me sera possible
  d'obtenir une carte bancaire?
- Je voyage fréquemment à l'étranger pour affaires et j'aimerais avoir une
  carte que je puisse utiliser et en France et à l'étranger.
- J'aimerais aussi faire le nécessaire pour que mes notes de gaz et
  d'électricité soient directement payées par la banque.
- C'est parfait. Je vous remercie beaucoup. Je vous renverrai le
  formulaire le plus vite possible.

BUSINESS GLOSSARY

A

abroad à l'étranger
accept accepter
account compte (*m.*)
   bank a. c. bancaire
   joint a. c. joint
accountant comptable (*m. f.*)
accounting comptabilité (*f.*)
acknowledge accuser réception de
add ajouter
additional supplémentaire
advance
   in advance à l'avance
advantage avantage (*m.*)
   take a. of profiter de
advertisement annonce, réclame (*f.*)
advertising publicité (*f.*)
advertising agency agence (*f.*) de publicité
advertising campaign campagne (*f.*) publicitaire
advertising medium support (*m.*) publicitaire
advise conseiller
after-sales service service (*m.*) après-vente
agenda ordre (*m.*) du jour
agent agent (*m.*)
agree se mettre d'accord
agricultural show exposition (*f.*) agricole
aim at viser
airfreight transporter par voie aérienne
amount montant (*m.*)
amount (to) s'élever (à)
annual paid holidays congés (*m.*) payés
answerphone répondeur (*m.*) téléphonique
application candidature (*f.*)
appoint nommer
appointment rendez-vous (*m.*)
approve (of) approuver
architect architecte (*m. f.*)

arrange fixer, organiser
arrange an appointment fixer un rendez-vous
arrange a meeting organiser une réunion
assembly shop atelier (*m.*) de montage
assets actif (*m.*)
   available a. a. disponible
attend assister à
attract attirer
automatic cash (teller) machine distributeur (*m.*) automatique (de billets)
available disponible
availability disponibilité (*f.*)
average moyen, -enne (*f.*)

B

balance solde (*m.*)
balance of payments balance (*f.*) des paiements
balance sheet bilan (*m.*)
bank banque (*f.*)
bank statement relevé (*m.*) de compte
bank transfer virement (*m.*) bancaire
bank draft traite (*f.*) bancaire
bankruptcy faillite (*f.*)
beneficial bénéfique
benefit bénéficier
bilingual bilingue
bill note, échéance (*f.*)
bill of lading connaissement (*m.*)
board of directors conseil d'administration
bonus prime (*f.*)
   productivity b. p. de rendement
book fair foire du livre
borrow emprunter
British britannique
brochure brochure (*f.*)
budget budget (*m.*)
   forecast b. b. prévisionnel
build bâtir, construire

business fonds (*m.*) (de commerce), affaires (*f. pl*)
   away on b. en déplacement
   on business pour affaires
business quarter quartier (*m.*) des affaires
business trip déplacement (*m.*) professionnel
businessman homme d'affaires
businesswoman femme d'affaires
buy acheter
buyer acheteur (*m.*)

C

calculate calculer
calculator calculatrice (*f.*)
campaign campagne (*f.*)
cancel annuler
capital capital (*m.*)
capital gains tax impôt (*m.*) sur les plus-values
   working c. fonds (*m. pl.*) de roulement
card carte (*f.*)
   credit c. c. de crédit
   bankers's c. c. bancaire
career carrière (*f.*)
case caisse (*f.*)
cash argent (*m.*) liquide
   to pay c. payer comptant
cash flow cash flow (*m.*)
cash dispenser distributeur (*m.*) automatique (de billets)
catalogue catalogue (*m.*)
chairman and managing director président-directeur général (PDG)
chairperson président, -ente (*f.*)
chamber of commerce chambre (*f.*) de commerce
change changer
   to change one's mind changer d'avis
charge faire payer
   person in charge responsable (*m. f.*)
check vérifier
cheque chèque (*m.*)
   bad c. c. sans provision

to pay by cheque payer par chèque
cheque book chéquier (*m.*)
clarify clarifier
client client, -e (*f.*)
collaborate collaborer
colleague collègue (*m. f.*)
commercial message (*m.*) publicitaire,
   spot (*m.*) publicitaire
commission commission (*f.*)
company société, compagnie (*f.*)
   finance c. société de crédit
   investment c. s. d'investissement
   limited liability c. s. à responsabilité limitée
   multinational c. s. multinationale
   parent c. s. mère
   public limited c. s. anonyme
company car voiture (*f.*) de fonction
compete rivaliser
competition concurrence (*f.*)
competitive compétitif, -ive (*f.*)
competitor concurrent (*m.*)
comprehensive complet, -ète (*f.*)
computer ordinateur (*m.*)
computer science informatique (*f.*)
computer expert informaticien, -ienne (*f.*)
computerize informatiser
conclude conclure
conclude the deal conclure le marché
conditions conditions (*f.*)
conference conférence (*f.*)
confirm confirmer
connection
   What is it in connection with?
     C'est à quel sujet?
consider considérer
consult consulter
consumer consommateur, -trice (*f.*)
consumer goods biens de consommation
contract contrat (*m.*)
copier copieur (*m.*)
copy copie (*f.*)
copy copier
copywriter rédacteur-concepteur (*m.*)
corporation tax impôt (*m.*) sur les

sociétés
correspondence correspondance (*f.*)
cost coût, prix (*m.*)
cost of living coût de la vie
cost, insurance, freight (CIF)
    coût, assurance, fret (CAF)
cost price prix de revient
costs coûts, frais (*m.*)
count compter
cover
    under separate cover sous pli
    séparé
credit crédit (*m.*)
    on credit à crédit
credit card carte (*f.*) de crédit
creditor créancier, -ière (*f.*)
crucial crucial
currency devises (*f. pl.*)

D

damage dommage (*m.*)
damage endommager, abîmer
damages dommages-intérêts (*m. pl.*)
data processing informatique (*f.*)
date date (*f.*)
sell-by date date de limite de vente
debt dette (*f.*)
debtor débiteur, -trice (*f.*)
decide décider
decrease diminuer
deduct déduire
deduction déduction
defective défectueux,-euse (*f.*)
delay retarder
deliver livrer
delivered free as far as French
    frontier livraison franco frontière
    française
delivery livraison
delivery date date (*f.*) de livraison
delivery free franco domicile
demonstration démonstration (*f.*)
deposit acompte (*m.*), arrhes (*f. pl.*)
desk bureau (*m.*)
diary agenda (*m.*)
dictate dicter
direct debit prélèvement (*m.*)
    automatique
director directeur,-trice (*f.*)

chairman and managing d.
    président-directeur général
board of d. conseil (*m.*)
    d'administration
disadvantage inconvénient (*m.*)
discontinued lines fins (*f.*) de série
discount remise
discuss discuter de
discussion discussion (*f.*)
dismiss renvoyer
dispatch expédition (*f.*)
dispatch expédier
disturb déranger
document document (*m.*)
duties fonctions (*f. pl.*)

E

economic économique
economize économiser
economy économie (*f.*)
effective efficace
efficient performant
electric électrique
electronic électronique
employee employé, -ée (*f.*)
employer employeur (*m.*)
employment emploi (*m.*)
enclosed
    please find enclosed veuillez
        trouver ci-joint
engage embaucher
engineer ingénieur (*m.*)
environment environnement (*m.*)
    international e. e. international
equip équiper
equipment équipement, matériel (*m.*)
espionage espionnage (*m.*)
    industrial e. e. industriel
essential essentiel, -elle (*f.*)
establish oneself s'établir,
        s'implanter
estate agent agent (*m.*) immobilier
estimate devis (*m.*)
estimate estimer
European Economic Community
    (EEC) Communauté (*f.*)
        Économique
        Européenne (CEE)
European Monetary System (E.M.S)

Système (*m.*) monétaire
européen (SME)

examine examiner
exceed dépasser
executive cadre (*m.*)
exhibition exposition (*f.*) , salon (*m.*)
exhibitor exposant (*m.*)
expansion expansion (*f.*)
expenses frais (*m. pl.*)
  incidental e. faux f.
  medical e. f. médicaux
  travelling e. f. de déplacement
expensive cher, chère (*f.*)
experience expérience (f)
  professional e. e. professionnelle
experienced expérimenté
export exporter
exports exportations (f.pl)

F

factory usine (*f.*)
fax télécopie (*f.*)
fax télécopier
fax machine télécopieur
fair foire (*f.*)
  trade f. f. commerciale
facilitate faciliter
fee(s) honoraires (*m. pl.*)
figure chiffre (*m.*)
file dossier (*m.*)
file classer
filing cabinet classeur (*m.*)
finance financer
financial financier, -ière (*f.*)
financing financement (*m.*)
finish finir
firm firme, entreprise (*f.*)
flexible hours horaires (*m.*)
  variables/mobiles
floppy disk disquette (*f.*)
folder dépliant (*m.*)
foreign exchange market marché
  (*m.*) des changes
form formulaire (*m.*)
  to complete a form remplir un
  formulaire
fortunately heureusement
fragile fragile

free franco, gratuit
free on board (FOB) franco à bord
  (FAB)
French français
fringe benefits avantages (*m.*) en
  nature
fruitful fructueux, -euse (*f.*)
function fonctionner
funds fonds (*m. pl*)

G

gap in the market créneau (*m.*)
German allemand
goods marchandises (*f.*)
grant accorder
growth croissance (*f.*)
growth rate taux (*m.*) de
croissance
guarantee garantie (*f.*)
guarantee garantir

H

head chef (*m.*)
head of a company chef
  d'entreprise
head of personnel chef du
  personnel
hereby par la présente
hire louer
hiring location (*f.*)

I

import importer
important important
imports importations (*f.*)
income revenu(s) (*m.*)
income tax impôt (*m.*) sur le revenu
increase augmentation (*f.*)
increase augmenter
independence indépendance (*f.*)
  financial i. i. financière
industry industrie (*f.*)
inflation inflation (*f.*)
inform informer
information renseignements (*m. pl.*)
  to obtain i. se renseigner, se
  documenter

install installer
insurance assurance (f.)
insurance policy police (f.)
  d'assurance
  comprehensive insurance
  assurance multirisques
life insurance assurance-vie
Italian italien,-ienne (f.)
interest rate taux (m.) d'intérêt
interview interview, entrevue (f.)
  entretien (m.)
interview interviewer
inventory inventaire (m.)
  to make an i. faire un i.
invest investir
investment investissement,
  placement (m.)
  foreign i. investissements
  étrangers
invoice facture (f.)
issue délivrer

J

Japanese japonais
journal revue (f.) professionnelle
job poste (m.), situation (f.), emploi (m.)

L

launch lancer
lawyer avocat, -e (f.)
letter lettre (f.)
licence licence (f.), permis (m.)
  under licence sous licence
loan prêt, emprunt (m.)
lorry camion (m.)
lorry driver camionneur (m.)
loss perte (f.)

M

machine machine (f.)
magazine magazine (m.)
  current affairs magazine
  magazine d'actualité
mail courrier (m.)
mail order selling vente (f.) par
  correspondance
management direction, gestion (f.)

manager directeur, -trice
managerial staff cadres (m. pl)
managing director directeur général
  chairman and managing director
  président-directeur général
manufacture fabrication (f.)
manufacture fabriquer
market marché (m.)
market research étude (f.) de
  marché
market commercialiser
marketing marketing
meet (bill) faire face à
meet (person) rencontrer
meeting réunion (f.)
merger fusion (f.)
message message (m.)
micro-computer micro-ordinateur (m.)
miss manquer
model modèle (m.)
modification modification (f.)
monopoly monopole (m.)
monthly mensuel, -elle (f.)
monthly payment mensualité (f.)
mortgage prêt (m.) immobilier,
  hypothèque (f.)

N

necessary nécessaire
  to do what is n. faire le n.
  it is n. il faut
negotiate négocier
negotiations négociations (f.)
negotiator négociateur, -trice (f.)
newspaper journal (m.)
notice (advance) préavis (m.)

O

office bureau (m.)
office automation bureautique (f.)
office furniture mobilier (m.) de
  bureau
office supplies fournitures (f.) de
  bureau
oil pétrole (m. energy), huile
  (f. lubricat.)
opportunity occasion (f.)
order commande (f.)

order commander
order form bon (*m.*) de commande
organize organiser
organizer organisateur, -trice (*f.*)
outlet débouché (*m.*)
owner propriétaire (*m. f.*)

P

packing emballage (*m.*)
participate (in) participer (à)
partner associé, -ée (*f.*)
paste-up maquette (*f.*)
pay payer, verser
payment paiement, règlement (*m.*)
percentage pourcentage (*m.*)
perfect perfectionner
perfectly parfaitement
personnel personnel (*m.*)
photocopier photocopieuse (*f.*)
plan planifier
plan projet (*m.*)
   cash flow plan plan (*m.*) de
     trésorerie
point point (*m.*)
   break-even point point mort
policy politique (*f.*)
portable portatif, -ive, (*f.*), portable
poster affiche (*f.*)
postpone remettre
potential potentiel, -elle (*f.*)
premium prime (*f.*)
   insurance p. p. d'assurance
prepare préparer
press presse (*f.*)
press conference conférence de
   presse
price prix (*m.*)
   introductory p. p. de lancement
   retail p. p. au détail
   wholesale p. p. de gros
print imprimer
printer imprimante (*f.*)
private secretary secrétaire (*m. f.*)
   de direction
problem problème (*m.*)
product produit (*m.*)
production production (*f.*)
productivity productivité (*f.*),
   rendement (*m.*)

profession profession (*f.*), métier (*m.*)
profit bénéfice (*m.*)
profit margin marge (*f.*)
   bénéficiaire
profit sharing intéressement (*m.*)
program programmer
project projet
property propriété (*f.*)
property tax taxe (*f.*) foncière
proposal proposition (*f.*)
purchase achat (*m.*)
purchase acheter
purchasing power pouvoir (*m.*)
   d'achat

Q

quality qualité
quotation devis (*m.*)

R

rail
   by rail par chemin de fer
rail link liaison (*f.*) ferroviaire
range gamme (*f.*)
rate taux (*m.*)
   birth rate taux de natalité
   death r. t. de mortalité
   exchange r. t. de change
   growth r. t. de croissance
   interest r. t. d'intérêt
   lending r. t. de prêt
raw materials matières (*f.*)
   premières
receive recevoir
recently récemment
recommend recommander
recruit recruter
redundancy licenciement (*m.*)
redundancy payment indemnité (*f.*)
   de licenciement
redundant
   to make r. licencier
refer (to) se reporter (à)
reference référence (*f.*)
   bank references références
     bancaires
refund remboursement (*m.*)
refuse refuser

renew renouveler
reliable fiable
repair réparer
repayment remboursement (*m.*)
reply réponse (*f.*)
reply répondre
report rapport (*m.*)
represent représenter
representative représentant, -ante (*f.*)
reserve réserver
responsible (for) responsable (de)
retire prendre sa retraite
retrain (oneself) se recycler
right droit (*m.*)
   to be right avoir raison
robot robot (*m.*)

S

salary salaire (*m.*); rémunération (*f.*)
salary claims revendications (*f.*)
   salariales
   gross s. salaire brut
   net s. s. net
   s. increase augmentation de s.
sale vente (*f.*)
   for s. en v.
sales manager directeur commercial
sales force force (*f.*) de vente
sales report relevé (*m.*) des ventes
sample échantillon (*m.*)
satisfaction satisfaction (*f.*)
   to give complete s. donner
   entière s.
saving économie (*f.*)
secretary secrétaire (*m. f.*)
securities titres (*m. pl.*)
   Government s. t. d'État
sell vendre
send envoyer
settle s'établir, s'installer
settle (bills) régler
shares actions (*f. pl.*)
   ordinary s. a. ordinaires
shortly prochainement
shorthand sténo(graphie) (*f.*)
shorthand typist sténodactylo (*m. f.*)
sign signer
signature signature (*f.*)
signing signature (*f.*)

single European currency
   monnaie (*f.*) unique européenne
Single European Market Marché
   unique européen
size taille (*f.*), dimensions (*f. pl.*)
solution solution (*f.*)
solve résoudre
spare parts pièces (*f. pl.*)
   détachées
Spanish espagnol
specialize se spécialiser
specification sheet fiche (*f.*)
   technique
staff personnel (*m.*)
stand stand (*m.*)
steps démarches (*f.*)
   to take the necessary s. faire
   les d. nécessaires
stock stock (*m.*)
   out of s. en rupture de s.
   le stock est épuisé
Stock Exchange Bourse (*f.*)
strike grève
   to go on s. se mettre en grève
subisidiary company filiale (*f.*)
subsidize subventionner
subsidy subvention (*f.*)
succeed (in) réussir (à)
success succès (*m.*)
suggest suggérer
supplier fournisseur (*m.*)
supply fournir
supply and demand l'offre et la
   demande
switchboard standard (*m.*)
switchboard operator
   standardiste (*m. f.*)

T

tape recorder magnétophone (*m.*)
target cible (*f.*)
target audience population (*f.*) cible
tax impôt (*m.*), taxe (*f.*)
   dwelling t. taxe d'habitation
   property t. t. foncière
   wealth t. impôt sur les grandes
   fortunes
tax collector percepteur (*m.*)
tax system système (*m.*) fiscal

team équipe (*f.*)
technology technologie (*f.*)
  advanced t. t. de pointe
telephone téléphone (*m.*)
telephone téléphoner
  t. conversation conversation
    téléphonique
  t. number numéro de téléphone
teleconference vidéo-conférence (*f.*)
telex télex (*m.*)
terms termes (*m.*), conditions (*f.*)
  terms of payment conditions de
    paiement
test tester
  psychology tests tests (*m.*)
    psychologiques
ticket billet (*m.*)
  air t. b. d'avion
time limit délai (*m.*)
touch
  in touch with en contact avec
trade échanges (*m. pl.*)
  commerciaux
trade balance balance (*f.*)
  commerciale
training formation (*f.*)
training period stage (*m.*)
transaction transaction (*f.*)
transfer (money) virement (*m.*)
transfer virer
translation traduction (*f.*)
translator traducteur, -trice (*f.*)
transport transport (*m.*)
transport transporter
turnover chiffre (*m.*) d'affaires
typewriter machine (*f*) à écrire
typist dactylo (*m. f.*)
  shorthand t. sténodactylo (*m. f.*)

U

unemployed chômeur (*m.*)
unfortunately malheureusement
union syndicat (*m.*)
  u. demands revendications (*f.*)
    syndicales
United States États-Unis (*m.*)
United Kingdom Royaume-Uni (*m.*)
urgent urgent

V

VAT TVA (*f.*)
video recorder magnétoscope (*m.*)

W

wage salaire (*m.*)
  index-linked minimum wage
    SMIC (*m.*)
warehouse entrepôt (*m.*)
welcome accueillir
  to w. clients accueillir les clients
withdraw retirer
word processing/processor
  traitement de texte
work travail (*m.*)
work travailler
  to w. overtime faire des heures (*f.*)
    supplémentaires
worker ouvrier, -ière (*f.*) travailleur,
  -euse (*f.*)
  unskilled w. ouvrier non-qualifié
workforce effectif (*m.*)
working conditions conditions (*f.*)
  de travail
works manager directeur technique
workshop atelier (*m.*)
wrong
  to be wrong avoir tort

IMITATED PRONUNCIATION

UNIT 1

1 ler
2 ler dee-rek-terr
3 rahng-day-voo
4 tay-lay-fon
5 bü-roh
6 lah
7 lah dee-rek-treess
8 so-syay-tay
9 kahrt
10 vahngt
11 mahrsh
12 err
13 lay
14 lay vahngt
15 bree-tah-neek
16 mong, mah
17 song, sah
18 zher swee
19 zhay
20 noo zah-vong
21 voo zah-vay tay-lay-fo-nay
22 el voo zah-tahng
23 eel/el ay
24 voo-lay voo
25 pah-say
26 pahr-dong
27 vwah-see
28 byang sür
29 seel voo play
30 ah-tahng-syong ah
31 ah-vek
32 dahng
33 pahr
34 ee-see, pahr ee-see
35 ee-yair
36 der
37 dü
38 day
39 ah
40 oh
41 ongz
42 wee
43 nong
44 bong-zhoor
45 mer-syer
46 mah-dam

47 mahd-mwah-zel

UNIT 2

48 tahng
49 kah-fay
50 sükr
51 pro-dwee
52 mahr-shay
53 mah-tay-ree-yel
54 ahng
55 ko-nay-sahngss
56 sü-kret
57 bü-roh-teek
58 mah-sheen ah ay-kreer
59 tek-no-lo-zhee der pwangt
60 krem
61 ang-tahng-syong
62 ahng-trer-preez
63 frahngss
64 ahng-shahng-tay
65 ay-lek-tro-neek
66 votr
67 voh
68 too, toot, too, toot
69 veet
70 vo-long-tyay
71 vray-mahng
72 sahng
73 sür
74 der
75 ahng
76 poor
77 ung per
78 poor-kwah
79 tyang
80 kom
81 ay byang
82 ness pah
83 ah-say-yay voo
84 day-zhah
85 say tah deer
86 ker
87 may
88 ahng-tray
89 ah-ree-vay

90 pah-say
91 ah-por-tay
92 fah-bree-kay
93 day-see-day
94 ser spay-syah-lee-zay
95 fairr, zher fay, eel fay, noo fer-
zong, voo fet, eel fong, zhay
fay
96 prahng-dr,zher prahng,eel
prahng,noo prer-nong, voo
prer-nay,eel pren zhay pree
97 poo-vwahr, zher per, eel per,
noo poo-vong, voo poo-vay,
eel perv, zhay pü
98 vwahr, zher vwah, eel vwah,
noo vwah-yong, voo vwah-
yay, eel vwah, zhay vü

UNIT 3

99 pay-ee
100 vwah-zang
101 mo-mahng
102 frahng-glay
103 frahng-say
104 ray-pü-tah-syong
105 dee-fee-kül-tay
106 frong-tyair
107 fah-bree-kah-syong
108 tek-no-lo-zhee
109 tair-mee-no-lo-zhee
110 gahm
111 mo-dee-fee-kah-syong
112 eks-pahng-syong
113 ang-flah-syong
114 o-kah-zyong
115 rwah-yohm ü-nee
116 ahng-glo sahk-song,son
117 plang
118 sair-tang
119 ay-ko-no-meek
120 prosh
121 see-mee-lair
122 nay-sess-air
123 fah-meel-yah-ree-zay (ah-vek)
124 bong, bon
125 mo-vay
126 zhay-o-grah-feek-mahng
127 sair-ten-mahng
128 boh-koo
129 ah kohz der
130 dongk

131 ner...pah
132 bref
133 plü
134 say sah
135 dü mwang
136 ah-pray too
137 byang-nay-tah-blee
138 ahng ser mo-mahng
139 ler/lah vohtr
140 lay vohtr
141 mahng-syo-nay
142 og-mahng-tay
143 pahng-say
144 ko-mahng-say
145 mahng-kay
146 ang-tay-gray
147 frahng-sheer
148 ah-vwahr ray-zong
149 ah-vwahr tor
150 fahl-wahr, eel foh, eel ah fah-lü
151 sah-vwahr, zher say, eel say,
noo sah-vong, voo sah-vay,
eel sahv, zhay sü

UNIT 4

152 pro-dwee
153 play-zeer
154 poor-sahng-tahzh
155 kah-myong
156 day-lay
157 pay-mahng
158 veer-mahng bahng-kair
159 mwah
160 rerl-vay day vahngt
161 sair-veess ah-pray vahngt
162 tek-nee-syang
163 koor
164 pwang
165 ahng-trer-poh
166 fray
167 deess-kü-syong
168 letr
169 ko-mee-syong
170 pü-blee-see-tay
171 pahr-tee-see -pah-syong
172 fwahr ko-mair-syahl
173 kahng-pan-yer pü-blee-see-
tair
174 lee-vray-zong
175 mahr-shahng-deez
176 ser-men

177 ray-sep-syo*ng*
178 ko-mah*ng*d
179 fahk-tür
180 bah*ng*k
181 day-dük-syo*ng*
182 for-mah-syo*ng*
183 ko-lah-bo-rah-syo*ng*
184 ah*ng*-tre*r*-preez
185 sah-lü-tah-syo*ng*
186 po-see-ble*r*
187 ray-spo*ng*-sah-ble*r* (de*r*)
188 bee-la*ng*-g
189 ay-sah*ng*-syel
190 shair
191 ay-vah*ng*-tü-el
192 mah*ng*-sü-el
193 frük-tü-e*r*, e*r*z
194 pro-shen-mah*ng*
195 dee-rek-te*r*-mah*ng*
196 ee-may-dyaht-mah*ng*
197 veev-mah*ng*
198 frah*ng*-koh
199 pahr
200 day
201 ah*ng*-tr
202 pahr lah pray-zah*ng*t
203 tray
204 kee
205 ke*r*
206 pweess-ke*r*
207 notr, noh
208 ah votr deess-poh-zee-syo*ng*
209 le*r*-kel, lah-kel, lay-kel, lay-kel
210 zhah*ng*-vyay
211 fay-vree-yay
212 mahrss
213 ah-vreel
214 may
215 zhwa*ng*
216 zhwee-yay
217 oot, (oo)
218 sep-tah*ng*-bre*r*
219 ok-to-bre*r*
220 no-vah*ng*-bre*r*
221 day-sah*ng*-bre*r*
222 va*ng*
223 va*ng*-tay u*ng*
224 va*ng*t de*r*
225 va*ng*t ne*r*f
226 trah*ng*t
227 trah*ng*t ay u*ng*
228 kah-rah*ng*t

229 sa*ng*-kah*ng*t
230 swah-sah*ng*t
231 lo*ng*-dre*r*
232 re*r*-mair-syay
233 ahk-sep-tay
234 re*r*-pray-zah*ng*-tay
235 ko-mair-syah-lee-zay
236 ko*ng*-feer-may
237 or-gah-nee-zay
238 ay-fek-tü-ay
239 ay-may
240 ah-gray-ay
241 ess-pay-ray, zhess-pair, eel
    ess-pair, noo zess-pay-ro*ng*,
    voo zess-pay-ray, eel zess-
    pair, zhay ess-pay-ray
242 eel se*r*-rah
243 voo se*r*-ray
244 eel/el se*r* fe*r*-rah
245 eel/el poo-rah
246 noo zay-merr-yo*ng*
247 ver-yay (vool-wahr)
248 ko*ng*-sah*ng*-teer, zhe*r* ko*ng*-
    sah*ng*, eel ko*ng*-sah*ng*, noo
    ko*ng*-sah*ng*-to*ng*,voo ko*ng*-
    sah*ng*-tay, eel ko*ng*-sah*ng*t,
    zhay ko*ng*-sah*ng*-tee
249 metr, zhe*r* may, eel may, noo
    met-o*ng*, voo met-ay, eel
    met, zhay mee
250 vool-wahr, zhe*r* ver, eel ve*r*,
    noo voo-lo*ng*, voo voo-lay,
    eel ve*r*l, zhay voo-lü, zhe*r*
    voo-dray
251 kong-prahng-dr

UNIT 5

252 no*ng*
253 pro-blem
254 do-mahzh
255 trah*ng*-spor
256 sük-say
257 a*ng*-stah*ng*
258 ah*ng*-bah-lahzh
259 ah-pah-ray-ee
260 leen-yer
261 shah*ng*ss
262 shohz
263 kess
264 eks-pay-dee-syo*ng*
265 mahr-shah*ng*-deez

266 per-tee
267 grah*ng*
268 nor-mahl
269 day-zo-lay
270 a*ng*-sür-mo*ng*-tah-bler
271. pray-fay-rah-bler
272 fü-tür
273 prerm-yay, prerm-yair
274 a*ng*-sü-fee-zah*ng*
275 frah-zheel
276 een-ah-day-kwah
277 ah-pah-rah*ng*
278 rah-peed-mah*ng*
279 ee-may-dyaht-mah*ng*
280 mahl-er-rerz-mah*ng*
281 veet
282 ma*ng*t-nah*ng*
283 ee-yair
284 oh-zhoor-dwee
285 der-ma*ng*
286 ah-pray der-ma*ng*
287 ser mah-ta*ng*
288 ah lahv-neer
289 mair-krer-dee
290 ah mee-dee
291 ah-meen-wee
292 eks-kü-zay mwah
293 ah mo*ng*-nah-vee, ah notr ah-vee
294 oh-see frah-zheel ker
295 der pray-fay-rah*ng*ss
296 lwa*ng* der lah
297 too mo*ng* po-see-bler
298 too tah fay
299 ner...oh-ku*ng*
300 see
301 er
302 ah-loh
303 do*ng*k
304 ker
305 kel-ker
306 ay bya*ng*
307 oh-tr shohz
308 pahr root
309 oh koor der
310 ner kee-tay pah
311 say der lah pahr der
312 ah-pray too
313 zhay ay-tay
314 eel sah*ng*-bler ee ah-vwahr
315 eel yah
316 yah-teel

317 fairr ler nay-sess-air
318 fahss
319 voo zay-merr-yay
320 swah-sah*ng*t ay u*ng*
321 swah-sah*ng*t der
322 swah-sah*ng*t deess
323 swah-sah*ng*t ay o*ng*z
324 swah-sah*ng*t dooz
325 swah-sah*ng*t trezz
326 swah-sah*ng*t-deez-nerf
327 kah-trer-va*ng*
328 sah*ng*-blay
329 kee-tay
330 pah-say
331 pah*ng*-say
332 ah-zhoo-tay
333 trah*ng*-spor-tay
334 ah-bee-may
335 ay-may
336 rah-play
337 ray-pay-tay, zher ray-pet, eel ray-pet, noo ray-pay-to*ng*, voo ray-pay-tay, eel ray-pet, zhay ray-pay-tay
338 ay-say-yay, zhay-say, eel ay-say, noo zay-say-yo*ng*, voo zay-say-yay, eel zay-say, zhay ay-say-yay
339 ah*ng*-do-mah-zhay, noo zah*ng*-do-mah-zho*ng*
340 rah*ng*-for-say, noo rah*ng*-for-so*ng*
341 ah-prah*ng*-dr,zhah-prah*ng*, eel ah-prah*ng*, noo zah-prer-no*ng*, voo zah-prer-nay, eel zah-pren, zhay ah-pree
342 ray-zoodr, zher ray-zoo,eel ray-zoo, noo ray-zol-vo*ng*, voo ray-zol-vay, eel ray-zolv, zhay ray-zo-lü

INDEX

The figures refer to Checknotes, *not* pages.